KU-176-337

Italian
phrase book

HOW TO USE THIS BOOK

We suggest that you start with the Pronunciation section (pp. 6–9), then turn to Basic Expressions (pp. 10–19). These sections give you some useful words, phrases, and short dialogs and help you get used to pronouncing and using the language.

Consult the Contents pages (pp. 3–5) for the section you need. In each chapter you'll find travel facts, hints, and useful information. Sample phrases are followed by translations and pronunciation.

Look for special YOU MAY HEAR and YOU MAY SEE boxes that highlight phrases that someone may say to you or signs you may see during your travels.

Read along with the dialog boxes (e.g. IN A CAFÉ) that present short, useful conversations. An audio recording of the dialogs in this book can be heard in the Cassette Pack and CD Pack versions.

If you want to know the meaning of a word, your fastest look-up is via the Dictionary section (pp. 168–199).

If you wish to learn about constructing sentences, check the Grammar in the Reference section (pp. 215–218).

Note the color margins are indexed to help you quickly locate the section you need.

If you have difficulty speaking and understanding the language, you can hand the phrase book to the Italian speaker; each of you can then point to the appropriate phrase or sentence.

Layout: Media Content Marketing, Inc.

CONTACTING THE EDITORS

Every effort has been made to provide accurate information in this publication, but changes are inevitable. The publisher cannot be responsible for any resulting loss, inconvenience or injury. We would appreciate it if readers would call our attention to any errors or outdated information by contacting Berlitz Publishing, PO Box 7910, London SE1 1WE, England. Fax: (44) 20 7403 0290. email: berlitz@apaguide.demon.co.uk

TABLE OF CONTENTS

PRONUNCIATION

This section is designed to make you familiar with the sounds of Italian using our simplified phonetic transcription. You'll find the pronunciation of the Italian letters and sounds explained below, together with their "imitated" equivalents. This system is used throughout the phrase book: simply read the pronunciation as if it were English, noting any special rules below.

THE ITALIAN LANGUAGE

Italian evolved from Latin, just as French, Spanish, Portuguese, and Romanian. What is known as standard Italian today dates back to last century, when the great Italian novelist Alessandro Manzoni (1785-1873) gave Italy a national language by resolving that it should basically be Tuscan Italian with a heavy contribution from the Italian used in the other regions of Italy. The language spoken and written in Tuscany had taken precedence over the regional forms from the twelfth century to Manzoni's times because of the political, artistic and social prominence of Florence.

There are approximately 64 million speakers of Italian. These are the countries where you can expect to hear Italian spoken (figures are approximate):

Italia Italy

Italian is the national language, spoken by almost the entire population (59 million). Other languages: Sardinian in Sardinia (1.5 million); Rhaeto-Romanic in Friuli, near the border with Slovenia and Austria.

Svizzera Switzerland

Italian is one of the four official languages, spoken by about 800,000 people in the southern part of the country, particularly the canton of Ticino (capital: Bellinzona). Other languages: German in the north (5 milllion); French in the west (1.3 million); Romansch in the east (50,000).

Italian is also spoken amongst large Italian emigré communities, particularly in the United States (**Stati Uniti**), with almost 1.5 million speakers, and Canada (**Canada**), with over half a million speakers.

The Italian alphabet is the same as English, with the addition of accents which indicate stress only (see below). However, the letters **j**, **k**, **w**, **x** and **y** only appear in foreign words.

English has absorbed numerous Italian words, for example: **balcony**, **studio**, **umbrella**, **volcano** as well as terms in the fields of food (e.g. **broccoli**, **maca-roni**, **pizza**, **spaghetti**) and music (e.g. **concerto**, **piano**, **solo**, **trio**, **viola**).

Consonants

Letter	Approximate pronunciation	Symbol	Example	
c	1) before **e** and **i**, like *ch* in *ch*ip	ch	**cerco**	_chayrko_
	2) elsewhere, like *c* in *cat*	k	**conto**	_konto_
ch	like *c* in *cat*	k	**che**	_kay_
g	1) before **e** and **i**, like *j* in *jet*	j	**valigia**	_valeeja_
	2) elsewhere, like *g* in *go*	g	**grande**	_granday_
gh	like *g* in *go*	g	**ghiaccio**	_geeacho_
gl	like *lli* in mi*lli*on	ly	**gli**	_lyee_
gn	like *ni* in o*ni*on	ny	**bagno**	_banyo_
h	always silent		**ha**	_ah_
r	trilled like a Scottish *r*	r	**deriva**	_dehreeva_
s	1) generally like *s* in *s*it	s	**questo**	_kwaysto_
	2) sometimes like *z* in *z*oo	z	**viso**	_veezo_
sc	1) before **e** and **i**, like *sh* in *sh*ut	sh	**uscita**	_oosheeta_
	2) elsewhere, like *sk* in *sk*in	sk	**scarpa**	_skarpa_
z/zz	1) generally like *ts* in hi*ts*	ts	**grazie**	_graatseeay_
	2) sometimes like *ds* in roa*ds*	dz	**romanzo**	_romandzo_

Vowels

a	1) short, like *a* in c*a*t	a	**gatto**	_gatto_
	2) long, like *a* in f*a*ther	aa	**casa**	_kaasa_
e	1) can always be pronounced like *ay* in w*ay*, but without moving tongue or lips	ay	**sera**	_sayra_
	2) in correct speech, it is sometimes pronounced like *e* in g*e*t or, when long, more like *ai* in h*ai*r	eh	**bello**	_behllo_
i	like *ee* in m*ee*t	ee	**vini**	_veenee_
o	can always be pronounced like *o* in g*o*	o	**sole**	_solay_
u	1. like *oo* in f*oo*t	oo	**fumo**	_foomo_
	2. like *w* in *w*ell	w	**buono**	_bwono_

b, d, f, k, l, m, n, p, q, t and **v** are pronounced as in English

Two or more vowels

In groups of vowels **a**, **e** and **o** are strong, and **i** and **u** are weak vowels. The following combinations occur:

two strong vowels	pronounced as two separate syllables	**beato**	*bay-aato*
a stong vowel and a weak vowel	1) the weak one is pronounced more quickly and with less stress than the strong one; such sounds are diphthongs and constitute only one syllable:	**piede**	*peeayday*
	2) if the weak vowel is stressed, then it is pronounced as a separate syllable	**due**	*doo-ay*
two weak vowels	pronounced as a diphthong; it is generally the second one that is more strongly stressed	**guida**	*gweeda*

STRESS

Stress has been indicated in the phonetic transcription by underlining the letters that should be pronounced louder than the others.

Generally, the vowel of the next to last syllable is stressed. When a final vowel is stressed, it has an accent written over it (**caffè**). Normally, when the stress falls on the syllable before the next to last one, it is not indicated by an accent.

PRONUNCIATION OF THE ITALIAN ALPHABET

A	*ah*		**N**	*ehnnay*
B	*bee*		**O**	*o*
C	*chee*		**P**	*pee*
D	*dee*		**Q**	*koo*
E	*ay*		**R**	*ehrray*
F	*ehffay*		**S**	*ehssay*
G	*jee*		**T**	*tee*
H	*aaka*		**U**	*oo*
I	*ee*		**V**	*voo*
J	*ee loongga*		**W**	*voo doppeea*
K	*kaappa*		**X**	*eeks*
L	*ehllay*		**Y**	*ee grayka*
M	*ehmmay*		**Z**	*dzaytah*

BASIC EXPRESSIONS

GREETINGS/APOLOGIES

ESSENTIAL		
Yes.	**Sì.** *see*	
No.	**No.** *no*	
Okay.	**D'accordo./Va bene.** *daakordo/va baynay*	
Please.	**Per favore.** *pehr favoray*	
Thank you (very much).	**(Mille) grazie.** *(meellay) graatseeay*	

Hello/Hi!	**Salve./Ciao!** *saalvay/chaao*
Good morning.	**Buongiorno.** *bwon jorno*
Good afternoon.	**Buonasera.** *bwona sayra*
Good evening.	**Buonasera.** *bwona sayra*
Good night.	**Buonanotte.** *bwona nottay*
Good-bye.	**Arrivederci.** *arreevaydehrchee*
Excuse me! *(getting attention)*	**Scusi!** *skoozee*
Excuse me. *(May I get past?)*	**Permesso?** *pehrmehsso*
Excuse me!/Sorry!	**Scusi!/Sono spiacente!** *skoozee/sono speeachehntay*
It was an accident.	**È stato un incidente.** *eh staato oon eencheedehntay*
Don't mention it.	**Prego.** *praygo*
Never mind.	**Non importa.** *non eemporta*

COMMUNICATION DIFFICULTIES

Do you speak English?	**Parla inglese?** _parla eengglaysay_
Does anyone here speak English?	**C'è qualcuno qui che parla inglese?** _cheh kwalkoono kwee kay parla eengglaysay_
I don't speak . (much) Italian	**Non parlo italiano (molto bene).** _non parlo eetaleeaano (molto baynay)_
Could you speak more slowly?	**Può parlare più lentamente?** _pwo parlaaray peeoo layntamayntay_
Could you repeat that?	**Può ripetere?** _pwo reepehtayray_
Pardon?/What was that?	**Prego?/Cosa ha detto?** _praygo/kosa ah daytto_
Could you spell it?	**Come si scrive?** _komay see skreevay_
Please write it down.	**Lo scriva, per piacere.** _lo skreeva pehr peeachayray_
Can you translate this for me?	**Può tradurre questo?** _pwo tradoorray kwaysto_
What does this/that mean?	**Cosa significa questo/quello?** _kosa seenyeefeeka kwaysto/kwayllo_
Please point to the phrase in the book.	**Per piacere, indichi la frase nel libro.** _pehr peeachayray eendeekee la fraazay nel leebro_
I understand.	**Capisco.** _kapeesko_
I don't understand.	**Non capisco.** _non kapeesko_
Do you understand?	**Capisce?** _kapeeshay_

ON THE STREET

Buongiorno! Come sta? _bwon jorno komay sta_
(Hi. How are you?)
Bene, grazie, e Lei? _baynay graatseeay ay layee_
(Fine, thanks. And you?)
Bene, grazie. _baynay graatseeay_
(Fine . Thanks.)

11

Where?

Where is it?	**Dov'è?** _do<u>veh</u>_
Where are you going?	**Dove va?** _<u>do</u>vay va_
to the meeting place	**al punto d'incontro** _al <u>poon</u>to deen<u>kon</u>tro_
[point] downstairs	**al piano inferiore** _al pee<u>aa</u>no eenfayree<u>o</u>ray_
from the U.S.	**dagli Stati Uniti** _<u>daa</u>lyee <u>staa</u>tee oo<u>nee</u>tee_
here	**qui** _kw<u>ee</u>_
in the car	**in automobile** _een owto<u>mo</u>beelay_
in Italy	**in Italia** _een ee<u>taa</u>leea_
inside	**dentro** _<u>day</u>ntro_
near the bank	**vicino alla banca** _vee<u>chee</u>no <u>a</u>lla <u>ban</u>ka_
next to the apples	**accanto alle mele** _ak<u>kan</u>to <u>a</u>llay <u>may</u>lay_
opposite the market	**di fronte al mercato** _dee <u>fron</u>tay al mayr<u>kaa</u>to_
on the left/right	**a sinistra/a destra** _ah see<u>nee</u>stra/ah <u>day</u>stra_
there	**là** _la_
to the hotel	**in albergo** _een al<u>behr</u>go_
toward Florence	**verso Firenze** _<u>vehr</u>so fee<u>rehn</u>zay_
outside the café	**fuori del bar** _<u>fwo</u>ree dayl baar_
upstairs	**al piano superiore** _al pee<u>aa</u>no soopayree<u>o</u>ray_

When?

When does the museum open?	**Quando apre il museo?** _kwando_ apray eel _moozeho_
When will the train arrive?	**Quando arriva il treno?** _kwando_ ar_ree_va eel _trayno_
in 10 minutes	**fra dieci minuti** frah dee-_eh_chee meen_oo_tee
after lunch	**dopo pranzo** _dopo_ _prandzo_
around midnight	**verso mezzanotte** _vehr_so mehdza_notte_tay
at 7 o'clock	**alle sette** _allay_ _sehtte_tay
before Friday	**prima di venerdì** _pree_ma dee vaynayr_dee_
by tomorrow	**entro domani** _ayntro_ do_maa_nee
early	**di buon'ora** dee bwo_nora_
every week	**ogni settimana/tutte le settimane** _onyee_ saytteе_maa_na/_toot_tay lay saytteе_maa_nay
for 2 hours	**per due ore** pehr _doo-ay_ oray
from 9 a.m. to 6 p.m.	**dalle nove alle diciotto** _dallay_ _nova_y _allay_ deecho_tto_
immediately	**immediatamente** eemaydeeata_mayn_tay
in 20 minutes	**fra venti minuti** frah _vayntee_ meen_oo_tee
always	**sempre** _sehm_pray
never	**mai** _maee_
not yet	**non ancora** non an_kora_
now	**ora/adesso** _ora_/a_dehsso_
often	**sovente/spesso** so_vayn_tay/_speh_sso
on March 8	**l'otto marzo** _lotto_ _martso_
on weekdays	**nei giorni feriali** _nayee_ _jornee_ fehree_aa_lee
sometimes	**qualche volta** _kwal_kay _volta_
soon	**presto/fra poco** _prehs_to/fra _poko_
then	**poi** _poee_
within 2 days	**entro due giorni** _ayntro_ _doo-ay_ _jornee_

What kind of ...?

I'd like something ...	**Vorrei qualcosa ...**	*vorrehee kwalkosa*
It's ...	**È ...**	*eh*
beautiful/ugly	**bello(-a)/brutto(-a)**	*behllo(-a)/brootto(-a)*
better/worse	**migliore/peggiore**	*meelyoray/paydjoray*
big/small	**grande/piccolo(-a)**	*granday/peekkolo(-a)*
cheap/expensive	**a buon prezzo/caro(-a)**	
	a bwon pretso/kaaro(-a)	
clean/dirty	**pulito(-a)/sporco(-a)**	
	pooleeto(-a)/sporko(-a)	
dark/light	**scuro(-a)/chiaro(-a)**	
	skooro(-a)/keeahro(-a)	
delicious/revolting	**delizioso(-a)/disgustoso(-a)**	
	dehleetzeeozo(-a)/deesgoostozo(-a)	
easy/difficult	**facile/difficile**	
	faacheelay/deeffeecheelay	
empty/full	**vuoto(-a)/pieno(-a)**	
	vwoto(-a)/peeayno(-a)	
good/bad	**buono(-a)/cattivo(-a)**	
	bwono(-a)/katteevo(-a)	
heavy/light	**pesante/leggero(-a)**	
	paysantay/laydjehro(-a)	
hot/warm/cold	**molto caldo(-a)/caldo(-a)/freddo(-a)**	
	molto kaldo(-a)/kaldo(-a)/frayddo(-a)	
modern/old-fashioned	**moderno(-a)/antiquato(-a)**	
	modayrno(-a)/anteekwato(-a)	
narrow/wide	**stretto(-a)/largo(-a)**	*straytto(-a)/lahrgo(-a)*
old/new	**vecchio(-a)/nuovo(-a)**	
	vehkkeeao(-a)/nwovo(-a)	
open/shut	**aperto(-a)/chiuso(-a)**	
	apehrto(-a)/keeooso(-a)	
pleasant/nice/unpleasant	**gradevole/bello(-a)/sgradevole**	
	grahdayvolay/behllo(-a)/zgradayvolay	

quick/slow	**veloce/lento(-a)** _vaylochay/laynto(-a)_
right/wrong	**guisto(-a)/sbagliato(-a)** _joosto(-a) zbalyaato(-a)_
tall/short	**alto(-a)/basso(-a)** _alto(-a)/basso(-a)_
vacant/occupied	**libero(-a)/occupato(-a)** _leebayro(-a)/okoopaato(-a)_

How much/many?

How much is that?	**Quanto costa?** _kwanto kosta_
How many are there?	**Quanti ce ne sono?** _kwantee cheh neh sono_
1/2/3	**uno(-a)/due/tre** _oono(-a)/doo-ay/tray_
4/5	**quattro/cinque** _kwattro/cheenkway_
none	**nessuno(-a)** _nayssoono(-a)_
about 20 euros	**circa venti euro** _cheerka vayntee ayooro_
a little	**un po'** _oon po_
a lot of traffic	**molto traffico** _molto traffeeko_
enough (adv./adj.)	**abbastanza/sufficiente** _abbastantsa/sooffeecheeayntay_
few/a few of them	**alcuni(-e)/alcuni(-e) di loro** _alkoonee(-ay)/alkoonee(-ay) dee loro_
more than that	**più di quello(-a)** _peeoo dee kwayllo(-a)_
less than that	**meno di quello(-a)** _mayno dee kwayllo(-a)_
much more	**molto di più** _molto dee peeoo_
nothing else	**nient'altro** _neeayntaltro_
too much	**troppo(-a)** _troppo(-a)_

Why?

Why is that?	**Perchè?** _pehrkay_
Why not?	**Perchè no?** _pehrkay no_
because of the weather	**a causa del tempo** _a kowsa dayl tehmpo_
because I'm in a hurry	**perchè ho fretta** _pehrkay o fraytta_
I don't know why	**non so perchè** _non so pehrkay_

Who?/Which?

Who's there?	**Chi è?**	*kee eh*
It's me!	**Sono io!**	*sono eeo*
It's us!	**Siamo noi!**	*seeamo noee*
someone	**qualcuno**	*kwalkoono*
no one	**nessuno**	*nayssoono*
Which one do you want?	**Quale vuole?**	*kwalay vwolay*
one like that	**uno(-a) come quello(-a)**	
	oono(-a) komay kwayllo(-a)	
that one/this one	**quello(-a)/questo(-a)**	
	kwayllo(-a)/kwaysto(-a)	
not that one	**non quello(-a)**	*non kwayllo(-a)*
something	**qualcosa**	*kwalkosa*
nothing	**niente**	*neeayntay*
none	**nessuno(-a)**	*nayssoono(-a)*

Whose?

Whose is that?	**Di chi è quello(-a)?**	
	dee kee eh kwayllo(-a)	
It's …	**È …** *eh*	
mine/ours	**mio(-a)/nostro(-a)**	
	meeo(-a)/nostro(-a)	
yours (*formal*)/	**Suo(-a)/tuo(-a)**	
yours (*familiar*)	*soo-o(-a)/too-o(-a)*	
his/hers/theirs	**suo(-a)/di lui (di lei)/loro**	
	soo-o(-a)/dee looee(di layee)/loro	

How?

How would you like to pay?	**Come desidera pagare?** *komay dayzeedayra pagaaray*	
by cash	**in contanti** *een kontantee*	
by credit card	**con carta di credito**	
	kon karta dee kraydeeto	
How are you getting here?	**Come arriva qui?**	
	komay arreeva kwee	

by car	**in automobile/macchina** *een owtomobeelay/makkeena*
by bus	**in autobus** *een owtobooss*
on foot	**a piedi** *a peeaydee*
extremely	**estremamente** *aystraymamayntay*
quickly	**presto** *prehsto*
slowly	**lentamente** *lehntamayntay*
too fast	**troppo veloce** *troppo vehlochay*
totally	**totalmente** *totalmayntay*
very	**molto** *molto*
with a friend	**con un amico/un'amica** *kon oon ameeko/ameeka*

Is it …?/Are there …?

Is it …?	**È …?** *eh*
Is it free? *(unoccupied)*	**È libero(-a)?** *eh leebayro(-a)*
It isn't ready.	**Non è pronto(-a)** *non eh pronto(-a)*
Is there …?	**C'è …?** *cheh*
Are there …?	**Ci sono …?** *chee sono*
Is there a bus into town?	**C'è un autobus per il centro?** *cheh oon owtobooss pehr eel chayntro*
Are there buses to the airport?	**Ci sono autobus per l'aeroporto?** *chee sono owtoboos pehr la-ayroporto*
Here it is/they are.	**Eccolo(-a)/eccoli(-e).** *ehkkolo/ehkkolee*
There it is/they are.	**È là/sono là** *eh la/sono la*

IN A STORE

Come desidera pagare? *komay dayzeedayra pagaaray*
(How would you like to pay?)
In contanti, per favore. *een kontantee pehr favoray*
(Cash, please.)

Can/May?

May I have …?	**Posso avere …?** _posso avayray_
May we have …?	**Possiamo avere …?** _posseeamo avayray_
Can you tell me?	**Può dirmi …?** _pwo deermee_
Can you help me?	**Può aiutarmi?** _pwo aeeootaarmee_
Can I help you?	**Posso aiutare?** _posso aeeootaaray_
Can you direct me to …?	**Può indicarmi la via per …?** _pwo eendeekaarmee la veea pehr_
I can't.	**Non posso.** _non posso_

What do you want?

I'd like …	**Vorrei …** _vorrehee_
Do you have …?	**Ha …?** _ah_
We'd like …	**Vorremmo …** _vorrehmmo_
Give me …	**Mi dia …** _mee deea_
I'm looking for …	**Cerco …** _chayrko_
I need to …	**Ho bisogno di …** _beezonyo dee_
go …	**andare …** _andaaray_
find …	**trovare …** _trovaaray_
see …	**vedere …** _vaydayray_
speak to …	**parlare a …** _parlaaray ah_

18

OTHER USEFUL WORDS

fortunately	**fortunatamente** *fortoonatamayntay*
hopefully	**con (la) speranza di** *kon (la) spayrantsa dee*
of course	**naturalmente** *natooralmayntay*
perhaps/possibly	**forse/possibilmente** *forsay/posseebeelmayntay*
probably	**probabilmente** *probabeelmayntay*
unfortunately	**sfortunatamente** *sfortoonatamayntay*

EXCLAMATIONS

At last!	**Finalmente!** *feenalmayntay*
Damn!	**Maledizione!** *malaydeetseeonay*
Go on.	**Continui.** *konteenooee*
Good Heavens!	**Santo Cielo!** *santo cheeaylo*
I can't believe it!	**Incredibile!** *eenkraydeebeelay*
I don't mind.	**Mi è indifferente.** *mee eh eendeeffayrayntay*
No way!	**Assolutamente no.** *assolootamayntay no*
Really?	**Davvero?** *davvayro*
Rubbish.	**Stupidaggini.** *stoopeedadjeenee*
That's enough!	**Basta!** *basta*
That's true.	**É vero.** *eh vayro*
How are things?	**Come vanno le cose?** *komay vanno lay kosay*
Fine, thanks.	**Bene, grazie.** *baynay graatseeay*
great/brilliant	**magnifico** *manyeefeeko*
great	**benissimo** *bayneesseemo*
fine	**bene** *baynay*
not bad	**non c'è male** *non cheh malay*
okay	**abbastanza bene** *abbastantza baynay*
not good	**non bene** *non baynay*

ACCOMMODATIONS

Early reservations are essential in most major tourist centers. If you haven't booked, most towns and arrival points have a tourist information office (**azienda di promozione turistica** or **ufficio turistico**).

The Italian tourist organization **E.N.I.T.** publishes an annual directory of all the 37,000 hotels in Italy, with details of prices and facilities.

There is a wide range of accommodation options available, from **locande** (country inns) and **rifugi alpini** (mountain huts) to converted historic buildings, and the following:

albergo/hotel *al<u>bayr</u>go/o<u>te</u>hl*

Hotels in Italy are classified as **di lusso** (luxury class), or **di prima, seconda, terza, quarta categoria** (first, second, third, fourth class).

Note: especially near railway stations, one often finds **alberghi diurni** ("daytime hotels"). These have no sleeping accommodations, but provide bathrooms, rest rooms, hairdressers, telecommunication, and other similar services. Most close at midnight.

motel *mo<u>te</u>hl*

Increasing in number and improving in service; the Automobile Association of Italy has a list of recommended motels.

pensione *paynsee<u>o</u>nay*

Corresponds to a guest house; it usually offers **pensione completa** (full board) or **mezza pensione** (half board). Meals are likely to be from a set menu. **Pensioni** are classified first, second, and third class.

ostello della gioventù *os<u>te</u>hllo <u>day</u>lla jovayn<u>too</u>*

Youth hostel. They are open to holders of membership cards issued by the International Youth Hostel Association. The Italian Association of Youth Hostels (**AIG**) publishes a complete guide of youth hostels in Italy. Information can also be obtained from any **CTS** (**Centro Turistico Studentesco**). Reservations are advisable.

RESERVATIONS

In advance

Can you recommend a hotel in …?	**Può consigliarmi un albergo a …?** *pwo konsil<u>yar</u>mee oon al<u>bayr</u>go ah*
Is it near the center of town?	**È vicino al centro?** *eh vee<u>chee</u>no al <u>chayn</u>tro*

How much is it per night?	**Quanto costa una notte?**
	kwanto kosta oona nottay
Is there anything cheaper?	**C'è qualcosa di più economico?** *cheh*
	kwalkosa dee peeoo aykonomeeko
Could you reserve me a room there, please?	**Può prenotarmi una camera, per piacere?** *pwo prehnotaarmee oona kamayra pehr peeachayray*
How do I get there?	**Come ci arrivo?** *komay chee arreevo*

At the hotel

Do you have a room?	**Avete camere libere?**
	avayteh kamayray leebayray
I'm sorry. We're full.	**Mi dispiace, siamo al completo.**
	mee deespeeachay seeamo al komplayto
Is there another hotel nearby?	**C'è un altro albergo qui vicino?**
	cheh oon altro kwee veecheeno
I'd like a single/. double room	**Vorrei una camera singola/doppia.**
	vorrehee oona kamayra seengola/doppeea
A room with …	**Una camera con …**
	oona kamayra kon
twin beds	**due letti**
	doo-ay lehttee
a double bed	**un letto matrimoniale**
	oon lehtto matreemoneeaalay
a bath/shower	**bagno/doccia**
	baanyo/dotcha

AT THE HOTEL RECEPTION

Avete camere libere? *avayteh kamayray leebayray*
(Do you have any vacancies?)
Mi dispiace, siamo al completo. *mee deespeeachay seeamo al komplayto (I'm sorry, we're full.)*
Grazie. *graatseeay (Thank you.)*

I have a reservation.	**Ho una stanza prenotata.** *o oona stahnzah prenoht**a**htah*
My name is …	**Sono …** *sono*
We've reserved a double and a single room.	**Abbiamo prenotato una camera doppia e una camera singola.** *abbee**a**amo prayno**taa**to oona **ka**mayra **do**ppeea ay oona **ka**mayra **see**ngola*
I confirmed my reservation by mail.	**Ho confermato la prenotazione per lettera.** *o konfehr**maa**to la praynotatsee**o**nay pehr **leh**ttayra*
Could we have adjoining rooms?	**Possiamo avere camere adiacenti?** *possee**a**mo a**vay**ray **ka**mayray adja**cheh**ntee*

Amenities and facilities

Is there (a) … in the room?	**C'è … nella camera?** *cheh **nay**lla **ka**mayra*
air conditioning	**l'aria condizionata** *l**a**reea kondeetsee**onaa**ta*
TV/telephone	**la televisione/il telefono** *la taylayveezee**o**nay/ eel tay**lay**fono*
Does the hotel have a(n)…?	**L'albergo ha …** *lal**bay**rgo ah*
laundry service	**il servizio di lavanderia** *eel sayr**vee**tseeo dee lavanda**yree**a*
satellite TV	**la televisione via satellite** *la taylayveezee**o**nay **vee**a sa**tay**lleetay*
solarium	**il solarium** *eel sol**a**reeoom*
swimming pool	**la piscina** *la pee**shee**na*
Could you put … in the room?	**Può mettere … nella camera?** *pwo **may**ttehrray … **nay**lla **ka**mayra*
an extra bed	**un letto supplementare** *oon **leh**tto sooplplaymayn**ta**ray*
a crib [child's cot]	**una culla** *oona **koo**lla*
Do you have facilities for children/the disabled?	**È attrezzato per i bambini/i disabili?** *eh attrayts**aa**to pehr ee bam**bee**nee/ ee deesabeelee*

22

How long?

We'll be staying …	**Ci fermeremo …** chee fehrmay<u>ray</u>mo
overnight only	**solo per una notte** <u>solo</u> pehr <u>oo</u>na <u>not</u>tay
a few days	**per alcuni giorni** pehr al<u>koo</u>nee <u>jor</u>nee
a week (at least)	**una settimana (minimo)** <u>oo</u>na saytee<u>maa</u>na (<u>mee</u>neemo)
I don't know yet.	**Non so ancora.** non so an<u>ko</u>ra
I'd like to stay an extra night.	**Vorrei fermarmi per un'altra notte.** vor<u>reh</u>ee fehr<u>maar</u>mee pehr oon<u>aal</u>tra <u>not</u>tay

YOU MAY SEE

SOLO CAMERA … EURO	room only … euros
COLAZIONE COMPRESA	breakfast included
RISTORANTE	meals available
COGNOME/NOME	last name/first name
INDIRIZZO/DOMICILIO/	home address/street/
VIA/NUMERO	number
NAZIONALITÀ/PROFESSIONE	nationality/profession
DATA/LUOGO DI NASCITA	date/place of birth
NUMERO DI PASSAPORTO	passport number
NUMERO DI TARGA DEL VEICOLO	license plate [registration] number
LUOGO/DATA	place/date (of signature)
FIRMA	signature

YOU MAY HEAR

Posso vedere il suo **passaporto, per piacere?**	May I see your passport, please?
Per piacere, compili **questo modulo/firmi qui.**	Please fill out this form/sign here.
Qual è il suo numero **di targa?**	What's your license plate [registration] number?

PRICE

How much is it …?	**Quant'è …?** _kwanteh_
per night/week	**per notte/per settimana** _pehr nottay/pehr saytteemaana_
for bed and breakfast	**per il pernottamento e la colazione** _pehr eel pehrnottamaynto ay la kolatseeonay_
excluding meals	**pasti esclusi** _paastee ayskloozee_
for American Plan (A.P.) [full board]	**per la pensione completa** _pehr la paynseeonay komplayta_
for Modified American Plan (M.A.P.) [half board]	**per la mezza pensione** _pehr la mehdza paynseeonay_
Does the price include …?	**Il prezzo include …?** _eel prehtso eengklooday_
breakfast	**la colazione** _la kolatseeonay_
sales tax [VAT]	**l'IVA (Imposta Valore Aggiunto)** _leeva (eemposta valoray adjoonto)_
Do I have to pay a deposit?	**Devo pagare un anticipo?** _dayvo pagaaray oon anteecheepo_
Is there a reduction for children?	**Ci sono sconti per i bambini?** _chee sono skontee pehr ee bambeenee_

DECISIONS

May I see the room?	**Posso vedere la camera?** _posso vaydayray la kamayra_
That's fine. I'll take it.	**Va bene. La prendo.** _va baynay. la prayndo_
It's too …	**È troppo …** _eh troppo_
dark/small	**buia/piccola** _booeea/peekola_
noisy	**rumorosa** _roomoroza_
Do you have anything …?	**Ha qualcosa di …?** _ah kwalkoza dee_
bigger/cheaper	**più grande/più economico** _peeoo granday/peeoo aykonomeeko_
quieter/warmer	**più tranquillo/più caldo** _peeoo trankweello/peeoo kaldo_
No, I won't take it.	**No, non la prendo.** _no non la prehndo_

PROBLEMS

The ... doesn't work.	**... non funziona.** *non foontseeona*
air conditioning	**L'aria condizionata** *laareea kondeetseeonaata*
fan	**Il ventilatore** *eel vaynteelatoray*
heat	**Il riscaldamento** *eel reeskaldamaynto*
light	**La luce** *la loochay*
I can't turn the heat [heating] on/off.	**Non posso accendere/spegnere il riscaldamento.** *non posso atchayndehray/spaynyehray eel reeskaldamaynto*
There is no hot water/ toilet paper.	**Non c'è acqua calda/carta igienica.** *non cheh akwa kalda/karta eejayneeka*
The faucet [tap] is dripping	**Il rubinetto perde.** *eel roobeenehto pehrday*
The sink/toilet is blocked.	**Il lavello/water è bloccato.** *eel lavehllo/vateyr eh blokaato*
The window/door is jammed.	**La finestra/porta è bloccata.** *la feenaystra/porta eh blokaata*
My room has not been made up.	**La mia camera non è stata rifatta.** *la meea kamayra non eh staata reefatta*
The ... is broken.	**... è rotto(-a).** *eh rotto(-a)*
blind	**la tapparella** *la tapparehlla*
lock	**la serratura** *la sehrratoora*
There are insects in our room.	**Ci sono insetti nella nostra camera.** *chee sono eensehtee naylla nostra kamayra*

Action

Could you have that taken care of?	**Può farlo(-a) controllare?** *pwo farlo(-a) kontrollaaray*
I'd like to move to another room.	**Vorrei cambiare camera.** *vorrehee kambeeaaray kamayra*
I'd like to speak to the manager.	**Vorrei parlare con il direttore.** *vorrehee parlaaray kon eel deeraytoray*

REQUIREMENTS

In the hotel

Where's the …?	**Dov'è …?** *doveh*
bar	**il bar** *eel baar*
restroom [toilet]	**la toilette** *la toehlehteh*
parking lot [car park]	**il parcheggio** *eel parkaydjo*
dining room	**la sala da pranzo** *la sala da prandzo*
elevator [lift]	**l'ascensore** *lashaynsoray*
shower	**la doccia** *la dotchaa*
swimming pool	**la piscina** *la peesheena*
tour operator's bulletin board	**la bacheca dell'agente di viaggio** *la bakayka dayllajayntay dee veeadjo*
Does the hotel have a garage?	**L'albergo ha un garage?** *lalbayrgo ah oon garazh*
What time is the front door locked?	**A che ora chiudete?** *ah kay ora keeoodayteh*
What time is breakfast served?	**A che ora è servita la colazione?** *a kay ora eh sayrveeta la kolatseeonay*
Is there room service?	**C'è servizio camera?** *cheh sayrveetseeo kamayra*

YOU MAY SEE

SOLO PER RASOI	shavers only
USCITA D'EMERGENZA	emergency exit
PORTA ANTINCENDIO	fire door
NON DISTURBARE	do not disturb
FARE … PER OTTENERE LA LINEA ESTERNA	dial … for an outside line

Personal needs

The key to my room, please.	**La chiave della camera, per piacere.** *la keeaavay daylla kamayra pehr peeaachayray*
I've lost my key.	**Ho perso la chiave.** *o pehrso la keeaavay*
I've locked myself out of my room.	**Mi sono chiuso(-a) fuori della camera.** *mee sono keeooso(-a) fworee daylla kamayra*
Could you wake me at …?	**Può svegliarmi alle …?** *pwo zvaylyaarmee allay*
I'd like breakfast in my room.	**Vorrei la colazione in camera.** *vorrehee la kolatseeonay een kamayra*
Can I leave this in the safe?	**Vorrei mettere questo in cassaforte.** *vorrehee mayttehray kwaysto een kassafortay*
Could I have my things from the safe?	**Vorrei ritirare le mie cose dalla cassaforte.** *vorrehee reeteeraaray lay meeay kosay daylla kassafortay*
Where is …?	**Dov'è …?** *doveh?*
a maid	**una cameriera** *oona kamareeehra*
a bellman [porter]	**un portiere** *oon porteeayray*
our tour representative	**il nostro rappresentante?** *eel nostro rappraysayntaantay*
Do you have a(n)/some …?	**Ha …?** *ah*
bath towel	**un asciugamano** *oon ashoogamaano*
blanket	**una coperta** *oona kopehrta*
hangers	**grucce portabiti** *grootchay portabeetee*
pillow	**un cuscino** *oon koosheeno*
soap	**del sapone** *dayl saponay*
Is there any mail for me?	**C'è posta per me?** *cheh posta pehr meh*
Are there any messages for me?	**Ci sono messaggi per me?** *chee sono mayssadjee pehr meh*

Renting

We've reserved an
apartment/cottage
in the name of …
**Abbiamo prenotato un appartamento/una
villa a nome di …** *abbeeamo praynotato
oon appartamaynto/oona veella ah
nomay dee*

Where do we pick up
the keys?
Dove passiamo a prendere le chiavi? *dovay
passeeamo a prayndehray lay keeaavee*

Where is/are the …?
Dov'è …?/Dove sono …? *doveh/doveh sono*

electric meter
il contatore dell'elettricità
eel kontatoray dayll aylehttreecheeta

fuses
i fusibili *ee foozeebeelee*

stopcock
il rubinetto di arresto
eel roobeenehtto dee arraysto

water heater
lo scaldaacqua *low skalda-akwa*

Are there any spare …?
Ci sono … di ricambio?
chee sono … dee reekambeeo

fuses
fusibili *foozeebeelee*

gas bottles
bombole di gas *bombolay dee gaz*

sheets
lenzuola *layntsoo-ola*

Which day does the maid
come?
Che giorno viene la cameriera?
kay jorno veeaynay la kamareeayra

Where/When do I put out
the trash?
Dove/Quando si mettono fuori i rifiuti?
*dovay/kwando see mehttono fworee ee
reefeeootee*

Problems?

Where can I contact you?
Dove posso contattarla?
dovay posso kontattaarla

How does the stove/
water heater work?
Come funziona la stufa/lo scaldaacqua?
komay foontseeona la stoofa/lo skalda-akwa

The … is dirty.
Il … è sporco. *eel … eh sporko*

The … has broken down.
La … non funziona. *la … non foontseeona*

We accidentally
broke/lost …
Abbiamo accidentalmente rotto/perso …
*abbeeamo acheedayntalmayntay
rotto/pehrso*

USEFUL TERMS

dishes [crockery]	**le stoviglie** *lay stoveelyay*
freezer	**il congelatore** *eel konjaylatoray*
frying pan	**la padella** *la padehlla*
kettle	**il bollitore** *eel bolleetoray*
lamp	**la lampada** *la lampada*
refrigerator	**il frigorifero** *eel freegoreefayro*
saucepan	**la pentola** *la payntola*
stove [cooker] (gas/electric)	**la cucina a gas/elettrica** *la koocheena a gaz/aylehttreeka*
utensils [cutlery]	**le posate** *lay posatay*
washing machine	**la lavatrice** *la lavatreechay*
water heater	**lo scaldaacqua** *lo skalda-akwa*

Rooms

balcony	**il balcone** *eel balkonay*
bathroom	**il bagno** *eel baanyo*
bedroom	**la camera da letto** *la kamayra da lehtto*
dining room	**la sala da pranzo/il tinello** *la saala da prandzo/eel teenehllo*
kitchen	**la cucina** *la koocheena*
living room	**il soggiorno** *eel sodjorno*
bathroom [toilet]	**la toilette** *la toaylehteh*

YOUTH HOSTEL

Do you have any places left for tonight?	**Avete posti liberi per questa notte?** *postee leebayree pehr kwaysta nottay*
Do you rent bedding?	**Noleggiate la biancheria da letto?** *nolehdjatay la beeankayreea da lehtto*
What time are the doors locked?	**A che ora chiudete?** *a kay ora keeoodaytay*

CAMPING

Reservations

Is there a campsite near here?
C'è un campeggio qui vicino?
cheh oon kampaydjo kwee veecheeno

Do you have space for a tent/trailer [caravan]?
Avete un posto per una tenda/una roulotte? *avaytay oon posto pehr oona tehnda/oona roolot*

What is the charge …?
Quanto costa …? *kwanto kosta*

per day/week
al giorno/alla settimana
al jorno/alla saytteemaana

for a tent/a car
per una tenda/un'auto(mobile)
pehr oona tehnda/oonowto (oon owtomobeelay)

for a trailer [caravan]
per una roulotte *pehr oona roolot*

Facilities

Are there cooking facilities on site?
Ci sono attrezzature per cucinare? *chee sono attraytsatooray pehr koocheenaaray*

Are there any electrical outlets [power points]?
Ci sono delle prese di corrente? *chee sono dayllay prayzay dee korrayntay*

Where is/are the …?
Dov'è/Dove sono …?
doveh/dovay sono

drinking water
l'acqua potabile *lakwa potabeelay*

trash cans [dustbins]
i bidoni dei rifiuti
ee beedonee day reefeeootee

laundry facilities
la lavanderia (sing.) *la lavandayreea*

showers
le docce *lay dotchay*

Where can I get some butane gas?
Dove si compra il gas?
dovay see kompra eel gas

YOU MAY SEE

CAMPEGGIO VIETATO	no camping
ACQUA POTABILE	drinking water
VIETATO ACCENDERE FUOCHI/	no fires/barbeques
CUCINARE ALL'APERTO	

Complaints

It's too sunny.	**È troppo esposto al sole.** *eh troppo aysposto al solay*
It's too shady/crowded.	**È troppo ombreggiato/affollato.** *eh troppo ombraydjaato/affollaato*
The ground's too hard/ uneven.	**Il terreno è troppo duro/in dislivello.** *eel tayrrayno eh troppo dooro/een deesleevehllo*
Do you have a more level spot?	**C'è uno spazio su terreno più livellato?** *cheh oono spatseeo soo tayrrayno peeoo leevehllaato*
You can't camp here.	**Qui non può campeggiare.** *kwee non pwo kampaydjaaray*

Camping equipment

air mattress	**il materassino di gomma** *eel matayrassino dee gomma*
butane gas	**il campingaz** *eel campingaz*
campbed	**il lettino da campeggio** *eel lehtteeno da kampaydjo*
charcoal	**il carbone** *eel karbonay*
flashlight [torch]	**la torcia** *la torcheea*
groundcloth [groundsheet]	**il telone impermeabile** *eel taylonay eempehrmeeaabeelay*
hammer	**il martello** *eel martehllo*
kerosene [primus] stove	**il fornello da campeggio** *eel fornayllo da kampaydjo*
knapsack/backpack	**lo zaino** *lo dzaaeeno*
mallet	**il maglio** *eel malyo*
matches	**i fiammiferi** *ee feeammeefayree*
sleeping bag	**il sacco a pelo** *eel sakko a paylo*
tent	**la tenda** *la taynda*
tent pegs	**i picchetti** *ee peekkehttee*
tent pole	**il palo della tenda** *eel palo daylla taynda*

Checking out

Customers are required by law to have a receipt (**ricevuta fiscale**) for any services or goods purchased in hotels, shops, and restaurants.

Tipping: a service charge is generally included in hotel and restaurant bills. However, if the service has been particularly good, you may want to leave an extra tip.

What time do we have to check out?	**A che ora dobbiamo lasciare libere le camere?** *a kay ora dobbeeaamo lashaaray leebayray lay kamayray*
Could we leave our baggagehere until …	**Possiamo lasciare i bagagli fino alle …?** *posseeaamo lashaaray ee bagalyee feeno allay …*
I'm leaving now.	**Parto ora.** *parto ora*
Could you call me a taxi, please?	**Può chiamarmi un tassì, per piacere?** *pwo keeamaarmee oon tassee pehr peeachayray*
It's been a very enjoyable stay.	**È stato un soggiorno molto piacevole.** *eh staato oon sodjorno molto peeachayvolay*

PAYING

May I have my bill, please?	**Vorrei il conto, per favore.** *vorrehee eel konto pehr favoray*
I think there's a mistake.	**Penso che ci sia un erroreo.** *paynso kay chee seea oon ayrroray*
I've made … telephone calls.	**Ho fatto … telefonate.** *oh fatto … taylayfonatay*
I've taken … from the minibar.	**Ho preso … dal minibar.** *oh prayzo … dal minibar*
Can I have an itemized bill?	**Vorrei un conto dettagliato, per favore.** *vorrehee oon konto dayttalyaato pehr favoray*

TIPPING		
Bellman [Porter]	Hotel maid (per week)	Waiter
€2–3	€5	5–10%

EATING OUT

RESTAURANTS

Autogrill _owtogreel_
A large restaurant on an expressway [motorway]; usually table and cafeteria service available.

Bar _bar_
Bar; can be found on virtually every street corner; coffee and drinks served. In most of them you first have to pay and get a ticket from the cashier. Then you go to the counter and order what you want.

Caffè _kaffeh_
Coffee shop; generally food isn't served there except for breakfast. If it offers panini (sandwiches) or toast you'll be able to get a snack. Coffee shops always serve alcoholic beverages.

Gelateria _jaylatayreea_
Ice cream parlor; Italian ice cream is very tasty, rich and creamy, often reminiscent of old-fashioned, homemade ice cream. Ice cream and pastries can also be bought and consumed in a **sala da tè.**

Locanda _lokanda_
Simple restaurant serving local dishes.

Osteria _ostayreea_
Inn; wine and simple food are served.

Paninoteca _paneenotayka_
A sort of coffee shop where you can find a great variety of sandwiches (**panini**) served hot or cold.

Ristorante _reestorantay_
You'll encounter restaurants classified by stars or forks and knives and endorsed by everyone including travel agencies, automobile associations and gastronomic guilds. Bear in mind that any form of classification is relative. Some restaurants are judged according to their fancy décor while others – linen and chandeliers aside – are rated merely by the quality of their cooking.

Trattoria _trattoreea_
A medium-priced restaurant serving meals and drinks. The food is simple but can be surprisingly good if you happen to hit upon the right place. A more modest type of **trattoria** is the **taverna.** Bear in mind that some very expensive restaurants may call themselves **Osteria, Trattoria** or **Taverna.**

Most restaurants display a menu in the window. Many offer a tourist menu (**menù turistico**), a fixed-price three- or four-course meal with limited choice, or the specialty of the day (**piatto del giorno**).

All restaurants, no matter how modest, must issue a formal bill (**la ricevuta fiscale**) with VAT, or sales tax (**I.V.A.**). A customer may actually be stopped outside the premises and fined if he or she cannot produce this receipt. The bill usually includes cover (**il coperto**) and service (**il servizio**) charges as well.

You may have difficulty finding a restaurant with a non-smoking area.

MEAL TIMES

la colazione *la kolatsee<u>o</u>nay*
Breakfast is usually served at the hotel from 7 to 10 a.m. Hotels usually offer coffee or tea, bread, butter and jam. Italians usually have just a cappuccino and a brioche for breakfast.

il pranzo *eel <u>pran</u>dzo*
Lunch is served from 12.30 to 2 p.m.

la cena *la <u>chay</u>na*
Dinner begins at 8 p.m., but hotels tend to open their dining rooms earlier just for foreign tourists. The names of meals can be confusing. Lunch is sometimes called **colazione** and dinner **pranzo**, especially in towns. If you are invited out, make sure of the time, so you don't turn up at the wrong meal.

ITALIAN CUISINE

Italian cuisine consists of a lot more than just pasta. You will be amazed at the rich variety available: tasty hors d'œuvres, long-simmered soups, traditional meat dishes, fresh fish and shellfish, high-quality poultry, an incredible number of cheeses, not to mention the magnificent cakes and ice cream.

Each of Italy's 18 regions has its own specialty, never lacking in flavor or originality, inspired by sun-drenched fruit and vegetables. Italian cooking is like the country itself: colorful, happy, generous, exuberant.

wine cellar	**la cantina**	pizza parlor	**la pizzeria**
take-out/take-away	**da portar via**	self-service	**il self-service**
pub/public house	**il pub**	cafeteria	**il caffé**
stall	**la bancarella**	snack bar	**il bar**
canteen	**la mensa**		

ESSENTIAL

A table for … 1/2/3/4_	**Un tavolo per …** oon _tavolo_ pehr **uno(-a)/due/tre/quattro** _oo_no(-a)/_doo_-ay/tray/_kwatt_ro
Thank you.	**Grazie.** _graat_seeay
The bill, please.	**Il conto, per piacere.** eel _kon_to pehr peea_chay_ray

FINDING A PLACE TO EAT

Can you recommend a good restaurant?	**Può consigliare un buon ristorante?** pwo konseel_yaa_ray oon bwon reesto_ran_tay
Is there a … near here?	**C'è … qui vicino?** cheh … kwee vee_chee_no
traditional local restaurant	**un ristorante con cucina tradizionale** oon reesto_ran_tay kon koo_chee_na tradeetseeo_naa_lay
Chinese/Greek restaurant	**un ristorante cinese/greco** oon reesto_ran_tay chee_nay_say/_gray_ko
inexpensive restaurant	**una trattoria** _oo_na tratto_ree_a
Turkish restaurant	**un ristorante turco** oon reesto_ran_tay _toor_ko
vegetarian restaurant	**un ristorante vegetariano** oon reesto_ran_tay vayjaytaree_aa_no
Where can I find a/an …?	**Dove si trova …?** _do_vay see _tro_va
burger stand	**un chiosco dove vendono hamburger** oon kee_os_ko _do_vay _vayn_dono hamburger
café	**un bar** oon bar
café with terrace/garden	**un bar con terrazza/giardino** oon bar kon tayr_rat_sa/jar_dee_no
fast-food restaurant	**una tavola calda (un self-service)** _oo_na _ta_vola _kal_da (oon self-service)
ice cream parlor [parlour]	**una gelateria** _oo_na jaylatay_ree_a
pizzeria	**una pizzeria** _oo_na peettsay_ree_a
steak house	**ristorante specializzato in bistecche** reesto_ran_tay spaychalee_dza_to een bee_stayk_kay

RESERVATIONS

I'd like to reserve a table for 2.
Vorrei prenotare un tavolo per due. *vorrehee praynotaaray oon tavolo pehr dooay*

For this evening/ tomorrow at ...
Per questa sera/domani alle ... *pehr kwaysta sayra/domanee allay*

We'll come at 8:00.
Arriveremo alle otto. *arreevayraymo allay otto*

A table for 2, please.
Un tavolo per due, per piacere. *oon tavolo pehr dooay pehr peeachayray*

We have a reservation.
Abbiamo una prenotazione. *abbeeamo oona praynotatseeonay*

YOU MAY HEAR

A che nome, prego?	What's the name, please?
Mi dispiace. Siamo al completo.	I'm sorry. We're very busy/full.
Avremo un tavolo libero fra ... minuti.	We'll have a free table in ... minutes.
Dovrà ritornare fra ... minuti.	You'll have to come back in ... minutes.

Where to sit

Could we sit over there?
Possiamo sederci là? *posseeaamo saydayrchee la*

in a non-smoking area
in una zona per non fumatori *een oona dzona pehr non foomatoree*

by the window
vicino alla finestra *veecheeno alla feenaystra*

IN A RESTAURANT

Scusi! *scoosee (Excuse me!)*
Sì, Signora. *see sinyohrah (Yes, m'am.)*
Il menù, per favore. *eel maynoo pehr favoray (The menu, please.)*
Certamente. *cherta menteh (Certainly.)*

E' pronto(-a) per ordinare?	Are you ready to order?
Che cosa prende/desidera?	What would you like?
Vuole ordinare prima le bibite?	Would you like to order drinks first?
Consiglio ...	I recommend ...
Non abbiamo ...	We haven't got ...
Ci vogliono ... minuti.	That will take ... minutes.
Buon appetito!	Enjoy your meal.

ORDERING

Excuse me!
Scusi!
scoosee

May I see the wine list, please?
Posso vedere la lista dei vini, per piacere? *posso vedayray la leesta dehee veenee pehr peeachayray*

Do you have a set menu?
Avete un menù fisso?
avaytay oon maynoo feesso

Can you recommend some typical local dishes?
Può consigliare dei piatti tipici della regione? *pwo konseelyaarmee dehee peeattee teepeechee daylla rayjonay*

Could you tell me what ... is?
Cos'è ...?
kozay

I'd like ...
Vorrei ... *vorrehee*

a bottle/glass/carafe of ...
una bottiglia/un bicchiere/una caraffa di ... *oona botteelya/oon beekkeeehray/oona karaffa dee*

IN A RESTAURANT

Un tavolo per due, per piacere. *oon tavolo per dooay pehr peeachayray (A table for two, please.)*
Fumatori o non fumatori? *foomatoree o non foomatoree (Smoking or non-smoking?)*
Non fumatori. *non foomatoree (Non-smoking.)*

Side dishes

I prefer … without the …	**Preferisco … senza …** *prayfayreesko … sayntsa*
With a side order of …	**Con contorno di …** *kon kontorno dee*
Could I have salad instead of vegetables, please?	**Si può avere insalata al posto della verdura?** *see pwo avayray eensalaata al posto daylla verdoora*
Does the meal come with vegetables/potatoes?	**Il piatto include legumi/patate?** *eel peeatto eenklooday laygoomee/patatay*
Do you have any sauces?	**Ha delle salse?** *ah dayllay salsay*
Would you like … with your dish?	**Vuole … con il Suo piatto?** *vwolay kon eel soo-o peeatto*
vegetables	**verdura** *vayrdoora*
mixed salad	**insalata mista** *eensalaata meesta*
potatoes/French fries [chips]	**patate/patatine fritte** *patatay/patateenay freettay*
sauce	**la salsa** *la salsa*
ice	**il ghiaccio** *eel geeatcho*
May I have some …?	**Mi può portare …?** *mee pwo portaaray*
bread	**del pane** *dayl panay*
butter	**del burro** *dayl boorro*
lemon	**del limone** *dayl leemonay*
mustard	**della senape** *daylla saynapay*
pepper	**del pepe** *dayl paypay*
salt	**del sale** *dayl salay*
seasoning (oil/vinegar)	**dei condimenti (olio/aceto)** *dehee kondeemayntee (olyo/achayto)*
sugar	**dello zucchero** *dayllo tsookkayro*
(artificial) sweetener	**del dolcificante** *dayl dolcheefeekantay*

General requests

Could you bring a(n) (clean) …, please?	**Può portare … (pulito), per piacere?** _pwo portaaray (pooleeto) pehr peeachayray_
ashtray	**un portacenere** _oon portachaynayray_
cup/glass	**una tazza/un bicchiere** _oona tattsa/oon beekkeeeehray_
fork/knife	**una forchetta/un coltello** _oona forkehtta/oon koltehllo_
napkin	**un tovagliolo** _oon tovalyolo_
plate/spoon/little spoon	**un piatto/un cucchiaio/un cucchiaino** _oon peeatto/oon kookkeeaeeo/oon kookkeeaeeno_
I'd like some more …, please.	**Vorrei ancora un po' di …, per piacere.** _vorrehee ankora oon poh dee … pehr peeachayray_
Nothing more, thanks.	**Nient'altro, grazie.** _neeehntaltro gratseeay_
Where are the restrooms [toilets]?	**Dov'è la toilette?** _dovay la toylayttay_

Special requirements

I can't eat food containing …	**Non posso mangiare piatti che contengono …** _non posso manjaaray peeattee kay kontayngono_
salt/sugar	**sale/zucchero** _salay/tsookkayro_
Do you have meals/ drinks for diabetics?	**Avete piatti/bevande per diabetici?** _avaytay peeattee/bayvanday pehr deeabayteechee_
Do you have vegetarian dishes?	**Avete piatti vegetariani?** _avaytay peeattee vayjaytareeanee_

For the children

Do you have children's portions?	**Fate porzioni per bambini?** _fatay portseeonee pehr bambeenee_
Could you bring a child's seat, please?	**Può portare un seggiolone per bambini, per piacere?** _pwo portaaray oon saydjolonay pehr bambeenee pehr peeachayray_

FAST FOOD

Bars and cafés play an important part in Italian life; there is one on almost every corner. They are an ideal place to meet people, revive weary feet, write postcards, study maps, or just watch the world go by while sipping a cappuccino or beer. Bar staff are usually friendly and a great source of local information.

Something to drink

I'd like …	**Vorrei …** *vorrehee*
a beer	**una birra** *oona beerra*
coffee	**un caffè** *oon kaffeh*
with milk	**con latte** *kon lattay*
tea	**un tè** *oon teh*
red/white wine	**del vino rosso/bianco** *dayl veeno rosso/beeanko*

And to eat …

A piece/slice of …, please.	**Un pezzo/una fetta di … , per piacere** *oon pehtso/oona fehtta dee … pehr peeachayray*
I'd like two of those.	**Vorrei due di quelli(e).** *vorrehee doo-ay dee kwehllee (ay)*
burger/French fries	**un hamburger/delle patatine fritte** *oon hamburger/dayllay patateenay freettay*
cake/sandwich	**una torta/un panino** *oona torta/oon paneeno*
bun/pastry	**una pasta** *oona pasta*
an ice cream	**un gelato** *oon jaylaato*

Ice cream; flavors include: **alla vaniglia** or **alla crema** (vanilla), **al cioccolato** (chocolate), **alla fragola** (strawberry), **al limone** (lemon), **misto** (mixed).

a sandwich	**un panino** *oon paneeno*

Sandwich; you may want yours **con il formaggio** (cheese), **con il prosciutto cotto** (ham), **con il prosciutto crudo** (Parma ham) or **con il al salame** (salami).

A … portion, please.	**Una porzione … , per piacere.** *oona portseeonay … pehr peeachayray*
small/medium/large	**piccola/media/grande** *peekkola/medeea/granday*

IN A CAFÉ

Due caffè, per piacere. _dooay kaffeh pehr peeachayray_
(Two coffees, please.)
Nient'altro? _neeayn taltro_ *(Anything else?)*
No, grazie. _no graatseeay_ *(No, thanks.)*

COMPLAINTS

I have no knife/ fork/spoon.	**Non ho il coltello/la forchetta/il cucchiaio.** _non oh eel koltayllo/la forkaytta/eel kookeeaeeo_
There must be some mistake.	**Deve esserci un errore.** _dayvay ehssayrchee oon ehrroray_
That's not what I ordered.	**Non ho ordinato questo.** _non oh ordeenaato kwaysto_
I ordered …	**Ho ordinato …** _oh ordeenaato_
The meat is …	**La carne è …** _la karnay eh_
overdone	**troppo cotta** _troppo kotta_
underdone	**non abbastanza cotta** _non abbastantsa kotta_
too tough	**troppo dura** _troppo doora_
This is too …	**Questo è troppo …** _kwaysto eh troppo_
bitter/sour	**amaro/aspro** _amaaro/aspro_
This … is cold.	**Questo … è freddo.** _kwaysto … eh frehddo_
This isn't fresh.	**Questo non è fresco.** _kwaysto non eh fraysko_
How much longer will our food be?	**Quanto dobbiamo aspettare ancora?** _kwanto dobbeeaamo aspayttaray ankora_
We can't wait any longer. We're leaving.	**Non possiamo più aspettare. Andiamo via.** _non posseeaamo peeoo aspehttaaray andeeaamo veea_
This isn't clean.	**Questo non è pulito.** _kwaysto non eh pooleeto_
I'd like to speak to the head waiter/manager.	**Vorrei parlare con il capocameriere/ il direttore.** _Vorrehee parlaaray kon eel kapokamayree-ehray/eel deeraytoray_

PAYING

A service charge (**il servizio**) is generally included in restaurant bills, but if the service has been especially good, an extra tip (**la mancia**) is appropriate and appreciated: 5–10%. You may also find the following items added to your bill: **coperto** (cover charge), **supplemento** (surcharge).

The check [bill], please.	**Il conto, per piacere.**
	eel konto pehr peeachayray
We'd like to pay separately.	**Vorremmo pagare separatamente.**
	vorrehmmo pagaaray
	sayparatamayntay
It's all together, please.	**Un conto unico, per piacere.**
	oon konto ooneeko pehr peeachayray
I think there's a mistake.	**Penso ci sia un errore.**
	paynso chee seea oon ehrroray
What is this amount for?	**Per cosa è questa cifra?**
	pehr kosa eh kwaysta cheefra
I didn't order that. I had …	**Non ho ordinato questo. Ho preso …**
	non oh ordeenaato kwaysto. oh prayzo
Is service included?	**Il servizio è compreso ?**
	eel sayrveetseeo eh komprayzo
I would like to pay with this credit card.	**Vorrei pagare con la carta di credito.**
	vorrehee pagaaray kon la karta dee kraydeeto
I haven't got enough cash.	**Non ho abbastanza contanti.**
	non oh abbastantsa kontantee
Could I have a receipt?	**Vorrei la ricevuta.**
	vorrehee la reechayvoota

IN A RESTAURANT

Il conto, per piacere. *eel konto pehr peeachayray*
(*The bill please.*)
Certamente. Ecco a Lei. *cherta menteh ekko a lay*
(*Of course. Here you are.*)
Grazie. *graatseeay* (*Thank you.*)

COURSE BY COURSE

Breakfast

I'd like …	**Vorrei …** *vorrehee*
bread	**del pane** *dayl paanay*
butter	**del burro** *dayl boorro*
eggs	**delle uova** *dayllay wova*
fried/scrambled	**fritte/strapazzate** *freettay/strapattsaatay*
fruit juice	**un succo di frutta** *oon sookko dee frootta*
grapefruit/orange	**un pompelmo/un'arancia** *oon pompaylmo/oon arancheea*
milk	**del latte** *dayl lattay*
jam	**della marmellata** *daylla marmayllaata*
marmalade	**della marmellata d'arance** *daylla marmayllaata daranchay*
honey	**del miele** *dayl mee-aylay*
rolls	**dei panini** *dehee paneenee*
toast	**del pane tostato** *dayl paanay tostaato*

Appetizers/Starters

anchovies	**acciughe** *achoogay*
assorted appetizer	**antipasto assortito** *anteepasto assorteeto*
artichoke hearts in olive oil	**carciofini sott'olio** *karchofeenee sottolyo*
cured pork shoulder	**coppa** *koppa*
Bologna sausage	**mortadella** *mortadehlla*
cured ham from Parma	**prosciutto crudo di Parma** *proshootto kroodo dee parma*
pickled vegetables	**sottaceti** *sottachaytee*

bagna cauda *baanya kaooda*
raw vegetables accompanied by a hot sauce made from anchovies, garlic, oil, butter and sometimes truffles (Northern Italy)

Pizza

Pizza (plural **pizze**) is one of Italy's best-known culinary exports. The variety of toppings is endless. A **calzone** has basically the same ingredients, but the pastry forms a sealed sandwich, with the filling inside.

con i funghi	*kon ee foonggee*	with mushrooms
capricciosa	*kapreetchosa*	the cook's specialty
siciliana	*seecheeleeaana*	with black olives, capers and cheese

margherita *margayreeta*
named after Italy's first queen, the pizza ingredients (tomato, cheese and basil or oregano) reflect the national colors

napoletana *napolaytaana*
the classic pizza with anchovies, tomatoes, and cheese

quattro formaggi *kwattro formadjee*
pizza with four types of cheese, usually including **gorgonzola** and **caciotta**

quattro stagioni *kwattro stajonee*
"four seasons", containing a variety of vegetables: tomatoes, artichokes, mushrooms, olives; plus cheese, and ham

Soups

An Italian meal always includes a **pastasciutta** or a soup; some of them are sufficient for a main course.

brodo di manzo	*brodo dee manzo*	beef broth
busecca	*boozaykka*	thick tripe, vegetable and bean soup
cacciucco	*kachookko*	spicy seafood chowder/stew
crema di legumi	*krehma dee laygoomee*	legumes cream soup
minestrone	*meenehstronay*	vegetable soup (sometimes with noodles) sprinkled with parmesan cheese
passato di verdura	*passaato dee vehrdoora*	mashed vegetable soup, generally with croutons
zuppa alla pavese	*tsooppa alla pavayzay*	consommé with poached egg, croutons and cheese
zuppa di vongole	*tsooppa dee vonggolay*	clams and white wine soup

Pasta

Pasta (or **pastasciutta**) constitutes the traditional Italian first course. In addition to the well-known **spaghetti**, pasta comes in a bewildering variety of sizes and shapes– **penne** (quills), **tagliatelle** (flat noodles), and the following examples:

cannelloni *kanaylonee*
tubular dough stuffed with meat, cheese or vegetables, covered with a white sauce and baked

cappelletti *kapaylayttee*
small ravioli filled with meat, ham, cheese and eggs

fettuccine *faytoocheenay*
narrow flat noodles made with eggs

lasagne *lazaanyay*
thin layers of white or green (**lasagne verdi**) dough alternating with tomato sauce and sausage meat, white sauce and grated cheese; baked in the oven

tortellini *tortehlleenee*
rings of dough filled with ground meat in broth or with a sauce

Fish and seafood

acciughe	*atchoogay*	anchovies
anguilla	*anggooeella*	eel
bianchetti	*beeangkayttee*	herring/whitebait
gamberi	*gambayree*	prawns
granchi	*grangkee*	crabs
merluzzo	*mayrloottso*	cod
polipo	*poleepo*	octopus
sogliola	*solyola*	sole

Fish specialties Specialità di pesce

anguilla alla veneziana *anggooeella alla vaynaytseeaana*
eel cooked in sauce made from tuna and lemon

fritto misto *freetto meesto*
fry of small fish and shellfish

lumache alle milanese *loomaakay allay meelanaysay*
snails with anchovy, fennel and wine sauce

stoccafisso *stokkafeesso*
dried cod cooked with tomatoes, olives and artichoke

Meat

Among small fowl considered gourmet dishes in Italy are lark (**allodola**), thrush (**tordo**) and ortolan (**ortolano**). They are usually grilled or roasted.

Vorrei …	vorrehee	I'd like some …
del manzo	dayl _manzo_	beef
del pollo	dayl _pollo_	chicken
dell'anatra	dayll_aa_natra	duck
dell'oca	dayll_o_ka	goose
del prosciutto	dayl pro_shoo_tto	ham
dell'agnello	dayllan_yeh_llo	lamb
del maiale	dayl maee_aa_lay	pork
delle salsicce	_dayl_lay sal_seet_chay	sausages
del vitello	dayl vee_teh_llo	veal

Meat dishes

bistecca alla fiorentina _beestaykka alla feeoraynteena_
grilled steak flavored with pepper, lemon juice and parsley

cima alla genovese _cheema alla jaynovaysay_
rolled veal stuffed with eggs, sausage and mushrooms

cotoletta alla milanese _kostolaytta alla meelanaysay_
breaded veal cutlet

fegato alla veneziana _faygato alla vaynaytseeaana_
thin slices of calf's liver fried with onions

filetto al pepe verde _feelaytto al paypay vehrday_
filet steak in a creamy sauce with green peppercorns

galletto amburghese _gallaytto amboorgaysay_
young tender chicken, oven-roasted

involtini _eenvolteenee_
thin slices of meat rolled and stuffed with ham

polenta e coniglio _polehnta ay koneelyo_
rabbit stew with cornmeal mush

pollo alla romana _pollo alla romaana_
diced chicken with tomato sauce and sweet peppers

saltimbocca alla romana _salteembokah alla romaana_
veal escalope braised in marsala wine with ham and sage

You'll recognize: **asparagi**, **broccoli**, **carote**, **patate**, **spinaci**, **zucchini**.

cavolo	_kaavolo_	cabbage
cipolle	_cheepollay_	onions
funghi	_foonggee_	mushrooms
insalata mista	_eensalaata meesta_	mixed salad
lattuga	_lattooga_	lettuce
piselli	_peesehllee_	peas
pomodoro	_pomodoro_	tomato
verdura mista	_vehrdoora meesta_	mixed vegetables

carciofi alla giudea _karchofee alla jeeoodeea_
deep-fried artichoke, originally a specialty of the old Jewish quarter in Rome

carciofi alla romana _karchofee alla romaana_
whole lightly stewed artichokes stuffed with garlic, salt, olive oil, wild mint
(**mentuccia**) and parsley

fagioli alla toscana _fajolee alla toskana_
Tuscan-style beans, seasoned with salt, black pepper and crude olive oil

fagioli in umido _fajolee een oomeedo_
all types of haricot beans cooked in tomato sauce and spices

funghi porcini arrosto _foonggee arrosto_
boletus mushrooms roasted or grilled with garlic, parsley and chili peppers

peperoni ripieni _paypayronee reepeeaynee_
stuffed sweet peppers (usually containing ground meat); similarly,
zucchini is also served this way (**zucchini ripieni**)

Sauces

Italian cooks are masters at making the sauces that make spaghetti and
macaroni taste so delicious.

al burro	_al boorro_	butter, grated parmesan
bolognese	_bolonyayzay_	tomatoes, ground meat, onions, herbs
carbonara	_karbonaara_	bacon, cheese, eggs, olive oil
pesto	_paysto_	basil leaves, garlic, cheese
al pomodoro	_al pommodoro_	tomatoes, garlic, basil

Cheese

bel paese	smooth cheese with delicate taste
caciotta	firm, usually mild cheese; some sharper varieties can be found
caciocavallo	firm, slightly sweet cheese from cow's or sheep's milk
gorgonzola	blue-veined cheese, rich with a tangy flavor
grana	a grained cheese similar to parmesan originating from Padova usually grated on pasta dishes
mascarpone	a thick, full-fat creamy cheese mostly used for desserts; similar to clotted cream
mozzarella	soft, unripened cheese with a bland, flavor, made from buffalo's milk in the south, elsewhere with cow's milk
parmigiano (-reggiano)	parmesan, a hard cheese generally grated for use in hot dishes and pasta but also eaten alone
pecorino	a hard cheese with a strong flavor made from sheep's milk usually grated on certain pasta dishes
provolone	a firm, tasty cheese
ricotta	soft cow's or sheep's milk cheese

Fruit

You'll recognize: **banane, dattero, limone, melone, pera**.

ciliege	*cheelee-ehjay*	cherries
uva	*oova*	grapes
arancia	*arancha*	orange
pesca	*pehska*	peach
prugna	*proonya*	plum
lamponi	*lamponee*	raspberries
fragole	*fraagolay*	strawberries
anguria	*angoorreea*	watermelon (northern Italy)
cocomero	*kokomayro*	watermelon (southern Italy)

Dessert

cassata siciliana *kassaata seecheeleeaana*
sponge cake garnished with sweet cream cheese, chocolate and candied fruit

tiramisù *teerameesoo*
mascarpone, eggs and sponge cake chocolate dessert

DRINKS

Aperitifs

Often bittersweet, some aperitifs have a wine and brandy base with herbs and bitters, while others may have a vegetable base.

americano *amayreekaano*: vermouth with bitters, brandy and lemon peel

aperol *_apayrol*: a non-alcoholic bitters

bitter analcolico *beettehr analkoleeko*: a non-alcoholic aperitif

Campari *kampaaree*: reddish-brown bitters with orange peel and herbs

Campari soda *kampaaree soda*: Campari diluted with soda

Cynar *cheenaar*: produced from artichoke

gingerino *jeenjehreeno*: ginger-flavored aperitif

Martini *marhteenee*: brand-name vermouth, sweet or dry

neat/straight	**liscio** *leesho*	
on the rocks	**con ghiaccio** *kon geeacho*	
with (seltzer or soda) water	**con acqua (di seltz)** *kon akwa (dee sehltz)*	

Beer

Do you have … beer?	**Avete della birra …?** *avayta daylla beerra*
bottled/draft/draught	**in bottiglia/alla spina** *een botteelya/alla speena*

Wine

Italy is one of the most important wine producers in Europe. Some of the country's best come from northwestern Italy (like *Barbaresco*, *Barbera* and *Barolo*). Italy's best-known wine abroad is Chianti, particularly **classico** and **riserva** (superior quality); the best is produced between Florence and Siena.

Quality bottled wine from the various regions is now easily available all over Italy in restaurants and specialized wine shops (*enoteche*).

Don't expect a trattoria to offer more than a few types of wine. In smaller places you may find **vino sfuso** (unbottled wine usually served as house wine) at a moderate price, served in one-quarter, one-half or one-liter carafes.

I'd like a bottle of white/red wine.	**Vorrei una bottiglia di vino bianco/rosso.** *vorrehee oona botteelya dee veeno beeanko/rosso*
I'd like the house wine, please.	**Desidero il vino della casa, per favore.** *dayzeedayro eel veeno dayllya kassa pehr favoray*

Italian wines may be named by place (e.g. *Chianti*, *Frascati*, *Asti*), descriptive term (e.g. **classico**, **dolce**, **riserva**, **superiore**), grape (e.g. **Barbera**, **Moscato**, **Pinot nero**), proprietary name or a combination of these elements.

Type of wine	*Examples*
sweet white wine	**Aleatico, Vino Santo (Tuscany); Marsala and Malvasia (Sicily), Moscato, Passito di Pantelleria**
dry white wine	**Frascati (Latium), Verdicchio dei Castelli di Jesi (Adriatic Marches), Orvieto (Umbria), Vermentino (Sardinia), Corvo bianco, Colombo Platino (Sicily); Cortese di Gavi (Liguria) Gavi dei Gavi (Piedmont) Chardonnay, Pinot bianco, Pinot grigio (Friuli); local white wine generally falls into this category**
rosé	**Lagrein (Trentino-Alto Adige)**
light-bodied red wine	**Bardolino, Valpolicella (Lake Garda); Vino Novello (in the Autumn); local red wine, including Italian-Swiss Merlot, usually fits into this category**
full-bodied red wine	**Barolo, Barbera, Barbaresco, Dolcetto, Gattinara, Nebbiolo (Piedmont); Amarone (Veneto); Brunello di Montalcino (one of the most famous wines in Italy), Chianti Classico, Vino Nobile di Montepulciano (Tuscany); Corvo Rosso (Sicily).**
sparkling wine	**Asti Spumante**
sparkling dry white wine	**Prosecco, Ferrari Brut Spumante; metodo champenoise in general**
sparkling sweet red wine	**Braghetto d'Acqui (Piedmont); Fragolino (made from "uva fragola" with a distinct strawberry flavour, Veneto region)**

Reading the label

abboccato semi-dry"	**leggero** light
amabile slightly sweet	**pieno** full-bodied
bianco white	**rosato/rosatello** rosé
DOC guarantee of origin	**rosso** red
DOCG highest quality wine	**secco** dry
dolce sweet	**spumante** sparkling
imbottigliato dal produttore	**vino del paese** local wine
all'origine bottled by producers	**vino tipico** basic table wine

Other drinks

You'll certainly want to take the opportunity to sip an after-dinner drink. If you'd like something that approaches French cognac try **Vecchia Romagna etichetta nera** or **Carpenet Malvolta Stravecchio**.

If you feel like an after-dinner drink (**un digestivo**), why not try the following:

amaro   *amaaro*

Bitter; three of the most popular being *Amaro Averna*, *Amaro Lucano* or *Amaro Montenegro* (bittersweet), or a glass of *Fernet-Branca* (very bitter) should fit the bill.

liquore   *leekworay*

Popular liqueurs include *Strega* (sweet herb), *Sambuca* (aniseed-flavored), *Amaretto* (almond), *Millefiori* (herb and alpine flower), *Silvestro* (herb and nut).

You'll recognize: **un brandy**, **un cognac**, **un gin e tonic**, **un porto**, **un rum**, **una vodka**.

Non-alcoholic drinks

I'd like ...	**Vorrei ...** *vorrehee*
hot chocolate	**una cioccolata calda** *oona chokkolaata kalda*
lemonade	**una limonata** *oona leemonaata*
milk shake	**un frullato** *oon froollaato*
mineral water	**dell'acqua minerale** *dayllakwa meenayraalay*
carbonated/non-carbonated	**gassata/naturale** *gassaata/natooraalay*
tonic water	**dell'acqua tonica** *dayllakwa toneeka*

un caffè   *oon kaffeh*

Any coffee drinker will be spoiled in Italy; try un **caffè** (**espresso**), strong and dark with a rich aroma, served in demi-tasses, or **un ristretto** (concentrated espresso); alternatively, ask for **un caffè lungo** (weaker coffee), which can be **con panna** (with cream), or **con latte** (with milk). **Un cappuccino** (coffee and hot milk, sometimes dusted with cocoa) is also a must; while in summer, **un caffè freddo** (iced coffee) is popular.

un succo di frutta   *oon sookko dee frootta*

Common juices include: **un succo di limone** (lemon), **di pompelmo** (grapefruit), **di pomodoro** (tomato) and **d'arancia** (orange); for a freshly squeezed fruit juice ask for **una spremuta**.

MENU READER

Italian cooking is essentially regional. Although there are many well-known dishes that are common to the whole of Italy, the terminology may vary from place to place. (There are at least half a dozen names for octopus or squid!) So, be prepared for regional variations to the terms appearing in this Menu Reader.

HOW IT IS COOKED

baked	**al forno**	*al forno*
breaded	**impanato(-a)**	*eempanaato(-a)*
boiled	**bollito(-a)**	*bolleeto(-a)*
braised	**stufato(-a)**	*stoofaato(-a)*
diced	**tagliato(-a) a cubetti**	*talyaato(-a) a koobayttee*
fried	**fritto(-a)**	*freetto(-a)*
grilled	**alla griglia**	*alla greelya*
roasted	**arrosto(-a)**	*arrosto(-a)*
poached	**in camicia**	*een kameecha*
marinated	**marinato(-a)**	*mareenaato(-a)*
sautéed	**saltato(-a)**	*saltaato(-a)*
smoked	**affumicato(-a)**	*affoomeekaato(-a)*
spicy	**speziato(-a)/piccante**	*spaytsaato(-a)/peekkantay*
steamed	**al vapore**	*al vaporay*
stewed	**in umido**	*een oomeedo*
stuffed	**ripieno(-a)**	*reepeeayno(-a)*
creamed	**in purè**	*een pooreh*
very rare	**quasi crudo(-a)**	*kwasee kroodo(-a)*
rare/underdone	**al sangue**	*al sanway*
medium	**a puntino**	*a poonteeno*
well-done	**ben cotto(-a)**	*behn kotto (a)*

A

a puntino medium
a scelta choice
abbacchio roast lamb; ~ **al forno con patate** with potatoes; ~ **alla**

cacciatora "hunting style": diced and cooked with white wine, garlic, rosemary, anchovy paste and peppers
abbacchio alla scottadito tender grilled lamb cutlets

(all')abruzzese Abruzzi style; with red peppers and sometimes ham
acciughe anchovies
aceto vinegar
acetosella sorrel
acqua water; ~ calda hot water; ~ minerale mineral water; ~ tonica tonic water
acquacotta soup of bread and vegetables, sometimes with egg and cheese
affettati cold cuts; ~ misti mixed cuts of pork
affogato poached
affumicato smoked
aglio garlic; ~ olio, peperoncino sauce of garlic, olive oil, sweet peppers, anchovies and parmesan
agnello lamb; ~ abbacchio very young lamb
agnolotti round-filled pasta
(all')agro dressing of lemon juice and oil
agrodolce sweet-sour dressing of caramelized sugar, vinegar and flour
aguglie garfish
ai ferri grilled
ai funghi (pizza) with mushrooms
ai funghi porcini sauce of boletus mushrooms
al burro with butter and grated parmesan
al forno baked
al sangue rare/underdone
al sugo with tomato sauce and grated parmesan
al tartufo sauce of grated truffle
al, all', alla in the style of; with
ala wing
albicocca apricot
alfredo dairy sauce
alice anchovy

alici al limone baked anchovies with lemon juice
alla boscaiola with eggplant, mushrooms and tomato sauce
alla carrettiera "cart driver style"; with hot peppers and pork
alla graticola barbequed
alla griglia grilled
alla milanese with marrow, white wine, saffron and parmesan (risotto)
alla Norma with spices and tomato sauce (Sicily)
alla pescatora with tomatoes and seafood
alla rustica with garlic, anchovies and oregano
alla spina draft/draught (beer)
alle vongole sauce of clams, garlic, parsley, pepper, olive oil, sometimes tomatoes
allo spiedo broiled; spit-roasted
allodola lark
alloro bay leaf
amaro after-dinner drink/digestive
amatriciana sauce of tomatoes, pancetta, onions, garlic and hot pepper
americano a vermouth
ananas pineapple
anelli small egg-pasta rings
anguilla eel; ~ alla veneziana cooked in sauce made from tuna and lemon
anguria watermelon (northern Italy)
animelle di vitello calf's sweetbreads fried in butter and Marsala
anitra duck; ~ selvatica wild duck
annegati slices of meat in white wine or Marsala

antipasti appetizers, hors d'oeuvres; **~ a scelta** of one's choice; **~ assortiti** assorted; **~ di mare** seafood

aperitivi aperitifs

Aperol a non-alcoholic bitters

arachidi peanuts

aragosta lobster

arancia orange

aranciata orangeade

arancini popular and tasty southern Italian rice snack specialties

aringa herring

arista loin of pork; **~ alla fiorentina** roast with garlic, cloves and rosemary

arrosto roast(ed)

arselle scallops

asparagi asparagus; **~ alla Fiorentina** with fried eggs and cheese

assortito assorted

astice lobster

attesa: 15 minuti waiting time: 15 minutes

B

baccalà dried salt cod; **~ alla romana** cooked with tomato sauce, garlic and parsley; **~ alla vicentina** cooked in milk

bagna cauda raw vegetables served with a hot sauce (*a specialty in northern Italy*)

barbabietola beet

basilico basil

bavette type of flat spaghetti

beccaccia woodcock

beccaccino snipe

bel paese smooth cheese with delicate taste

ben cotto well-done

bevande drinks; **~ analcoliche** non-alcoholic drinks

bianchetti herring/whitebait

bianco white (wine)

bibita soft drink

bicchiere glass

bieta swiss chard

bionda light (beer)

birra beer; **~ rossa** stout (dark beer)

biscotti cookies/biscuits

bistecca steak; **~ di cinghiale** wild boar in a sweet-sour sauce; **~ alla fiorentina** grilled and flavored with pepper, lemon juice and parsley; **~ di filetto** rib steak

bitter analcolico a non-alcoholic aperitif

bollito boiled

bollito misto mixed boiled meats

bologna smooth, mild, slightly smoked sausage, usually of pork or beef, occasionally of veal or chicken

bolognese sauce of tomatoes, ground meat, onions and herbs

bottiglia bottle

braciola chop or cutlet

branzino (sea) bass

brasato braised

briciolata olive oil, black pepper and crisp breadcrumb sauce

broccoli broccoli; **~ al burro e formaggio** with butter and cheese; **~ alla romana** sauteed in olice oil and braised in wine

brodo bouillon, broth, soup

bruidda fish soup

bucatini thick spaghetti; **~ con le sarde alla palermitana** with fresh sardines

budino pudding; **~ di ricotta** souffle with ricotta cheese and candied fruits

burrida fish stew with dogfish and skate *(Sardinia)*

burro butter; **~ e salvia** butter and sage sauce

busecca thick tripe, vegetable and bean soup

C

cacciagione game

cacciucco spicy seafood chowder/stew

cachi persimmon

caciocavallo firm, slightly sweet cheese

caciotta firm, mild cheese

caffè coffee

caffè freddo iced coffee

calamaretti baby squid

calamari squid

caldo hot

camoscio chamois

Campari reddish-brown bitters, flavored with orange peel and herbs; has a quinine taste; **~ soda** *campari* diluted with soda, one of the most common Italian apertifis

canederli bread, ham and salami dumplings

cannariculi fried honey biscuits

cannella cinnamon

cannelloni stuffed tubular pasta baked with a white sauce; **~ alla partenopea** with ricotta, mozzarella and ham

cannoli sweetened ricotta cheese stuffed in deep-fried pastry shells

canoe di mele canoe-shaped pastry boats with rum pastry cream and glazed apples

canoe salate savory canoes

capellini thin type of spaghetti

caponata olives, eggplants and anchovies *(Sicily)*

capone apparecchiate mahi mahi fish fried with tomatoes, capers, olives *(Sicily)*

cappelletti "little hats" filled pasta

capperi capers

cappone capon

capretto kid goat; **~ ripieno al forno** stuffed with herbs and oven-roasted

capricciosa the cook's specialty (pizza)

capriolo roebuck

carbonara sauce of bacon, pepper, pecorino, cheese, eggs and olive oil

carciofi artichokes; **~ alla giudea** deep-fried; **~ alla romana** lightly stewed and stuffed

carciofini sott'olio artichoke hearts in olive oil

carne meat; **~ ai ferri** grilled

carota carrot; **~ rossa** beet

carpa carp

carrettiera sauce of tuna, mushrooms, tomato purée, freshly ground pepper

cassata ice cream with candied fruit (spumone); **~ siciliana** garnished sponge cake

castagna chestnut

castagnaccio chestnut cake with sultanas and pine nuts *(Tuscany)*

caviale caviar

cavolfiore cauliflower; **~ stracciato** boiled and fried in olive oil and garlic

cavolini di Bruxelles Brussels sprouts

cavolo cabbage
ceci chickpeas
cedro citron
cereali cereal
cervello brains
cervo deer
cetriolini pickles/gherkins
cetriolo cucumber
chiodi di garofano cloves
cicoria chicory
ciliege cherries
cima alla genovese rolled veal stuffed with eggs, sausage and mushrooms
cima genovese cold veal stuffed with onions, herbs and calf's brains
cinghiale wild boar
cioccolata (calda) (hot) chocolate
cipolle onions
cipollina spring onion
clementino seedless mandarin orange
cocomero watermelon (*Rome, southern Italy*)
colazione breakfast
con with
con acqua (di seltz) with (seltzer or soda) water
con briciolata with toasted breadcrumbs
con i funghi with mushrooms
con ghiaccio on the rocks (with ice)
con il sugo di melanze e peperoni sauce with pepper and eggplant
con il latte with milk
con le lumache with snails and parsley
con il limone with lemon
con la panna with cream
con le polpettine with tiny meatballs

con la porchetta with tasty cold pork (sandwich)
con la salsa di noci with walnut sauce
conchiglie conch shell-shaped pasta
coniglio rabbit; **~ ai capperi** cooked with capers
contorno a scelta choice of vegetables
coppa cured pork shoulder
cosciotto leg
costata al prosciutto filled chop
costola rib
costolette di maiale al finocchio braised pork chops with white wine and fennel seed
cotechino con lenticchie sausage-like spicy pork mix
cotogna quince
cotoletta cutlet; **~ alla milanese** breaded veal cutlet
cotto cooked; **~ a vapore** steamed
cozze mussels
crema custard; **~ di legumi** legumes cream soup; **~ di pomodori** tomato cream soup
crespelle di farina dolce chestnut-flour crepes with ricotta and rum
crostacei shellfish
crostata pie; **~ di mele** apple pie; **~ di ricotta** cheesecake with raisins and Marsala
crudo di Parma cured ham from Parma
cumino cumin
cuscus couscous
Cynar aperitif produced from artichoke

D

---

d', di of
datteri dates

decaffeinato decaffeinated
dentice type of sea bream
digestivo after-dinner drink
ditali pasta thimbles
dolce cake; dessert; mild (cheese); sweet (wine)
doppio double (a double shot)

E

elicoidali short, twisted pasta tubes
eperlano smelt

F

fagiano pheasant; ~ **al tartufo** stuffed with truffles
fagioli (haricot) beans; ~ **all'uccelletto** cooked in tomatoes and black olives; ~ **in umido** cooked in tomato sauce
fagioli alla toscana Tuscan-style beans, simmered for hours and garnished with salt, black pepper and crude olive oil
fagiolini French (green) beans
faraona guinea fowl
farcito stuffed
farfalle butterfly-shaped pasta
farfallini small bow-shaped egg-pasta
favata beans and port stew *(Sardinia)*
fave broad beans
fazzoletti salati savory turnovers
fegato liver; ~ **alla veneziana** thin slices fried with onions; ~ **alla salvia** with tomatoes, garlic and sage
fesa round cut from the rump
fetta di pizza slice of pizza
fettuccine egg-pasta ribbons; ~ **Alfredo** with parmesan and cream
fico fig

filetto fillet; ~ **al pepe verde** fillet steak served in a creamy sauce with green peppercorns
finocchio fennel
focaccia savory flatbread; ~ **alla salvia** sage bread; ~ **alla salsiccia** sausage bread; ~ **alle noci** walnut bread; ~ **genovese** savory bread with sage and olive oil
focaccia al gorgonzola warm yeast flatbread topped with cheese
fonduta hot dip of Fontina cheese, egg yolks and truffles
formaggio cheese
fragole strawberries
fragoline di bosco wild strawberries
freddo cold
frittata omelet; ~ **campagnola** with onion, grated cheese, milk and cream; ~ **primaverile** with vegetables
fritte al buro nero brains with black butter
fritte alla fiorentina marinated, breadcrumbed, fried brains served with spinach
fritto fried
fritto misto a fry of various small fish and shellfish or meat and vegetables
frullato milk-shake
frustenga cornmeal fruit cake
frutta fruit
frutti di mare seafood
funghi mushrooms; ~ **alla parmigiana** stuffed with breadcrumbs, Parmesan, garlic, herbs; ~ **porcini arrosto** roasted or grilled with chili peppers
fusilli pasta twists

G

galletto amburghese young tender chicken, oven-roasted

gallina stewing fowl
gallo cedrone grouse
gamberetti shrimps
gamberi prawns
gassata carbonated/fizzy (water)
gelato ice cream
gianduia cold chocolate pudding
gin e tonic gin and tonic
gingerino ginger-flavored aperitif
(also sold in small bottles)
gnocchi alla genovese dumplings
with pesto sauce
gnocchi di patate potato dumplings
gorgonzola blue-veined cheese
granchi crabs
granita coarse sorbet ice cream
gronghi conger eel

I

**i nostri piatti di carne sono
serviti con contorno** our meat
dishes are accompanied by
vegetables
in bianco without tomato sauce
in bottiglia bottled (beer)
in casseruola in casserole
in umido stewed
indivia endive
insalata salad
insalata di frutti di mare prawns
and squid with lemon, pickles and
olives
insalata di pollo chicken salad
with green salad, lemon and cream
insalata mista mixed salad
insalata russa diced boiled
vegetables in mayonnaise
involtini thin slices of meat (beef,
veal or pork) rolled and stuffed

L

lamponi raspberries

lamprede lampreys
lasagne thin layers of pasta lined
with meat and tomato sauce with
Bel Paese and Mozzarella cheeses;
~ al forno oven baked lasagna; **~
con l'anitra** with duck; **~ con le
verdure** vegetable lasagna
lasagnette del lucchese lasagna
with sauce of spinach, ricotta,
chicken livers
lattaiolo cinnamon custard
latte milk
lattuga lettuce
lauro bay
leggero light (wine)
lenticchie lentils
lepre hare; **~ in agrodolce** with
pine kernels, sultanas and
chocolate; **~ piemontese** cooked in
Barbera wine, sprinkled with herbs
and bitter chocolate
lesso boiled
limonata lemonade
limone lemon
lingua tongue
linguine type of flat spaghetti
liquore liqueur
liscio straight/neat
lo chef consiglia the chef
recommends …
lombata/lombo loin
lombo di maiale al forno garlic-
roasted pork loin
lombo di maiale al prosciutto
grilled pork loin with prosciutto
luccio pike
luganeghe fresh pork sausages
sold by the length
lumache snails; snail shell-shaped
pasta
lumache alle milanese snails with
anchovy, fennel and wine sauce

lumache di mare sea snails
lunette half-moon-shaped stuffed pasta

M

maccheroni alla chitarra handmade pasta cut into strips
macchiato with milk (coffee)
maggiorana marjoram
maiale pork
malfatti thin pasta strips
mandarino tangerine
mandorle almonds
manzo beef
margherita tomato, cheese and basil pizza
marinara sauce of tomatoes, olives, garlic, clams and mussels
marinato marinated
marmellata jam; ~ **d'arance** marmalade
mascarpone a thick, full-fat creamy cheese mostly used for desserts, similar to clotted cream
Martini a brand-name vermouth, sweet or dry; not to be confused with a martini cocktail
medaglioni round fillet
mela apple
melanzane eggplant/aubergine
mele apples
melone melon
menta mint
menù a prezzo fisso set menu
merlano whiting
merluzzo cod
mezzo pollo arrosto half a roasted chicken
midollo marrow
miele honey
minestra soup; ~ **di funghi** cream of mushroom soup; ~ **di sedano e**

riso celery and rice; ~ **in brodo** with noodles or rice
minestrone a thick vegetable soup (sometimes with noodles) sprinkled with parmesan cheese
mirtilli blueberries
misto mixed
molle soft (egg)
montone mutton
more blackberries
mortadella Bologna sausage
mostaccioli chocolate biscuits
mozzarella soft, unripened cheese; ~ **con i pomodori** with tomatoes

N

napoletana anchovies, tomatoes, cheese (pizza topping)
nasello coal-fish
naturale still (water)
nero black (coffee)
nocciole hazelnuts
noce di cocco coconut
noce moscata nutmeg
noci walnuts
nodini veal chops

O

oca goose
odori herbs
olio (d'oliva) (olive) oil
olive olives
orata type of sea bream
orecchiette ear-shaped pasta
origano oregano
ortolano ortolan
osso buco braised veal knuckles and shins
ostriche oysters

P

palombacce allo spiedo wood pigeon, spit-roasted

pan di Spagna sponge cake

pancetta affumicata smoked bacon

pandorato alla crema di formaggio fried bread with cream cheese

pandoro large, Cristmas sponge cake served with powdered vanilla on top

pane bread; **~ al latte** milk bread: **~ all'olio** olive oil white bread: **~ tostato** toast

pane, grissini e coperto bread, breadsticks (**grissini**) and table cover charge

panettone butter-enriched Christmas bread with candied fruit, sultanas and raisins

panforte similar to **pangiallo**

pangiallo fairly hard nut and honey cake

panini rolls

panino imbottito sandwich

panna cotta delicious Italian adaptation of blancmange and creme brulé

panpepato very spicy nut cake

pansotti con salsa di noci alla ligure triangles stuffed with greens in walnut sauce

pappardelle fat ribbons of egg-pasta; **~ alla lepre** with hare sauce

papriot thick spinach soup

parmigiana breaded aubergine slices with tomato sauce and mozzarella

parmigiano (-reggiano) parmesan

passato di verdura mashed vegetable soup, generally with croutons

pasta pasta, noodles; **~ e ceci** with chickpeas; **~ e fagioli** with beans

pasta Maddalena plain génoise cake

pastasciutta pasta

pasticcini pastries

pasticcio macaroni, white sauce, meat and tomato

pastiera ricotta cake with wheat berries

pastina small pasta pieces; **~ in brodo** in broth

patate potatoes

patatine fritte French fries, chips

pecorino hard sheep's cheese

penne pasta quills

peperonata peppers sauteed with tomato and onion

peperoni peppers; **~ ripieni** stuffed

pera pear

pernice partridge

pesca peach

pescanoce nectarine

pesce all'acqua pazza fish cooked in seawater

pesce persico perch

pesce spada swordfish

pesche peaches

pesce fish; **~ al cartoccio** baked in a parchment envelope; **~ in carpione** boiled and cooked in vinegar, served cold with lemon

pestingolo rich fruit cake with figs and honey

pesto sauce of basil leaves, garlic, cheese and sometimes pine kernels *(Liguria)* and marjoram

piatti di carne meat dishes

piatti freddi cold dishes

piatto del giorno dish of the day

piccante sharp (cheese)

piccata al marsala thin

\veal escalope braised in marsala sauce

piccione pigeon

pieno full-bodied (wine)

pinoli pine nuts

piselli peas; ~ **al prosciutto** cooked slowly with Parma ham and bacon

piviere plover

pizelle fried bread with tomato sauce

pizza pizza

polenta mush made from cornmeal; ~ **alla piemontese** layered with meat; ~ **e coniglio** with rabbit stew; ~ **e uccelli** with roasted small birds *(northern Italy)*

pollame poultry

pollo chicken; ~ **all'abruzzese** with sweet peppers; ~ **alla romana** diced and served with tomato sauce and sweet peppers; ~ **alla diavola** highly spiced and grilled chicken; ~ **novello** spring chicken

polpette meatballs

polpettone meat loaf of seasoned beef or veal

polpo octopus

pomodori tomatoes

pomodori e capperi salad with capers

pompelmo grapefruit

porcellino da latte suckling pig

porcetto arrosto suckling spit-roasted pig *(Sardinia)*

porchetta roasted whole pig with fennels and sausages

porcini boletus mushrooms

porrata bacon and leeks in yeast dough crust

porro leek

porto port

prezzemolo parsley

primo piatto first course

prosciutto ham

prosciutto crudo con melone/ con fichi sliced melon or figs with cured ham from Parma

provolone firm cheese

prugna plum

prugna secca prune

puttanesca sauce of capers, black olives, parsley, garlic, olive oil, black pepper

Q

quaglia quail

quattro formaggi four types of cheese (pizza topping) or sauce

quattro stagioni vegetables, cheese, ham and bacon (pizza topping)

R

radicchio a kind of bitter red and white lettuce

ragù sauce like bolognese

ravanelli radishes

ravioli alla piemontese ravioli with beef and vegetable stuffing

razza ray

ribes red currants

ribes nero black currants

ricci sea urchins

ricciarelli delicate honey and almond biscuit *(Tuscany)*

ricotta soft cow's or sheep's milk cheese

rigatoni short, wide pasta tubes; ~ **alla pagliata** with veal guts

risi e bisi rice with peas and bacon

riso rice

riso con le seppie rice cooked with the ink from squid

riso in bianco boiled rice with butter and grated parmesan

risotto rice casserole;
~ con fegatini with chicken livers;
~ con gamberetti in bianco with prawns and wine

rognoncini trifolatti kidneys sauteed with Marsala

rognoni kidneys

rombo turbot

rosato rosé (wine)

rosbif roast beef

rosmarino rosemary

rosso red (wine)

ruote wheel-shaped pasta

salame spicy sausages made with uncooked beef or pork, often flavored with pepper and garlic

salciccia small sausage, country-style pork mixture

sale salt

salmone salmon

salse sauces

saltimbocca veal escalopes with prosciutto ham; **~ alla romana** braised in marsala wine with sage

salumi assorted pork products

salvia sage

sardine sardines; **~ all'olio** in oil

sauersuppe sour tripe soup marinated in white wine vinegar

scalogno shallot

scaloppina veal escalope;
~ alla valdostana filled with cheese and ham; **~ al marsala** with Marsala wine

scampi prawns

sciule pieuno onions stuffed with macaroons, breadcrumbs, cheese, spices and sultanas

scorfano sea-scorpion, sculpin

scura dark (beer)

secco dry (wine)

secondo piatto second (main) course

sedano celery

selvaggina venison

semifreddo ice cream cake

senape mustard

seppia cuttlefish

seppie con piselli baby squid and peas

sfogliatelle sweet Ricotta cheese turnovers

sgombri in umido stewed mackerel in white wine with green peas

sgombro mackerel

siciliana with black olives, capers and cheese (pizza)

sodo hard (egg)

sogliola sole

sogliole alla mugnaia sole sautéed in butter, garnished with parsley and lemon

solubile instant (coffee)

sottaceti pickled vegetables

spaghetti all'amatriciana spaghetti with tomato, bacon and Pecorino cheese sauce

spalla shoulder

specialità della casa specialties of the house

specialità di pesce fish specialties

specialità locali local specialties

spezie spices

spezzatino meat or poultry stew

spezzatino di cinghiale alla cacciatora diced wild boar stewed in white wine with garlic and bay leaves

spezzato di tacchino turkey casserole with olives *(Umbria)*

spiedino pieces of meat grilled or roasted on a skewer

spigola sea bass

spinaci spinach

spremuta di ... freshly squeezed (juice)

spumante sparkling (wine)

stecca di cioccolato chocolate bar

stelline small pasta stars

stoccafisso dried cod

storione sturgeon

stracciatella clear egg and cheese soup

stracotto meat stew with sausages, beef and vegetables in white wine, slowly cooked for several hours *(Tuscany)*

strangola preti bread and spinach dumpling

straniera foreign (beer)

su ordinazione made to order

succo di frutta fruit juice

supplemento extra charge

supplì very popular and tasty Italian rice croquettes with Mozzarella cheese and minced meat, breadcrumbed and fried

susina plum (yellow) or greengage

T

tacchino turkey

tagliatelle egg-pasta ribbons

tartufi truffles

tartufi di cioccolata chocolate truffles

timballo con le sarde macaroni, sardines, pine nuts, fennel, raisins

timo thyme

tiramisù sponge cake, mascarpone, eggs and chocolate dessert

tisana herb tea

tonno tuna

tonno alla livornese fried tuna in slices, stewed in garlic and tomato

tordo thrush

torrone delicious Italian nougat which can be found hard and crispy or soft, also chocolate flavored.

torta cake; pie

torta di cioccolata chocolate cake

torta di frutta fruit cake

torta di mandorle almond pie

torta di mele apple pie

torta di ricotta delicious pie made with ricotta cheese (roughly similar to cheese cake)

torta manfreda liver pate with Marsala and Parmesan

torta margherita layered cake with meringue, fresh fruit and whipped cream

tortelli di zucca big tortellini with pumpkin stuffing

tortellini stuffed egg-pasta rings; ~ **alla panna con tartufi** with cream and truffles; ~ **di piccioncello** with pigeon stuffing

tortino di zucchine zucchini with white sauce

triglie red mullet; ~ **alla livornese** baked; ~ **alla siciliana** grilled with orange peel and white wine

trippa tripe; ~ **alla fiorentina** and beef braised in a tomato sauce and served with cheese *(Tuscany)*; ~ **verde** in green sauce

trota trout: ~ **alla brace** grilled

tutto mare seafood sauce

tè tea; ~ **freddo** iced tea

U

uova eggs
uova alla romana omelet with beans, onions and herbs
uova e pancetta bacon and eggs
uova e prosciutto ham and eggs
uova fritte fried eggs
uova strapazzate scrambled eggs
uovo alla coque boiled egg
uva bianca/nera white/black grapes
uva passa raisins
uva spina gooseberries

V

vaniglia vanilla
veneziana sweet bread with whole almonds
verde with creamed green vegetables
verdura mista mixed vegetables
verdure vegetables; **~ di stagione** vegetables in season
vermicelli thin spaghetti
verza green cabbage
vincisgrassi cooked pasta with cream sauce and gravy
vino wine
vitello veal; **~ alla bolognese** cutlet cooked with Parma ham and cheese; **~ tonnato** cold with tuna fish sauce; **~ valdostana** stuffed with soft cheese
vongole clams

W

whisky (e soda/con seltz) whisky (and soda)
würstel frankfurters

Z

zabaglione egg yolks, sugar and Marsala wine

zafferano saffron
zampone pig's foot/trotter filled with seasoned pork, boiled and served in slices
zenzero ginger
ziti long, solid eggless-pasta tubes
zucca pumpkin, gourd; **~ gialla al forno** baked and served with parmesan cheese (winter only)
zucchero sugar
zucchini ripieni stuffed zucchini (usually containing mince meat)
zuppa soup; **~ alla cacciatora** meat soup with mushrooms; **~ alla marinara** spicy fish chowder/stew; **~ alla pavese** consommé with poached egg, croutons and grated cheese; **~ alla senese** sausages with lentils; **~ alla veneta** vegetable soup with white wine and noodles; **~ di bue con spaghettini** spaghetti in beef soup; **~ di cipolle** onion soup with brandy; **~ di cozze** mussels soup; **~ di datteri di mare** sea dates (kind of mussel) soup; **~ di frutti di mare** seafood soup; **~ di pesce** spicy fish chowder/stew; **~ di vongole** clams and white wine soup
zuppa inglese sponge cake steeped in rum with custard or whipped cream

TRAVEL

ESSENTIAL

1/2/3 for …	**Uno/due/tre per …** _oono/doo-ay/tray pehr_
A ticket to …	**Un biglietto per …** _oon beelyaytto pehr_
one-way [single]	**solo andata** _solo andaata_
round-trip [return]	**andata e ritorno** _andaata ay reetorno_
How much …?	**Quanto … ?** _kwanto_

SAFETY

Would you accompany me …?	**Le dispiace accompagnarmi?** _lay disspeeachay akkompanyaarmee_
to the bus stop	**alla fermata dell'autobus** _alla fayrmaata dayllowtobooss_
to my hotel	**al mio albergo** _al meeo albayrgo_
I don't want to … on my own.	**Non voglio … da solo(-a).** _non volyo … da solo(-a)_
stay here	**rimanere qui** _reemaneray kwee_
walk home	**rientrare a piedi** _reeayntraaray ah peeaydee_
I don't feel safe here.	**Non mi sento sicuro(-a) qui.** _non me saynto seekooro(-a) kwee_

IN A TRAIN STATION

Due biglietti per Roma, per favore. _dooay beelyayttee per roma pehr favoray (Two tickets to Rome, please.)_
Solo andata o andata e ritorno? _solo andaata o andaata ay reetorno (One way or round trip?)_
Andata e ritorno. _andaata ay reetorno (Round trip.)_

ARRIVAL

Most visitors, including citizens of all EU{European Union} countries, the US, Canada, Eire, Australia and New Zealand, require only a valid passport for entry to Italy.

Import restrictions between EU countries have been relaxed on items for personal use or consumption which are bought duty-paid within the EU. Suggested maximum: 90L. wine or 60L. sparkling wine, 20L. fortified wine, 10L. spirits and 110L. beer.

There are duty-free shops at the following airports: Bologna, Genova, Milan, Naples, Pisa, Rimini, Rome Ciampino, Rome Fiumicino, Turin, and Venice.

Passport control

We have a joint passport.	**Abbiamo un passaporto comune.** _abbeeamo oon passaporto komoonay_
The children are on this passport.	**I bambini sono su questo passaporto.** _ee bambeenee sono soo kwaysto passaporto_
I'm here on vacation [holiday]/business.	**Sono qui in vacanza/per lavoro.** _sono kwee in vakantsa/ pehr lavoro_
I'm just passing through.	**Sono solo di passaggio.** _sono solo dee passadjo_
I'm going to …	**Vado a …** _vado a_
I'm …	**Sono …** _sono_
on my own	**da solo(-a)** _da solo(-a)_
with my family	**con la mia famiglia** _kon la meea fameelya_
with a group	**con un gruppo** _kon oon groopo_

Customs

I have only the normal allowances.	**Ho solo beni in esenzione fiscale.** _oh solo baynee een ayzentseeonay feeskalay_

It's a gift.	**È un regalo.**
	eh oon raygaalo
It's for my personal use.	**È per uso personale.**
	eh pehr oozo pehrsonaalay
I would like to declare …	**Vorrei dichiarare …**
	vorrehee deekeearaaray
I don't understand.	**Non capisco.**
	non kapeesko
Does anyone here speak English?	**C'è qualcuno che parla inglese?**
	cheh kwalkoono kay parla eengglaysay

Duty-free shopping

What currency is this in?	**In che valuta è?**
	een kay valoota eh
Can I pay in …	**Posso pagare in …**
	posso pagaaray een
dollars	**dollari** *dollaree*
euros	**euro** *ayooro*
pounds	**sterline** *stayrleenay*

YOU MAY SEE

IL CONTROLLO PASSAPORTI	passport control
LA FRONTIERA	border crossing
LA DOGANA	customs
NIENTE DA DICHIARARE	nothing to declare
MERCI DA DICHIARARE	goods to declare
ESENTE DA DAZIO	duty-free

YOU MAY HEAR

Ha qualcosa da dichiarare?	Do you have anything to declare?
Per questo deve pagare la dogana.	You must pay duty on this.
Dove l'ha comprato?	Where did you buy this?
Apra questa borsa, per favore.	Please open this bag.
Ha altri bagagli?	Do you have any more luggage?

PLANE

Italian cities and major islands are well connected by air. This includes a shuttle service (**Arcobaleno**) between Rome and Milan every 20 minutes. Domestic flights can be expensive. However, cheaper rates can be obtained off-peak, and special fares are generally available for family groups, young people/students and senior citizens.

Tickets and reservations

When is the ... flight to ...?	**Quando parte il volo ... per ...?**
	kwando partay eel volo ... pehr
first/next/last	**il primo/il prossimo/l'ultimo**
	eel preemo/eel prosseemo/loolteemo
I'd like 2 tickets to ...	**Vorrei due biglietti per ...**
	vorrehe doo-ay beelyayttee ... pehr
one-way [single]	**di andata** _dee andaata_
round-trip [return]	**di andata e ritorno** _dee andaata ay reetorno_
first class	**prima classe** _preema klassay_
economy class	**classe turistica** _klassay tooreesteeka_
business class	**business class** _business klass_
How much is a flight to ...?	**Quanto costa il volo per ...?**
	kwanto kosta eel volo pehr
I'd like to ...	**Vorrei ... la mia prenotazione per il**
my reservation	**volo numero ...** _vorrehe ... la meea_
for flight number ...	_praynotatseeonay pehr eel volo noomayro_
cancel	**annullare** _annoollaaray_
change	**cambiare** _kambeeaaray_
confirm	**confermare** _konfayrmaaray_

Enquiries about the flight

How long is the flight?	**Quanto dura il volo?** _kwanto doora eel volo_
What time does the plane leave?	**A che ora decolla l'aereo?**
	ah kay ora daykolla la-ayrayo
What time will we arrive?	**A che ora arriveremo?**
	ah kay ora arreevayraymo

68

| What time do I have to check in? | **A che ora devo registrare i bagagli?** *ah kay ora dayvo rayjeestraaray ee bagaalyee* |

Checking in

Where is the check-in counter for flight ...?	**Dov'è il banco accettazione per il volo ...?** *dovay ell banko achaytatseeonay pehr eel volo*
I have ...	**Ho ...** *oh*
3 suitcases to check in	**tre valige da registrare** *treh valeejay da rayjeestraaray*
2 pieces of hand luggage	**due borse a mano** *doo-ay borsay ah mano*

YOU MAY HEAR

Il suo biglietto/passaporto/ la sua carta d'imbarco.	Your ticket/passport/ boarding card.
Preferisce un posto vicino al finestrino o al corridoio?	Would you like a window or an aisle seat?
Fumatori o non fumatori?	Smoking or non-smoking?
Si accomodi nella sala partenze.	Please go through to the departure lounge.
Quanti pezzi/quante valige ha?	How many pieces of luggage do you have?
Ha un eccesso di bagaglio.	You have excess luggage.
Deve pagare un supplemento di ... euro per ogni chilo in più.	You'll have to pay a supplement of euros per kilo of excess luggage.
Questo bagaglio a mano è troppo pesante/grande?	That's too heavy/ large for hand luggage.
Ha fatto i bagagli personalmente?	Did you pack these bags yourself?
Ci sono articoli elettrici o taglienti?	Do they contain any sharp or electrical items?

YOU MAY SEE

ARRIVI	arrivals
PARTENZE	departures
I CONTROLLI DI SICUREZZA	security check
TENERE CON SÉ I BAGAGLI	do not leave luggage unattended

Information

Is there any delay on flight …?	**C'è un ritardo sul volo …?** *cheh oon reetardo sool volo*
How late will it be?	**Di quanto ritarderà?** *dee kwanto reetardayra*
Has the flight from … landed?	**È atterrato il volo da …?** *eh attayrraato eel volo da*
Which gate does flight … leave from?	**Da quale uscita parte il volo …?** *da kwalay oosheeta partay eel volo*

Boarding/In-flight

Your boarding pass, please.	**La sua carta d'imbarco, per favore.** *la sooa karta deembarko pehr favoray*
Could I have a drink/something to eat, please?	**Può portarmi qualcosa da bere/da mangiare, per favore?** *pwo portaarmee kwalkosa da bayray/da manjaaray pehr favoray*
Please wake me for the meal.	**Mi svegli per il pasto, per favore.** *mee svaylyee pehr eel pasto pehr favoray*
What time will we arrive?	**A che ora arriveremo?** *ah kay ora arreevayraymo*
An airsick bag, quick, please.	**Presto un sacchetto di carta, per favore.** *praysto oon sakkaytto dee karta pehr favoray*

Arrival

Where is/are the …?	**Dov'è/Dove sono …?** *doveh/dovay sono*
currency exchange	**l'ufficio cambio** *looffeecho kambeeo*
buses	**gli autobus** *lyee owtobooss*
car rental	**il noleggio auto** *eel nolaydjo owto*
exit	**l'uscita** *loosheeta*
taxis	**i tassì** *ee tassee*
Is there a bus into town?	**C'è un autobus per il centro?** *cheh oon owtobooss pehr eel chayntro*
How do I get to the … Hotel?	**Come si arriva all' albergo …?** *komay see arreeva allalbayrgo*

Luggage/Baggage

Tipping: The suggested rate for the porter is €1–2 per bag; in railway stations, tariffs are generally displayed.

Porter! Excuse me!	**Facchino! Scusi!** *fakkeeno. skoozee*
Could you take my luggage to …?	**Può portarmi i bagagli fino …?** *pwo portaarmee ee bagalyee feeno*
a taxi/bus	**al tassì/alla fermata dell'autobus** *al tassee/ alla faymaata daylowtobooss*
Where is/are …?	**Dov'è/Dove sono …?** *doveh /dovay sono*
luggage carts [trolleys]	**i carrelli** *ee karrayllee*
baggage lockers	**il deposito bagagli automatico** *eel dayposeeto bagalyee owtomateeko*
baggage check [left-luggage office]	**il deposito bagagli** *eel dayposeeto bagalyee*
Where is the luggage from flight …?	**Dove sono i bagagli del volo …?** *dovay sono ee bagalyee dayl volo*

Loss, damage and theft

My luggage has been lost.	**Ho smarrito i bagagli.** *oh smarreeto ee bagalyee*
My luggage has been stolen.	**Il mio bagaglio è stato rubato.** *eel meeo bagaalyo eh staato roobaato*
My suitcase was damaged.	**La mia valigia è stata danneggiata** *la meea valeeja eh staata dannaydjaata*

YOU MAY HEAR

Può descrivere i suoi bagagli?	What does your luggage look like?
Ha l'etichetta di ricupero bagagli?	Do you have the claim check/ reclaim tag?
I suoi bagagli …	Your luggage …
potrebbero essere stati mandati a …	may have been sent to …
potrebbero arrivare più tardi	may arrive later
Ritorni domani, per favore.	Please come back tomorrow.
Chiami questo numero per controllare se i suoi bagagli sono arrivati.	Call this number to check if your luggage has arrived.

TRAIN

EuroCity (EC) _ayoorosseetee_
International express connecting main European cities; first and second class. A supplement is payable and reservations are obligatory.

Pendolino-ETR 450 (P) _pehndoleeno_
High-speed train connecting major Italian cities. Luxury first class and second class; tickets include hostess service and a meal. Reservations are obligatory.

Rapido _raapeedo_
Long-distance express train stopping at major cities only; first and second class.

Intercity (IC) _"intercity"_
Intercity express with very few stops; luxury, international service with first and second class. Seat reservations are essential and a special supplement is charged.

Espresso (EXP) _aysprehsso_
Long-distance express train, stopping at major stations.

Diretto (D) _deerehtto_
Slower than the Espresso, it stops at most stations.

Interregionale (IR) _eentehrrayjeeonalay_
Train stopping at main stations within a region.

Regionale (R) _rayjeeonalay_
Local train stopping at many smaller locations. Not very fast, but an excellent means of visiting small hilltop towns that abound in Italy. Marked by a white "**R**" on a black background (to distinguish it from the **Rapido**).

carrozza ristorante _karrottsa reestorantay_
Dining car. Some services include self-service restaurant cars. In addition, most trains have snacks and refreshments available.

vagone letto _vagonay lehtto_
Sleeping car with individual compartment and washing facilities. Sleeping cars containing berths with blankets and pillows (**carrozza cuccette**) are also available on some lines.

The National Railways (**Ferrovie dello Stato** – **FS**) publishes a free, easy-to-consult pocket timetable of the major trains running throughout Italy. Italy's trains can be crowded; if you haven't booked, it's wise to arrive at the station at least 30 minutes before departure to be sure of a seat.

Check out the various reductions and travel cards available. These include: **Biglietto turistico di libera circolazione** (for extensive "travel-at-will," only available outside Italy).

To the station

How do I get to the (main) rail station?
Come si arriva alla stazione ferroviaria (principale)? _komay see arreeva alla statseeonay fayrroveeaareea (preencheepaalay)_

Do trains to … leave from … Station?
I treni per … partono dalla stazione di …? _ee traynee pehr … partono dalla statseeonay dee_

Is it far?
È lontano? _ay lontano_

Can I leave my car there?
Posso lasciare la macchina alla stazione? _posso lashaaray la makkeena alla statseeonay_

At the station

Where is/are …?
Dov'è/Dove sono …? _doveh /dovay sono_

currency exchange office
l'ufficio cambio _looffeecho kambeeo_

information desk
lo sportello informazioni _lo sportayllo eenformatseeonay_

baggage check [left-luggage office]
il deposito bagagli _eel dayposeeto bagaalyee_

lost-and-found [lost property office]
l'ufficio oggetti smarriti _looffeecho odjayttee smarreetee_

luggage lockers
il deposito bagagli automatico _eel dayposeeto bagaalyee owtomaateeko_

platforms
i binari _ee beenaaree_

snack bar
il bar _eel bar_

ticket office
la biglietteria _la beelyayttayreea_

waiting room
la sala d'aspetto _la sala daspaytto_

YOU MAY SEE

ENTRATA	entrance
USCITA	exit
AI BINARI	to the platforms
INFORMAZIONI	information
PRENOTAZIONI	reservations
ARRIVI	arrivals
PARTENZE	departures

Tickets

It is very important to validate tickets before commencing your journey by inserting them in machines (generally yellow) positioned on platforms; otherwise you will be liable for a fine.

I'd like a ticket to …	**Vorrei un biglietto per …** *vorrehee oon beelyayto pehr*
one-way [single]	**andata** *andaata*
round-trip [return]	**andata e ritorno** *andaata ay reetorno*
first/second class	**prima/seconda classe** *preema/saykonda klassay*
I'd like to reserve a …	**Vorrei prenotare …** *vorrehee praynotaaray*
window/aisle seat	**un posto vicino al finestrino/ al corridoio** *oon posto veecheeno al feenaystreeno/al korreedoyo*
Is there a sleeping car [sleeper]?	**C'è un vagone letto?** *cheh oon vagonay laytto*
I'd like a … berth.	**Vorrei una cuccetta …** *vorrehee oona koochaytta*
upper/lower	**in alto/in basso** *in altoh/in bassoh*

Price

How much is that?	**Quant'è?** *kwanteh*
Do you offer a cheap same-day round-trip ticket?	**C'è una tariffa economica per andata e ritorno in giornata?** *che oona tareeffa aykonomeeka pehr andaata ay reetorno een jornaata*
Is there a discount for …?	**C'è una riduzione per …?** *cheh oon reedootseeonay pehr*

children/families	**bambini/famiglie**
	bambeenee/fameelyay
senior citizens	**anziani** *antseeanee*
students	**studenti** *stoodayntee*

Queries

Do I have to change trains?	**Devo cambiare treno?** *dayvo kambeeaaray trayno*
You have to change at …	**Deve cambiare a …** *dayvay kambeeaaray ah*
How long is this ticket valid for?	**Per quanto tempo è valido questo biglietto?** *pehr kwanto taympo eh valeedo kwaysto beelyayto*
Can I return on the same ticket?	**Posso ritornare con lo stesso biglietto?** *posso reetornaaray kon lo staysso beelyaytto*
Which car [coach] is my seat in?	**In quale carrozza è il mio posto?** *een kwalay karrotsa eh eel meeo posto*
Is there a dining car on the train?	**C'è il vagone ristorante sul treno?** *cheh eel vagonay reestorantay sool trayno*

Train times

Could I have a timetable, please?	**Ha l'orario, per favore?** *ah lorareeo pehr favoray*
When is the … train to … ?	**Quando parte … treno per …** *kwando paartay … trayno pehr*
first/next/last	**il primo/il prossimo/l'ultimo** *eel preemo /eel prosseemo/ loolteemo*
How frequent are the trains to …?	**Che frequenza hanno i treni per …?** *kay fraykwayntsa anno ee traynee pehr*
once/twice a day	**una volta/due volte al giorno** *oona volta/dooay voltay al jorno*

75

5 times a day	**cinque volte al giorno**
	cheenkweh voltay al jorno
every hour	**ogni ora**
	onyee ora
What time do they leave?	**A che ora partono?**
	ah kay ora partono
on the hour	**ad ogni ora precisa**
	ad onyee ora praycheesa
What time does the train stop at …?	**A che ora ferma il treno a …?**
	ah kay ora fayrma eel trayno ah
What time does the train arrive in …?	**A che ora arriva il treno a …?**
	ah kay ora arreeva eel trayno ah
How long is the trip [journey]?	**Quanto dura il viaggio?**
	kwanto doora eel veeadjo
Is the train on time?	**Il treno è in orario?**
	eel trayno eh een orareeo

Departures

Which platform does the train to … leave from?	**Da quale binario parte il treno per …?**
	da kwalay beenaareeo partay eel trayno pehr
Where is platform 4?	**Dov'è il binario quattro?**
	doveh eel beenaareeo kwattro
over there	**laggiù** *ladjoo*
on the left/right	**a sinistra/a destra**
	ah seeneestra/ah daystra
Where do I change for …?	**dove cambio per …?**
	dovay kambeeo pehr
How long will I have to wait for a connection?	**Quanto devo aspettare per la coincidenza?**
	kwanto dayvo aspayttaaray pehr la koeencheedayntsa

YOU MAY SEE

FRENI D'EMERGENZA	emergency brake
PORTE AUTOMATICHE	automatic doors
SEGNALE D'ALLARME	alarm signal

Boarding

Is this the right platform for the train to …?	**È questo il binario del treno per …?** *eh kwaysto eel beenaareeo dayl trayno pehr*
Is this the train to …?	**È questo il treno per …?** *eh kwaysto eel trayno pehr*
Is this seat taken?	**Questo posto è occupato?** *kwaysto posto eh okoopaato*
I think that's my seat.	**Questo è il mio posto, credo.** *kwaysto eh eel meeo posto kraydo*
Are there any seats/berths available?	**Ci sono posti liberi/cuccette libere?** *chee sono postee leebayree/ koochayttay leebayray*
Do you mind …?	**Le dispiace …?** *lay dispeeachay*
if I sit here	**se mi siedo qui** *say mee seeaydo kwee*
if I open the window	**se apro la finestra** *say apro la feenaystra*

During the trip

How long are we stopping here?	**Per quanto tempo ci fermiamo a …?** *pehr kwanto taympo che fayrmeeaamo ah*
When do we get to …?	**Quando arriviamo a …?** *kwando arreeveeaamo ah*
Have we passed …?	**Abbiamo passato …?** *abbeeaamo passaato*
Where is the dining/ sleeping car?	**Dov'è la carrozza ristorante/il vagone letto?** *doveh la karrotsa reestorantay/eel vagonay lehtto*
Where is my berth?	**Dov'è la mia cuccetta?** *doveh la meea koo\chaytta*
I've lost my ticket.	**Ho perso il biglietto.** *oh payrso eel beelyaytto*

LONG-DISTANCE BUS

Bus travel can be a convenient way of traveling to smaller towns and a cheaper way to reach major cities. You'll find information on destinations and timetables at bus terminals, usually situated near railway stations. Main companies include *A.M.T.* (Genoa), *Appian Line* (Rome), *Autostradale*, *Lazzi*, *Pesci*, *Sadem*, *Sita*.

Where is the bus [coach] station?	**Dov'è la stazione delle corriere/ dei pullman?** *doveh la statseeonay dayllay korreeehray/dayee pullman*
When's the next bus [coach] to …?	**Quando parte il prossimo pullman per …?** *kwando partay eel prosseemo pullman pehr*
Which terminal does it leave from?	**Da quale piazzola parte?** *da kwalay piatsola partay*
Where are the bus [coach] stops?	**Dove sono le piazzole di sosta?** *dovay sono ley piatsolay dee sosta*
Does this bus [coach] stop at …?	**Questo pullman ferma a …?** *kwaysto pullman fayrma ah*
How long does the trip [journey] take?	**Quanto dura il viaggio?** *kwanto doora eel veeadjo*

YOU MAY HEAR

Deve andare a quella fermata lì	You need that stop over there.
Deve prendere quella strada.	You need to go down that road.
Deve prendere l'autobus numero …	You need bus number …
Deve cambiare autobus a …	You must change buses at …

YOU MAY SEE

LA FERMATA DELL'AUTOBUS	bus stop
LA FERMATA A RICHIESTA	request stop
VIETATO FUMARE	no smoking
USCITA (D'EMERGENZA)	(emergency) exit

BUS

Many cities have introduced an automatic system of fare-paying. Instructions are usually also given in English. Most machines now give change, though usually limited to €1–2.

Bus or subway tickets are valid for 75 minutes and the fare is standard, irrespective of distance. If you're planning to travel extensively in one city, enquire about special runabout tickets, such as **biglietto giornaliero** (one-day ticket).

Buying tickets

Where can I buy tickets?	**Dove si comprano i biglietti?** _dovay see komprano ee beelyaytee_
A ... ticket to ..., please.	**Un biglietto per ..., per favore.** _oon beelyaytto pehr ... pehr favoray_
one-way/round-trip [single/return]	**di corsa semplice/circolare** _dee korsa saympleechay/cheerkolaaray_
bus pass	**per corse multiple** _pehr korsay moolteeplay_
day/weekly/monthly	**giornaliero/settimanale/mensile** _jornaleeehro/saytteemanaalay/maynseelay_
A book of tickets, please.	**Un blocchetto di biglietti, per favore.** _oon blokkaytto dee beelyaytee pehr favoray_
How much is the fare to ...?	**Quant'è il biglietto per ...?** _kwanteh eel beelyaytto pehr_

Traveling

Is this the right bus/tram to ...?	**È questo l'autobus/il tram per ...?** _eh kwaysto lowtobooss/eel tram pehr_
Could you tell me when to get off?	**Può dirmi quando devo scendere?** _pwo deermee kwando dayvo shayndayray_
Do I have to change buses?	**Devo cambiare autobus?** _dayvo kambeeaaray owtobooss_
How many stops are there to ...?	**Quante fermate ci sono per ...?** _kwantay fayrmaatay chee sono pehr_
Next stop, please!	**La prossima fermata, per favore!** _lah prosseema fayrmaata pehr favoray_

AT A BUS STATION

E' questo l'autobus per il centro? _eh kwaysto lowtobooss pehr eel chentro_ (Is this the bus to downtown?)
Sì, il numero otto. _see eel noomero otto_ (Yes, bus number 8.)
Grazie. _graatseeay_ (Thank you.)

SUBWAY

The **metropolitana** in Rome and Milan provide big maps in every station to make the system easy to use. The fare is standard, irrespective of the distance traveled.

General Inquiries

Where's the nearest subway [metro] station?	**Dov'è la fermata della metropolitana più vicina?** *doveh la fayrmaata daylla maytropoleetaana peeoo veecheena*
Where can I buy a ticket?	**Dove si comprano i biglietti?** *dovay see komprano ee beelyayttee*
Could I have a map of the subway [metro]?	**Ha una carta/mappa della metropolitana?** *ah oona karta/mappa daylla maytropoleetaana*

Traveling

Which line should I take for …?	**Che linea devo prendere per …?** *kay leeneea dayvo prayndayray pehr*
Is this the right line for …?	**È questa la linea per …?** *eh kwaysta la leeneea pehr*
Which stop is it for …?	**Che fermata è per …?** *kay fayrmaata eh pehr*
How many stops is it to …?	**Quante fermate ci sono per arrivare a …?** *kwantay fayrmaatay chee sono pehr arreevaaray ah*
Is the next stop …?	**La prossima/fermata è …?** *la prosseema (fayrmaata) eh*
Where are we?	**Dove siamo?** *dovay seeaamo*
Where do I change for …?	**Dove devo cambiare per …?** *dovay dayvo kambeeaaray pehr*
What time is the last train to …?	**A che ora è l'ultimo treno per …?** *ah kay ora eh loolteemo trayno pehr*

FERRY

Regular boat, ferry and hydrofoil services run to the Italian islands. In addition to the large state-owned services such as *Tirrenia* (esp. services to

Sicily and Sardinia), there are many other operators that access islands such as Capri, Ischia, Ponza, Ventotene, the Tremiti Islands, Elba and Giglio.

When is the … car ferry to …?	**Quando c'è … traghetto auto per …?** _kwando cheh tragaytto owto pehr_
first/next/last	**il primo/il prossimo/l'ultimo** _eel preemo/ eel prosseemo/ loolteemo_
hovercraft	**l'aliscafo** _laleeskaafo_
ship	**la nave** _la navay_
A round-trip [return] ticket for …	**Un biglietto di andata e ritorno per …** _oon beelyaytto andaata ay r eetorno pehr_
1 car and 1 trailer [caravan]	**un'auto e una roulotte** _oonowto ay oona roolot_
2 adults and 3 children	**due adulti e tre bambini** _doo-ay adooltee ay tray bambeenee_
I want to reserve a … cabin.	**Vorrei prenotare una cabina …** _vorrehee praynotaaray oona kabeena_
single/double	**singola/doppia** _seenggola/ doppeea_

BOAT TRIPS

Travelers to Venice can take tours on a myriad of canals, organized by the *Gondola Cooperative Service*. The price is usually quoted per gondola, which can seat 6 to 8 people, per 45 minutes, but you may be able to bargain.A cheaper, but less romantic, way of getting around are the water bus services: **vaporetti** (slow) and **diretti** (express).

Is there a …?	**C'è …?** _cheh_
boat trip	**una gita in barca** _oona jeeta een baarka_
Where can we buy tickets?	**Dove si comprano i biglietti?** _dovay see komprano_

YOU MAY SEE

VIETATO L'ACCESSO AL PONTE AUTO	no access to car decks
LA SCIALUPPA DI SALVATAGGIO	life boat
LA CINTURA DI SALVATAGGIO	life preserver [life belt]
PUNTO DI RACCOLTA	meeting point

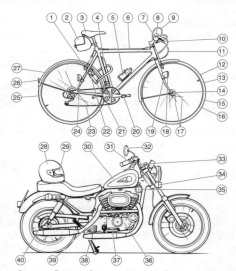

1 brake pad **il pattino/la pastiglia**	21 lock **la serratura**
2 bicycle bag **il borsello**	22 generator [dynamo] **la dinamo**
3 seat [saddle] **il sellino**	23 chain **la catena**
4 pump **la pompa**	24 rear light **il fanalino posteriore**
5 water bottle **la bottiglia dell'acqua**	25 rim **il cerchione**
6 frame **il telaio**	26 reflectors **il catarinfrangente**
7 handlebars **il manubrio**	27 fender [mudguard] **il parafango**
8 bell **il campanello**	28 helmet **il casco**
9 brake cable **il cavo dei freni**	29 visor **l'antiabbagliante**
10 gear shift [lever] **la leva del cambio**	30 fuel tank **il serbatoio**
11 gear [control] cable **il cambio**	31 clutch **la leva della frizione**
12 inner tube **la camera d'aria**	32 mirror **lo specchietto**
13 front/back wheel **la ruota anteriore/posteriore**	33 ignition switch **la leva dell'avviamento**
14 axle **l'asse**	34 turn signal [indicator] **l'indicatore di posizione**
15 tire **il pneumatico**	35 horn **il claxon**
16 wheel **la ruota**	36 engine **il motore**
17 spokes **i raggi**	37 gear shift **la leva del cambio**
18 bulb **la lampadina**	38 kick stand **il cavalletto**
19 headlamp **il fanalino anteriore**	39 exhaust pipe **la marmitta**
20 pedal **il pedale**	40 chain guard **il paracatena**

BICYCLE/MOTORBIKE

I'd like to rent a …	**Vorrei noleggiare …** *nolaydjaaray*
3-/10-gear bicycle	**una bici(cletta) a tre/dieci marce** *oona beechee(beecheeklaytta) ah tray/deeaychee marchay*
moped	**un motorino** *oon motoreeno*
mountain bike	**una mountain bike** *oona mountain bike*
motorbike	**una moto(cicletta)** *oona moto (motocheeklaytta)*
How much does it cost per day/week?	**Quanto costa al giorno/alla settimana?** *kwanto kosta al jorno/alla saytteemaana*
Do you require a deposit?	**Vuole una caparra?** *vwolay oona kaparra*
The brakes don't work.	**I freni non funzionano.** *ee fraynee non foontseeonano*
There are no lights.	**Non ci sono i fanalini.** *non chee sono ee fanaleenee*
The front/rear tire has a flat [puncture].	**il pneumatico anteriore/posteriore è bucato.** *eel pnayoomateeko antayreeoray/postayreeoray ay bookato*

HITCHHIKING

Where are you heading?	**In che direzione va?** *een kay deeraytseeonay va*
I'm heading for …	**Vado verso …** *vado vayrsoh*
Is that on the way to …?	**È sulla strada per …?** *eh soolla straada pehr*
Could you drop me off …?	**Può farmi scendere …?** *pwo faarmee shayndayray*
here	**qui** *kwee*
at the … exit	**all'uscita** *alloosheeta*
in the town center	**in centro** *een chayntro*
Thanks for the lift.	**Grazie per il passaggio.** *gratseeay pehr eel passadjeeo*

TAXI/CAB

All cabs must be metered by law, but it is still wise to ask the fare for longer trips. All rates, including supplements for Sundays, holidays, night trips (11 p.m. – 6 a.m.), airport trips, baggage, are indicated on an official chart, which should be posted inside the taxi. When arriving at or from an airport, remember there is a return trip surcharge to be added to what you read on the meter.

Beware of unlicensed cabs ("**abusivi**") touting for business at airports and stations – they charge greatly over the normal tariffs.

Tipping suggestions: 10-15% for the taxi driver.

Where can I get a taxi?	**Dove si trovano i tassi?** _dovay see trovano ee tassee_
Do you have the number for a taxi?	**Ha il numero dei tassi?** _ah eel noomayro dayee tassee_
I'd like a taxi …	**Vorrei un tassì …** _vorrehee oon tassee_
now/in an hour	**subito/fra un'ora** _soobeeto/ fra oonora_
for tomorrow at 9:00 am	**per domani alle nove** _pehr domaanee allay novay_
The address is …	**L'indirizzo è …** _leendeereetzo eh …_
Please take me …	**Per favore, mi porti …** _pehr favoray mee portee_
to the airport	**all'aeroporto** _allaayroporto_
to the train station	**alla stazione ferroviaria** _alla statseeonay fayrrooveeareea_
this address	**a questo indirizzo** _ah kwaysto eendeereetso_
How much will it cost?	**Quanto costerà?** _kwanto kostayra_
On the meter it's …	**Il tassemetro segna …** _eel tasseemaytroa saynya_

AT A TAXI STAND

Per favore, mi porti all'aeroporto. _pehr favoray mee portee allaayroporto (Please, take me to the airport)_
Certo. _cherto (Certainly.)_

CAR/AUTOMOBILE

While driving, the following documents must be carried at all times: valid full driver's license, vehicle registration document and insurance documen-

84

tation. If you don 't hold an EC format license, a translation of the license is also required. Visitors must carry their vehicle registration book/logbook and, if it is not their car, written consent from the owner.

Insurance for minimum Third Party risks is compulsory in Europe. It is recommended that you take out International motor insurance (or a "*Green Card*") through your insurer.

The most common crime against tourists in Italy is theft from rental cars. Always look for secure parking areas overnight and never leave valuables in your car at any time.

Essential equipment: warning triangle, nationality plate. Wearing seat-belts is compulsory. Children under 13 must travel in seats with special restraints.

Traffic on main roads has priority; where 2 roads of equal importance merge, traffic from the right has priority. On 3-lane roads, the central lane is for passing.

Minimum driving age: 18.

Tolls (**il pedaggio**) are payable on expressways (**autostrada**).

Traffic police can give on-the-spot fines (ask for a receipt). The use of horns is prohibited in built-up areas except for emergencies. Alcohol limit in blood: max. 80mg/100ml..

Conversion Chart

km	1	10	20	30	40	50	60	70	80	90	100	110	120	130
miles	0.62	6	12	19	25	31	37	44	50	56	62	68	74	81

Road network

Italy	**autostrada** – toll expressway [motorway]; **superstrada** – non-toll expressway [motorway]; **strata statale** – main road; **strada provinciale** – secondary road; **stada comunale** – local road
Switzerland	**A** – expressway [motorway] toll free; **N** – main road; **E** – secondary road

Speed limits *mph (kmph)*	Built-up area	Outside built-up area	(Toll) expressway/ highway [motorway]
Italy	31 (50)	69 (110) main roads 55 (90) sec. roads	81 (130)
car with trailer/ caravan	31 (50)	44 (70)	50 (80)
Switzerland	31 (50)	50 (80)	62–74 (100–120)

Car rental

Third-party insurance (**R.C.A.**) is included in the basic rental charge, usually with a Collision Damage Waiver.

If you are traveling by air or train, you may want to take advantage of special inclusive arrangements for car rental. Small local firms are generally cheaper than international or major Italian rental companies, but cars can only be booked locally. Some firms require a minimum age of 21; a valid license held for at least one year is a standard requirement.

Where can I rent a car?	**Dove si noleggia un'auto(mobile)?** _dovay see nolaydjaa oonowto (oonowtomobeelay)_
I'd like to rent ...	**Vorrei noleggiare ...** _vorrehee nolaydjaaray_
a 2-/4-door car	**un'auto a due/a quattro porte** _oonowto ah doo-ay/ah kwattro portay_
an automatic car	**un'auto con il cambio automatico** _oonowto kon eel kambeeo owtomaateeko_
with air conditioning	**con aria condizionata** _kon areea kondeetseeonaata_
I'd like it for a day/a week	**Vorrei noleggiarla per un giorno/una settimana.** _vorrehee nolaydjaaray pehr oon jorno/oona saytteemaana_
How much does it cost per day/week?	**Quanto costa al giorno/alla settimana?** _kwanto kosta al jorno/ alla saytteemaana_
Are mileage and insurance included?	**Il chilometraggio e l'assicurazione sono inclusi?** _eel keelomaytradjo ay lasseekooratseeonay sono eengkloosee_
Can I leave the car at ...?	**Posso lasciare la macchina a ...?** _posso lashaaray la makkeena ah_
What kind of fuel does it take?	**Che tipo di benzina prende?** _kay teepo dee bayndzeena praynday_
Where is the high/ low beam?	**Dove sono gli abbaglianti/anabbaglianti?** _dovay sono lyee abbalyeeantee/ anabbalyeeantee_
Could I have full insurance, please?	**Vorrei una polizza di assicurazione completa.** _vorrehee oona poleetsa dee asseekooratseeonay komplayta_

Gas station

Where's the next gas [petrol] station?	**Dov'è la prossima stazione di servizio?** *doveh la prosseema statseeonay dee sayrveetseeo*
Is it self-service?	**È un distributore automatico?** *eh oon deestreebootoray owtomateeko*
Fill it up, please.	**Il pieno, per favore.** *eel peeayno pehr favoray*
… liters of … , please.	**… litri di benzina …, per favore.** *leetree dee bayndzeena … pehr favoray*
super/regular	**super/normale** *super/normaalay*
lead-free/diesel	**verde/il diesel** *vayrday/eel diesel*
Where is the air pump/ water?	**Dov'è la pompa per l'aria/l'acqua?** *doveh la pompa pehr lareea/lakwa*

Parking

Most street parking is limited in town centers. Tokens (**dischi orari**) for parking (up to 1 hour) in blue zones are obtained from tourist organizations, automobile clubs and service stations. Set the disc to show when you arrived and when you must leave.

In Rome, central parking (in the **zona tutelata**) on weekdays is prohibited; punishable by a fine and prison sentence.

Is there a parking lot [car park] nearby?	**C'è un parcheggio qui vicino?** *cheh oon parkaydjo kwee veecheeno*
What's the charge per hour/per day?	**Quanto costa all'ora/al giorno?** *kwanto kosta allora/ al jorno*
Do you have some change for the parking meter?	**Ha qualche moneta per il parchimetro?** *ah kwalkay monayta pehr eel parkeemaytro*
My car has been booted [clamped]. Who do I call?	**La mia auto è stata bloccata con il bloccaruote. A chi devo rivolgermi?** *la meea owto ay staata blokkaata kon eel blokkaroo-otay. a kee dayvo reevoljayrmee*

YOU MAY SEE

PREZZO AL LITRO	price per liter/litre

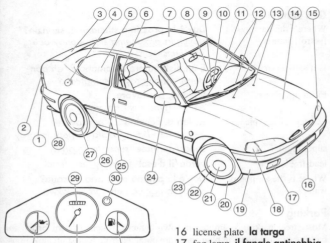

16 license plate **la targa**
17 fog lamp **il fanale antinebbia**
18 turn signals [indicators]
   gli indicatori di posizione
19 bumper **il paraurti**
20 tires **i pneumatici**
21 hubcap **la coppa**
22 valve **la valvola**
23 wheels **le ruote**
24 outside mirror **lo specchietto
   retrovisore esterno**
25 automatic locks **la chiusura
   centralizzata**
26 lock **la chiusura**
27 wheel rim **il cerchione**
28 exhaust pipe **il tubo di
   scappamento**
29 odometer **il contachilometri**
30 warning light **le luci
   d'emergenza**
31 fuel gauge **l'indicatore della
   benzina**

1 tail lights [back lights]
   i fanali posteriori
2 brakelights **le luci dei freni**
3 trunk [boot] **il portabagagli**
4 gas cap **il tappo del serbatoio**
5 window **il lunotto**
6 seat belt **la cintura di sicurezza**
7 sunroof **il tetto apribile**
8 steering wheel **il volante**
9 ignition/starter **l'accensione**
10 ignition key **la chiave
   dell'accensione**
11 windshield **il parabrezza**
12 windshield [windscreen] wipers
   il tergicristallo
13 windshield [windscreen]
   washers **i lavacristalli**
14 hood **il cofano**
15 headlights **i fari/gli abbaglianti**

88

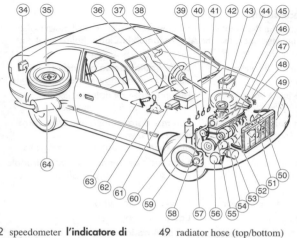

32 speedometer **l'indicatore di velocità**

33 oil gauge **l'indicatore del livello dell'olio**

34 backup lights **le luci di retromarcia**

35 spare tire [wheel] **il pneumatico/ la gomma di ricambio**

36 choke **la valvola d'aria**

37 heater **l'impianto di riscaldamento**

38 steering column il **piantone**

39 accelerator **l'acceleratore**

40 pedal **il pedale**

41 clutch **la frizione**

42 carburetor **il carburatore**

43 battery **la batteria**

44 alternator **l'alternatore**

45 camshaft **l'albero a camme**

46 air filter **il filtro dell'aria**

47 distributor **il distributore**

48 points **le candele**

49 radiator hose (top/bottom) **il tubo del radiatore**

50 radiator **il radiatore**

51 fan **il ventilatore**

52 engine **il motore**

53 oil filter **il filtro dell'olio**

54 starter motor **il motorino d'avviamento**

55 fan belt **la cinghia del ventilatore**

56 horn **il claxon**

57 brake pads **la ganascia dei freni**

58 transmission/gearbox **il cambio di velocità**

59 brakes **i freni**

60 shock absorbers **gli ammortizzatori**

61 fuses **i fusibili**

62 gear shift **la leva del cambio**

63 handbrake **il freno a mano**

64 muffler **la marmitta**

Breakdown

For help in the event of a breakdown refer to your breakdown assistance
documents; or contact the **ACI (Automobile Club d'Italia)** breakdown
service: Italy: ☎ 116.

Where is the nearest garage?	**Dov'è l'autorimessa più vicina?** *doveh lowtoreemayssa peeoo veecheena*
I've had a breakdown.	**Ho un guasto all'automobile.** *o oon goosto allowtomobeelay*
Can you send a mechanic/ tow [breakdown] truck?	**Può mandare un meccanico/un carro attrezzi?** *pwo mandaaray oon maykkaneeko/ oon karro attraytzee*
I belong to ... rescue service.	**Sono socio del servizio soccorso stradale ...** *sono socho dayl sayrveetseeo sokkorso stradaalay*
license plate number	**La targa ...** *la targa*
The car is ...	**L'auto è ...** *lowto eh*
on the highway [motorway]	**sull'autostrada** *soollowtostraada*
2 km from ...	**a due chilometri da ...** *ah doo-ay keelomaytree da*
How long will you be?	**Fra quanto tempo arriva?** *fra kwanto taympo arreeva*

What's wrong?

My car won't start.	**L'auto non parte.** *lowto non partay*
The battery is dead.	**La batteria è scarica.** *la battayreea eh skareeka*
I've run out of gas [petrol].	**Ho finito la benzina.** *oh feeneeto la bayndzeena*
I have a flat [pucture].	**Ho forato.** *oh foraato*
There is something wrong with ...	**C'è qualcosa che non funziona nel ...** *cheh kwalkosa kay non foontseeona nell*
I've locked the keys in the car.	**Ho lasciato le chiavi in macchina.** *o lashyatoh lay keeaavee in makkeena*

Repairs

Do you do repairs?	**Fa riparazioni?** *fa reeparatseeonee*
Can you repair it (temporarily)?	**Può fare una riparazione (provvisoria)?** *pwo faaray oona reeparatseeonay (provveezoreea)*
Please make only essential repairs.	**Faccia solo le riparazioni essenziali, per favore.** *fatcha solo lay reeparatseeonay ayssayntseeaalee pehr favoray*
Can I wait for it?	**Posso aspettare?** *posso aspayttaaray*
Can you repair it today?	**Può ripararla oggi?** *pwo reeparaarla odjee*
When will it be ready?	**Quando sarà pronta?** *kwando sara pronta*
How much will it cost?	**Quanto costerà?** *kwanto kostayra*
That's outrageous!	**Non esageriamo!** *non aysajayreeaamo*
Can I have a receipt for the insurance?	**Mi dia una ricevuta per l'assicurazione, per favore.** *mee deea oona reechayvoota pehr lasseekooratseeonay pehr favoray*

YOU MAY HEAR

… non funziona.	The … isn't working.
Non ho i pezzi di ricambio necessari.	I don't have the necessary parts.
Devo ordinare i pezzi di ricambio.	I will have to order the parts.
Posso solo fare una riparazione provvisoria.	I can only repair it temporarily.
La sua macchina è inservibile.	Your car is totaled/a write-off.
Non si può riparare.	It can't be repaired.
Sarà pronta …	It will be ready …
oggi più tardi	later today
domani	tomorrow
fra … giorni	in … days

Accidents

In the event of an accident:
1. put your red warning triangle about 100 meters [metres] behind your car;
2. report the accident to the police (compulsory if there is personal injury); don't leave before they arrive;
3. show your driver's license and green card;
4. give your name, address, insurance company to the other party;
5. report to the appropriate insurance bureaus of the third party and your own company;
6. don't make any written statement without advice of a lawyer or automobile club official;
7. note all relevant details of the other party, any independent witnesses of the accident.

There has been an accident.	**C'è stato un incidente.** *cheh staato oon eencheedayntay*
It's …	**È …** *eh*
on the highway [motorway]	**sull'autostrada** *soollowtostraada*
near …	**vicino a …** *veecheeno ah*
Where's the nearest telephone?	**Dov'è il telefono più vicino?** *doveh eel taylayfono peeoo veecheeno*
Call …	**Chiami …** *keeaamee*
the police	**la polizia/i carabinieri** *la poleetseea/ee karabeenyehree*
an ambulance	**un'ambulanza** *oon amboolantsa*
a doctor	**un medico** *oon maydeeko*
the fire department [brigade]	**i pompieri** *ee pompeeehree*
Help me, please!	**Mi aiuti, per favore!** *mee aeeootee pehr favoray*

Injuries

There are people injured.	**Ci sono dei feriti.** *chee sono day fayreetee*
No one is hurt.	**Non ci sono feriti.** *non chee sono fayreetee*
He is seriously injured.	**È gravemente ferito.** *eh gravaymayntay fayreeto*
She's unconscious.	**Ha perso conoscenza.** *ah payrso konoshayntsa*

Legal matters

What's your insurance company?	**Qual è la sua compagnia d'assicurazione?** *kwaleh la sooa kompanyeea dasseekooratseeonay*
What's your name and address?	**Qual è il suo nome e il suo indirizzo?** *kwaleh eel soo-o nomay ay eel soo-o eendeereetso*
He ran into me.	**Mi ha investito.** *mee ah eenvaysteeto*
She was driving too fast/ too close.	**Andava troppo veloce/era vicino.** *andaava troppo vaylochay/ era veecheeno*
I had the right of way.	**Avevo la precedenza.** *avayvo la praychaydayntsa*
I was only driving ... km/h.	**Andavo solo a ... chilometri all'ora.** *andaavo solo ah ... keelomaytree allora*
I'd like an interpreter.	**Vorrei un interprete.** *vorrehee oon eentayrpraytay*
I didn't see the sign.	**Non ho visto il segnale.** *non oh veesto eel saynyaalay*
The license plate [registration] number was ...	**Il numero di targa era ...** *eel noomayro dee targa ayra*

YOU MAY HEAR

Mi faccia vedere ..., per favore.	Can I see your ..., please?
la patente di guida	driver's license/licence
la polizza d'assicurazione	insurance certificate
i documenti del veicolo.	vehicle registration
A che ora è successo?	What time did it happen?
Dove è successo?	Where did it happen?
C'erano altre persone coinvolte?	Was anyone else involved?
Ci sono testimoni?	Are there any witnesses?
Deve pagare un'ammenda/ una multa subito.	You'll have to pay a fine (on the spot).
Deve fare una dichiarazione in Commissariato.	You have to make a statement at the station.

ASKING DIRECTIONS

Excuse me, please.	**Scusi, per favore.** _skoozee pehr favoray_
How do I get to …?	**Come si arriva a …?** _komay see arreeva ah_
Where is …?	**Dov'è … ?** _doveh_
Can you show me on the map where I am?	**Può indicarmi dove sono sulla cartina?** _pwo eendeekaarmee dovay sono soolla karteena_
I've lost my way.	**Mi sono perso/smarrito.** _mee sono payrso/ smarreeto_
Can you repeat that, please?	**Può ripetere, per favore?** _pwo reepaytayray pehr favoray_
Thanks for your help.	**Grazie (per il Suo aiuto).** _graatseeay (pehr eel soo-o aeeooto)_

Traveling by car

Is this the right road for …?	**È questa la strada per …?** _eh kwaysta la straada pehr_
How far is it to … from here?	**Quant'è lontano/a … da qui?** _kwanteh lontaano/a … da kwee_
Where does this road lead?	**Dove porta questa strada?** _dovay porta kwaysta straada_
How do I get onto the highway [motorway]?	**Come si entra in autostrada?** _komay see ayntra een owtostraada_
What's the next town called?	**Come si chiama la prossima città?** _komay see keeaama la prosseema cheetta_
How long does it take by car?	**Quanto tempo ci vuole in macchina?** _kwanto taympo chee vwolay een makkeena_

ON THE STREET

Scusi, la stazione è lontana da qui? _skoozee la statseeonay eh lontaana da kwee_ (Excuse me, is the train station far from here?)

No. È a dieci minuti a piedi. _no eh a deeehchee ah peeaydee_ (No. It's 10 minutes on foot.)

Mille grazie. _meelay graatseeay_ (Thank you very much.)

Prego. _praygo_ (You're welcome.)

Town plans

YOU MAY SEE	
aeroporto (m)	airport
passaggio (m) pedonale	pedestrian crossing
chiesa (f)	church
cinema (m)	movie theater [cinema]
città (f) storica	old town
commissariato (m)	police station
edifici (mpl) pubblici	public building
fermata (f) d'autobus	bus stop
gabinetti (mpl)	restrooms [toilets]
lei è qui	you are here
parcheggio (m)	parking lot [car park]
parco (m)	park
percorso (m) d'autobus	bus route
posteggio (m) dei tassì	taxi stand [rank]
sottopassaggio (m)	underpass
stadio (m)	stadium
stazione (f) (metropolitana)	subway [metro] station
ufficio (m) postale	post office
via (f) principale	main [high] street
zona (f) pedonale	pedestrian zone

YOU MAY HEAR	
È ... da qui	It's ... of here.
al nord/al sud	north/south
all'est/all'ovest	east/west
Prenda la strada per ...	Take the road for ...
È sulla strada sbagliata.	You're on the wrong road.
Deve ritornare a ...	You'll have to go back to ...
Segua le indicazioni per ...	Follow the signs for ...

Road signs

SOLO ACCESSO	access only
PERCORSO ALTERNATIVO	alternative route
DEVIAZIONE	detour [diversion]
METTERSI IN CORSIA	get in lane
DARE LA PRECEDENZA	yield [give way]
PONTE BASSO	low bridge
SENSO UNICO	one-way street
STRADA CHIUSA	road closed
SCUOLA	school
ACCENDERE I FARI	use headlights

YOU MAY HEAR

È ...	It's ...
vicino/lontano	close/a long way
a cinque minuti a piedi	5 minutes on foot
a dieci minuti in auto	10 minutes by car
a circa dieci chilometri	about 10 km away
È ...	It's ...
(sempre) diritto	straight ahead
a sinistra/a destra	on the left/on the right
dall'altro lato della strada	on the other side of the street
all'angolo	on the corner
dietro l'angolo	around the corner
in direzione di ...	in the direction of ...
di fronte .../dietro...	opposite .../behind ...
vicino a .../dopo ...	next to .../after ...
Scenda ...	Go down the ...
la strada (laterale/principale)	street (side/main)
Attraversi ...	Cross the ...
la piazza/il ponte	square/bridge
Prenda la terza svolta a destra.	Take the third turn to the right.
Giri a sinistra ...	Turn left ...
dopo il primo semaforo	after the first traffic light
al secondo incrocio	at the second intersection [crossroad]

SIGHTSEEING

TOURIST INFORMATION OFFICE

Tourist information offices are often situated in the town center; look for **Ufficio turistico**.

Where's the tourist office?	**Dov'è l'Ufficio turistico?** *dov<u>eh</u> loof<u>fee</u>cho too<u>ree</u>steeko*
booking office	**l'ufficio prenotazioni** *luf<u>ee</u>chio prenotats<u>ee</u>oni*
inquiry	**la richiesta d'informazioni** *la rik<u>ye</u>sta deenformats<u>ee</u>oni*
What are the main points of interest?	**Quali sono i principali punti d'interesse?** *<u>kwa</u>lay <u>so</u>no ee preencheep<u>aa</u>lay <u>poo</u>ntee deentay<u>ray</u>ssay*
We're here for …	**Siamo qui per …** *see<u>aa</u>mo kw<u>ee</u> pehr*
only a few hours	**solo poche ore** *<u>so</u>lo <u>po</u>chay <u>o</u>ray*
a day	**un giorno** *oon <u>jo</u>rno*
a week	**una settimana** *<u>oo</u>na saytteem<u>aa</u>na*
Can you recommend …?	**Può consigliare …?** *pwo konseely<u>aa</u>ray*
a sightseeing tour	**un giro turistico** *oon <u>jee</u>ro too<u>ree</u>steeko*
an excursion	**un'escursione** *<u>oo</u>n ayskoorsee<u>o</u>nay*
a boat trip	**una gita in barca** *<u>oo</u>na <u>jee</u>ta een b<u>aa</u>rka*
Do you have any information on …?	**Avete informazioni su …?** *a<u>vay</u>tay eenformatsee<u>o</u>nay soo*
Are there any trips to …?	**Ci sono gite per …?** *chee <u>so</u>no <u>jee</u>tay pehr*

Excursions

How much does the tour cost?	**Quanto costa il giro?** *kwanto kosta*
Is lunch included?	**Il pranzo è compreso?** *eel pranzo eh komprayzo*
Where do we leave from?	**Da dove si parte?** *da dovay partay*
What time does the tour start?	**A che ora comincia la gita?** *ah kay ora komeencha la jeeta*
What time do we get back?	**A che ora si ritorna?** *ah kay ora see reetorna*
Do we have free time in …?	**C'è del tempo libero a …?** *cheh dayl taympo leebayro ah*
Is there an English-speaking guide?	**C'è una guida di lingua inglese?** *cheh oona gooeeda dee eengglayzay*

On tour

Are we going to see …?	**Andiamo a vedere …?** *andeeaamo ah vaydayray*
We'd like to have a look at the …	**Vorremmo dare un'occhiata a …** *vorrehmmo daaray oonokeeaata ah*
Can we stop here …?	**Possiamo fermarci qui …?** *posseeaamo fayrmaarchee kwee*
to take photographs	**per fare fotografie** *pehr faaray fotografeea*
to buy souvenirs	**per comprare dei souvenirs** *pehr kohmpraaray dayee souvenirs*
to go to the restroom	**per andare alla toilette** *pehr andahray allah toaylaytte*
Would you take a photo of us, please?	**Le dispiace farci una fotografia?** *lay deespeeachay farzee oona fotografeea*
How long do we have here/in …?	**Quanto tempo abbiamo qui/a …?** *kwanto taympo abbeeaamo kwee/ah*
Wait! … isn't back yet.	**Aspetti! … non è ancora ritornato(-a).** *aspayttee non eh ankora reetornaato(-a)*

98

SIGHTS

Town maps are on display in city centers, train, tram and many bus stations, and at tourist information offices.

Where is/are the …?	**Dov'è …?** *doveh*
abbey	**l'abbazia** *labbatseea*
art gallery	**la galleria d'arte** *la gallayreea dartay*
battleground	**i luoghi della battaglia** *ee looogee daylla battalya*
botanical garden	**il giardino botanico** *eel jardeeno botaneeko*
castle	**il castello** *eel kastayllo*
cathedral	**la cattedrale** *la kattaydraalay*
cemetery	**il cimitero** *eel cheemeetayro*
church	**la chiesa** *la keeayza*
downtown area	**il centro** *eel chayntro*
fountain	**la fontana** *la fontaana*
market	**il mercato** *eel mayrkaato*
monastery	**il monastero** *eel monastayro*
museum	**il museo** *eel moozayo*
old town	**la città vecchia** *la cheetta vaykeea*
opera house	**il teatro dell'opera** *eel teeatro dayllopayra*
palace	**il palazzo** *eel palaatso*
park	**il parco/il giardino** *eel parko/eel jordeeno*
parliament building	**il palazzo del Parlamento** *eel palaatso dayl parlamaynto*
ruins	**le rovine** *lay roveenay*
shopping area	**la zona dei negozi** *la dzona dayee naygotsee*
viewpoint	**il punto(m) panoramico** *eel poonto panoraameeko*
Can you show me on the map?	**Può indicarmi sulla cartina?** *pwo eendeekahrmee soollah kahrteenah*

ADMISSION

Check opening times to avoid disappointment: some museums close at 2 p.m. Churches usually close between midday and 4 p.m.

Is the … open to the public?	**… è aperto(-a) al pubblico?** *eh apayrto(-a) al poobleeko*
What are the hours?	**Qual è l'orario di apertura?** *kwaleh loraareeo dee apayrtoora*
When does it close?	**A che ora chiude?** *ah kay ora keeooday*
Is … open on Sundays?	**… è aperto(-a) la domenica?** *eh apayrto(-a) la domayneeka*
When's the next guided tour?	**Quando c'è la prossima visita guidata?** *kwando cheh la prosseema veezeeta gooeedaata*
Do you have a guide book (in English)?	**C'è una guida (in inglese)?** *cheh oona gooeeda (een eengglayzay)*
Can I take photos?	**Posso fare fotografie?** *posso faaray fotograafeeay*
Is there access for the handicapped?	**C'è accesso per disabili?** *cheh achaysso pehr deesaabeelee*
Is there an audio guide in English?	**C'è una guida registrata in inglese?** *cheh oona gooeeda rayjeestraata een eengglaysay*

Paying/Tickets

How much is the entrance/ entry fee?	**Quant'è il biglietto d'ingresso?** *kwanteh eel beelyaytto deenggraysso*
Are there any discounts for …?	**Ci sono riduzioni/tariffe speciali per …?** *chee sono reedootseeonee/ tareeffay spaychaalee pehr*
children	**bambini** *bambeenee*
groups	**gruppi** *grooppee*
the handicapped	**disabili** *deesaabeelee*
senior citizens	**anziani** *antseeaanee*
1 adult and 2 children, please.	**Un adulto e due bambini, per piacere.** *oon adoolto ay doo-ay bambeenee pehr peeachayray*

AT THE TICKET COUNTER

Due adulti, per piacere. _dooay_ a_doo_ltee pehr pee_a_chayray _(Two adults, please.)_

Fa trentacinque euro. faa _tray_nta _cheeng_kweh a_yoo_ro _(That's 35 euros.)_

Ecco a Lei. _ekk_o a lay _(Here you are.)_

YOU MAY SEE

INGRESSO GRATUITO	free entry
CHIUSO	closed
APERTO	open
ARTICOLI DA REGALO/SOUVENIR	gift shop
L'ULTIMO INGRESSO È ALLE ORE DICIASSETTE.	last entry at 5 p.m.
LA PROSSIMA VISITA ALLE ...	next tour at ...
INGRESSO VIETATO	no entry
VIETATO USARE IL FLASH.	no flash photography

IMPRESSIONS

It's ...	È ... _eh_
amazing	**meraviglioso(-a)** mayraveelee_o_so(-a)
beautiful	**bello(-a)** _bayl_lo(-a)
boring	**noioso(-a)** noee_o_zo(-a)
breathtaking	**sensazionale** saynsatseeo_naa_lay
brilliant	**splendido(-a)** _splayn_deedo(-a)
great fun	**molto divertente** _molt_o deevayr_tayn_tay
interesting	**interessante** eentayrayss_saan_tay
magnificent	**magnifico** man_yee_feeko
romantic	**romantico(-a)** ro_man_teeko(-a)
strange	**strano(-a)** _straa_no(-a)
superb	**stupendo(-a)** stoo_payn_do(-a)
terrible	**terribile** tayr_ree_beelay
ugly	**brutto(-a)** _broot_to(-a)
It's a good value.	**Ne vale la spesa.** nay _val_ay la _spay_za
It's a rip-off.	**È una bidonata.** eh _oo_na beedo_naa_ta
I like it.	**Mi piace.** mee pee_a_chay

101

TOURIST GLOSSARY

acquaforte f etching
acquarello m watercolor
affresco m fresco
ala f wing of building
altare m altarpiece
altorilievo m high relief
antichità fpl antiquities
appartamenti mpl **reali**
royal apartments
arazzi mpl tapestry
arco m arch
arco m **rampante** buttress
arco m **trionfale** triumphal arch
argenteria f silverware
argento silver
arma f weapon
armeria f armory
artigianato m **d'arte** crafts
atrio m atrium
auriga f charioteer
badia f abbey
basso m **rilievo** bas-relief
biblioteca f library
biga f chariot
campanile m bell tower
camposanto m churchyard
cancello m gate
capolavoro m masterpiece
L'Ultima Cena The Last Supper
ceramica f ceramic
ceramiche fpl pottery
chiesa f church
collezione f collection
completato nel ... completed in
conferenza f lecture
contrafforte f buttress
cornicione m eaves
coro m choirstall

corona f crown
cortile m courtyard
costruito(-a) built in
cupola f dome
d'oro golden
da by person
dagherrotipo m daguerreotype
decorato(-a) da decorated by
decorazione f decoration
dettaglio m detail
dipinto m picture
dipinto(-a) da painted by
disegnato(-a) da designed by
disegno m design, drawing
distrutto(-a) da destroyed by
donato(-a) da donated by
dorato(-a) gilded
duomo m dome
edificio m building
eretto(-a) nel/in erected in
facciata facade
fibula f brooch
finestra f **con vetro colorato**
stained-glass window
fondato(-a) nel founded in
fonte f font
foro m forum
fossato m moat
fregio m frieze
frontone m pediment
garguglia f gargoyle
giardino f **formale**
formal garden
gioielli mpl jewelry
guglia f spire
imperatore m emperor
imperatrice f empress
in prestito a on loan to
incisione f carving, engraving
ingresso m foyer

iniziò nel started in
liberto m freedman
Maestà Madonna and Child
in majesty
marmo m marble
mattone m brick
mobilia f/**mobili** mpl furniture
moneta f coin
morto(-a) nel died in
mostra f display, exhibition
muro m wall
nato(-a) nel ... a ...
born in ... (year) in ... (town)
navata f nave
oggetto m **esposto/in mostra**
exhibit
orecchini mpl earrings
orologio m clock
padiglione m pavilion
paesaggio m landscape (painting)
palcoscenico m stage
paliotto m altar frontal
Papato m Papacy
pastello m pastel
Pietà f Virgin with crucified Christ
pietra f stone
pietra f **angolare** cornerstone
pietra f **preziosa** gemstone
pietra f **tombale** headstone
pilastro m pillar
pittore m, **pittrice** f painter
pittura f **murale** mural
pitture fpl **a olio** oils
placca f plaque
ponte m bridge
porta f **d'ingresso** doorway
ponte m **levatoio** drawbridge
primo livello m level 1
quadro m painting

rappresenta represents
re m king
regina f queen
regno m reign
restaurato nel restored in
ricostruito nel rebuilt in
ritratto m portrait
rocca m fortress/stronghold
rosone m rose window
rovine f ruins
ruderi fpl ruins
sagrestia sacristy
salone m **per cerimonie** stateroom
scala uno:cento scale 1:100
scala f staircase
scavi mpl excavations
schiavo m slave
schizzo m sketch
scoperto(-a) nel discovered in
scultore m, **scultrice** f sculptor
scuola f **di** school of
secolo m century
sette colli fpl Seven Hills
spalti mpl battlement
a spina f **de pesce** herringbone
sporgente overhanging
statua f **di cera** waxwork
tableau f tableau
tapezzerie fpl tapestry
tela f canvas
terme fpl baths
tetto m roof
tomba f grave, tomb
torre f tower
trittico m triptych
vetro m glass
visse lived
volta f vault
zoccolo m molding

Who/What?

What's that building?	**Cos'è quell'edificio?** _koseh kwayllaydeefeecho_
Who was the …?	**Chi era …?** _kee ayra_
architect	**l'architetto** _larkeetaytto_
artist	**l'artista** _larteesta_
What style is that?	**Che stile è?** _kay steelay eh_

Roma repubblicana 753–27 b.c.

After periods of Etruscan (**etrusco**) and Greek (**ellenistico**) influence in Italy, Rome was founded in 753 b.c. The Republic was declared in 509 b.c.; the city expanded its empire across the known world (esp. in Punic Wars against the Carthaginians, ca. 2nd b.c.; and the military successes of Julius Caesar). Caesar's assassination (44 b.c.) brought civil war.

Roma imperiale 27 b.c.–467 a.d.

Caesar's adopted son, Octavius (Augustus), became the first emperor. His descendants (Tiberius, Caligula, Claudius, Nero) were followed by the Flavian, Antonine and Severus dynasties. This period of expansion saw great artistic and architectural achievements. In 382 a.d. Christianity was recognized as the state religion. However, decline set in, the Empire split into two and power was moved to Constantinople. Goths and Vandals plundered Rome, which fell to the Ostrogoths.

Medioevo 467–1300

Italy remained fractured, featuring powerful families such as the Medicis, independent city states like Venice, and increasing Papal power (with Rome as the capital of Western Christianity) through the Holy Roman Empire (**Sacro Romano**). Foreign involvement (Norman, German, French, Spanish and Austrian) continued in Italy beyond the Middle Ages into the nineteenth century.

Impero Risorgimento 1815–1870

The reunification of Italy as one kingdom was achieved by Victor Emmanuel II of Piedmont in 1861, with assistance from his minister Cavour and the exploits of Garibaldi. The final piece came when Rome was captured (1870).

Novecento 20th century

Italy fought with the Allies in World War I, but Benito Mussolini allied with Hitler in World War II with devastating consequences. The Democratic Republic was established in 1946, with numerous fragile governments following. Italy was one of the founding members of the European Economic Community in 1957.

Rulers

What period is that?   **Che periodo è ...?** *kay payree__o__do eh*

Romano(-a) 500 b.c.–467 a.d.

Ruins remain throughout Italy and Western Europe of their forums, basilicas, arenas, theaters, amphitheaters, markets, circuses, libraries, triumphal arches, catacombs, baths, temples, aqueducts, bridges, city walls and mausoleums.

Bizantino 400–1100

Byzantine influence from the Eastern Christian Empire emphasized grandeur and mystery with splendid mosaic-decorated interiors (esp. Ravenna; also later influence in St Mark's in Venice, Sicily and Rome).

Gotico 1300–1400

Gothic style used complex architectural forms, using pointed arches and rib vaults (esp. cathedrals in Genoa and Siena, ornate window openings of Venetian houses, artistic work of Giotto in Padua, Assisi and Florence).

Rinascimento 1400–1650

The Renaissance was a hugely significant cultural and artistic movement, with a fascination with antiquity and admiration of beauty, colors, light, stability and poise. It saw stunning artistic creativity in the Quattrocento (ca. 15th cent.) esp. statues of Donatello, paintings of Botticelli; and Cinquecento (ca. 16th cent.) esp. Michelangelo (statues of David and Moses; Sistine Chapel ceiling), Leonardo da Vinci, Raphael, and the Venetian School (Titian, Tintoretto and El Greco).

Manierismo 1550–1650

Mannerism enjoyed frivolities and exaggerated use of Renaissance features (esp. Tivoli and Bomarzo; artists Caravaggio and Palladio).

Barocco e Rococò 1640–1789

Baroque emphasized movement, using scrolls and ornate embellishments (e.g. Bernini's facade of St Peter's in Rome; artists Canaletto and Bellotto).

CHURCHES

Predominantly Roman Catholic, Italy is rich in cathedrals and churches. Ask permission before taking photographs; cover bare shoulders before entering.

Catholic/Protestant church	**la chiesa cattolica/protestante** *la kee-__eh__za kat__o__leeka/protay__stan__tay*
mosque	**la moschea** *la mosk__ee__ah*
synagogue	**la sinagoga** *la seena__go__ga*
What time is ...?	**A che ora è ....?** *ah kay __oa__ra eh*

IN THE COUP

I'd like a map of …	**Vorrei una cartina di …** *vorrehee oona karteena dee*
this region	**questa regione** *kwaysta rayjonay*
walking routes	**percorsi a piedi** *pehrkorsee ah pee-ehdee*
cycle routes	**percorsi per ciclisti** *pehrkorsee pehr cheekleestee*
How far is it to …?	**Quanto dista …?** *kwanto deesta*
Is there a trail/scenic route to …?	**C'è un sentiero/una strada panoramica per …?** *cheh oon saynteeehro/oona straada panorameeka pehr*
Can you show me on the map?	**Puo indicarmi sulla cartina?** *pwo eendeekaarmee soolla karteena*
I'm lost.	**Mi sono smarrito(-a).** *mee sono smareeto(-a)*

Organized walks

When does the guided walk start?	**A che ora comincia la passeggiata/l'escursione?** *ah kay ora komeencha la passaydjaata/layskoorseeonay*
When will we return?	**Quando ritorneremo?** *kwando reetornayrehmo*
What is the walk like?	**Com'è la passeggiata?** *komeh la passaydjaata*
gentle/medium/tough	**facile/di media difficoltà/difficile** *facheelay/dee maydeea deeffeekolta/deeffeecheelay*
I'm exhausted.	**Sono esausto(-a).** *sono aysaoosto(-a)*
What kind of … is that?	**Che tipo di … è quello?** *kay teepo dee … eh kwayllo*
animal/bird	**animale/uccello** *aneemaalay/oochayllo*
flower/plant/tree	**fiore/pianta/albero** *feeoray/peeanta/albayro*

106

Geographic features

bridge	**il ponte** *eel pontay*
cave	**la caverna/la grotta** *la kavayrna/la grotta*
cliff	**la scogliera/la rupe** *la sholee-ehra/ la roopay*
field	**il campo** *eel kampo*
foot path	**il sentiero** *eel sayntee-ehro*
forest	**la foresta** *la foraysta*
hill	**la collina** *la kolleena*
lake	**il lago** *eel lago*
mountain	**la montagna** *la montaanya*
mountain pass	**il passo di montagna** *eel passo dee montaanya*
mountain range	**la catena di montagne** *la katayna dee montaanyay*
nature reserve	**l'oasi naturale** *loazee natooraale*
panorama	**il panorama/la vista** *eel panoraama/ la veesta*
park	**il parco** *eel parko*
peak	**il picco/la cima** *eel peeko/la cheema*
picnic area	**l'area da pic nic** *laraya da peekneek*
pond	**lo stagno** *lo staanyo*
rapids	**le rapide** *lay rapeeday*
river	**il fiume** *eel feeoomay*
sea	**il mare** *eel maaray*
stream	**il ruscello/il torrente** *eel rooshayllo/ eel torrayntay*
valley	**la valle** *la vallay*
viewpoint	**il punto panoramico** *eel poonto panorameeko*
village	**il paese** *eel pa-ehsay*
winery [vineyard]	**le vigne** *lay veenyay*

LEISURE

EVENTS

Local papers and, in large cities, weekly entertainment guides will tell you what's on.

Do you have a program of events?	**Ha un programma delle manifestazioni?** *ah oon programa dayllay maneefaystatseeonee*
Can you recommend ? a good …	**Può consigliare un(a) buon(a) …?** *pwo konseelyaaray oon(a) bwon(a)*
Is there a … somewhere?	**C'è …?** *cheh*
ballet/concert	**un balletto/un concerto** *oon ballaytto/oon konchayrto*
movie [film]	**un film** *oon film*
opera	**un'opera** *oonopayra*

Tickets for concerts, theater, and other cultural events are on sale at special ticket agencies (e.g. Anteprima, Prenoticket, Prontobiglietto) or major music stores (e.g. Messaggerie Musicali, Ricordi).

Availability

When does it start?	**A che ora comincia?** *ah kay ora komeencha*
When does it end?	**A che ora finisce?** *ah kay ora feeneeshay*
Are there any seats for tonight?	**Ci sono posti per questa sera?** *chee sono postee pehr kwaysta sayra*
Where can I get tickets?	**Dove si comprano i biglietti?** *dovay see kompraano ee beelyayttee*
There are … of us.	**Siamo in …** *see-aamo een*

Tickets

How much are the seats?	**Quanto costano i posti?** *kwanto kostano ee postee*
Do you have anything cheaper?	**Ha qualcosa di meno caro?** *ah kwalkosa dee mayno karo*
I'd like to reserve ...	**Vorrei prenotare ...** *vorrehee praynotaaray*
3 for Sunday evening	**tre posti per domenica sera** *tray postee pehr domayneeka sayra*
May I have a program, please?	**Ha un programma, per piacere?** *ah oon programma pehr peeachayray*
Where's the coat room?	**Dov'è il guardaroba?** *doveh eel goo-ardaroba*

YOU MAY HEAR

... della sua carta di credito?	What's your credit card ...?
il numero	number
il tipo	type
la data di scadenza	expiration date
Ritiri i biglietti ... per favore.	Please pick up the tickets ...
alle ... di sera	by ... p.m.
al banco prenotazioni	at the reservation desk

YOU MAY SEE

PRENOTAZIONI	Bookings
TUTTO ESAURITO	Sold out
BIGLIETTI PER LO SPETTACOLO DI OGGI	Tickets for today's show

AT THE BOX OFFICE

Avete un programma delle manifestazioni?
avaytay oon programa dayllay maneefaystatseeonee
(Do you have a program of events?)

Certo. Ecco a Lei. *cherto ekko a lay*
(Of course. Here you are.)

Grazie. *graatseeay (Thank you.)*

Movies

Foreign films are always dubbed into Italian, but a few movie houses show films in the original version. Italy has a film industry of its own, with famous directors such as Fellini, Antonioni and Visconti, Bertolucci, the Taviani Brothers, Roberto Benigni, Salvatores and Nanni Moretti. For a view of Italian humor, try a film by Carlo Verdone.

Is there a movie theater [cinema] near here?	**C'è un cinema qui vicino?** *cheh oon cheenayma kwee veecheeno*
What's playing at the movies tonight?	**Cosa danno al cinema questa sera?** *kosa danno al cheenayma*
Is the film dubbed/subtitled?	**Il film è doppiato/ha i sottotitoli?** *eel film eh doppeeaato/af ee sottoteetolee*
Is the film in the original English?	**Il film è in lingua originale (inglese)?** *eel film eh een leengwa oreejeenaalay eengglayzay*
A ..., please.	**..., per favore.** *pehr favoray*
box of popcorn	**un pacchetto di popcorn** *oon pachetto dee popcorn*
chocolate ice cream	**un cremino** *oon kremeeno*
hot dog	**un hot dog** *oon hot dog*
soft drink/soda	**una bibita** *oona beebeeta*
small/regular/large	**piccolo(-a)/medio(-a)/grande** *peekolo(a)/maydeeo(-a)/graanday*

Theater

What's playing at the ... Theater?	**Cosa danno al teatro ...?** *...kosa danno al teeatro*
Who's the playwright?	**Di chi è?** *dee kee eh*
Do you think I'd enjoy it?	**Pensa che mi piacerà?** *paynsa kay mee peeachayra*
I don't know much Italian.	**Non so bene l'italiano.** *non so baynay eetaleeaano*

Opera/Ballet/Dance

In addition to the La Scala in Milan, excellent productions are found at the opera houses in Bologna, Florence, Naples, Parma, Rome and Turin. Also look for open-air productions in the summer, often held in Greek and Roman ruins.

Where's the opera house? **Dov'è il teatro dell'Opera?**
doveh eel teeatro dayllopayra

Is formal dress required? **È necessario l'abito da sera?**
eh naychayssaareeo labeeto da sayra

Who's dancing? **Chi sono i ballerini?**
kee sono ee ballayreenee

I'm interested in
contemporary dance.
Mi interessa la danza contemporanea.
mee eentayraysa la dantsa kontaymporaaneha

Music/Concerts

Where's the concert hall? **Dov'è la sala concerti?**
doveh la sala konchayrtee

Which orchestra/
band is playing?
Che orchestra/gruppo sta suonando?
kay orkaystra/groopo sta soo-onando

What are they playing? **Cosa stanno suonando?**
kosa stanno soo-onando

Who is the
conductor/soloist?
Chi è il direttore d'orchestra/il (la) solista? *kee eh eel deerayttoray dorkaystra/eel (la) soleesta*

Who is the support band? **Chi è il gruppo di supporto?**
kee eh eel grooppo dee soopporto

I really like … **Mi piace molto…** *mee peeachay molto*

country music **la musica country** *la moozeeka country*

folk music **la musica folk**
la moozeeka folk

jazz **il jazz** *eel djaz*

pop **la musica pop** *la moozeeka pop*

rock music **il rock** *eel rock*

soul music **il soul** *il soul*

NIGHTLIFE

What is there to do in the evenings?	**Cosa si può fare la sera?** *kosa see pwo faaray la sayra*
Can you recommend a …?	**Può consigliare …?** *pwo konseelyaaray*
Is there a … in town?	**C'è … in città?** *cheh een cheetta*
bar	**un bar** *oon bar*
casino	**un casinò** *oon kazeeno*
discotheque	**una discoteca** *oona deeskotayka*
gay club	**un locale gay** *oon lokaalay gay*
nightclub	**un nightclub** *oon nightclub*
restaurant	**un ristorante** *oon reestorantay*
What type of music do they play?	**Che tipo di musica suonano?** *kay teepo dee moozeeka soo-onano*
How do I get there?	**Come ci si arriva?** *komay chee see arreeva*

Admission

What time does the show start?	**A che ora comincia lo spettacolo?** *ah kay ora komeencha lo spayttakolo*
Is evening dress required?	**È necessario l'abito da sera?** *eh naychayssareeo labeeto da sayra*
Is there a cover charge?	**Si paga il coperto?** *see paga eel kopayrto*
Is a reservation necessary?	**Si deve prenotare?** *see dayvay praynotaaray*
Do we need to be members?	**Bisogna essere soci?** *eh beesonya ayssayray sochee*
How long will we have to stand in line [queue]?	**Quanto tempo si deve aspettare/ fare la coda?** *kwanto taympo see dayvay aspayttaaray/faaray la koda*
I'd like a good table.	**Vorrei un buon tavolo.** *vorrehee oon bwon tavolo*

YOU MAY SEE

È COMPRESA UNA BIBITA	includes 1 complimentary drink

112

CHILDREN

Can you recommend
something for the children?
Può consigliare qualcosa per i bambini? *pwo konseelyaaray kwalkosa pehr ee bambeenee*

Are there changing facilities
here for infants?
Dove si possono cambiare i pannolini? *dovay see possono kambeeaaray ee pannoleenee*

Where are the restrooms
[toilets]?
Dove sono le toilette/i bagni? *dovay sono lay toaylayttay/ ee bannee*

amusement arcade **la sala da giochi** *la sala dah jokee*

fairground **la fiera** *la fee-ehra*

kiddie [paddling] pool **la piscina per bambini** *la peesheena pehr bambeenee*

playground **il parco giochi** *eel parko jokee*

zoo **lo zoo** *lo dzoh*

Baby-sitting

Can you recommend a
reliable baby-sitter?
Può consigliare una buona babysitter? *pwo konseelyaaray oona bwona babysitter*

Is there constant
supervision?
La sorveglianza è continua? *la sorvaylyaantsa eh konteenoo-a*

Are the helpers properly
trained?
Gli assistenti sono professionisti? *lyee asseestayntee sono professioneestee*

When can I drop
them off?
Quando posso lasciarli(-le)? *kwando posso lashaarlee(-lay)*

I'll pick them up at … **Li (Le) passo a prendere alle …** *lee (lay) passo ah prayndayray allay*

We'll be back by … **Ritorniamo alle …** *reetrneeamo allay*

She's 3 and he's
18 months.
Lei ha tre anni e lui diciotto mesi. *layee ah tray annee ay looee deechotto mayzee*

SPORTS

Soccer [football], tennis, boxing, wrestling, windsurfing and bicycle, car and horseracing are the most popular sports.

il calcio *eel kalcho*

Soccer is the overriding passion in Italy, which boasts probably the best league in the world (Serie A) with teams of the calibre of Juventus (Turin), Inter, Milan, Roma and Lazio. The intensity with which fans support their team creates a thrilling atmosphere during matches. In addition, the stadiums in Rome (Stadio Olimpico), Milan (Stadio San Siro) and Naples (Stadio San Paolo) are particularly striking.

Spectator Sports

Is there a soccer game [football match] this Saturday?	**C'è una partita di calcio stasera** *cheh oona parteeta dee kalcho stasayra*
Which teams are playing?	**Che squadre giocano?** *keh skwadray jokano*
Can you get me a ticket?	**Può comprarmi un biglietto?** *pwo kompraaray oon beelyaytto*
What's the admission charge?	**Quanto costa l'entrata?** *kwanto kosta layntraata*
Where's the racetrack [race course]?	**Dov'è l'ippodromo?** *doveh leeppodromo*
Where can I place a bet?	**Dove si scommette?** *dovay see skommayttay*
What are the odds on ...?	**Qual è il pronostico su ....?** *kwaleh eel pronosteeko soo*
athletics	**l'atletica** *l'atlayteeka*
basketball	**la pallacanestro** *la pallakanaystro*
cycling	**il ciclismo** *eel cheekleesmo*
golf	**il golf** *eel golf*
horseracing	**l'ippica** *leepeeka*
soccer [football]	**il calcio** *eel kalcho*
swimming	**il nuoto** *eel noo-oto*
tennis	**il tennis** *eel tennis*
volleyball	**la pallavolo** *la pallavollo*

Playing

Where's the nearest …?	**Dov'è … più vicino(-a)?** *doveh peeoo veecheeno(-a)*
golf course	**il campo da golf** *eel kampo da golf*
sports club	**la palestra** *la palaystra*
Where are the tennis courts?	**Dove sono i campi da tennis?** *dovay sono ee kampee da tennis*
What's the charge per …?	**Quanto costa a/al/all' …?** *kwanto kosta a/aal/al*
day/round/game/hour	**giorno/giro/partita/ora** *jorno/jeero/parteeta/ora*
Where can I rent …?	**Dove posso noleggiare …?** *dovay posso nolaydjaaray*
boots	**gli scarponi** *lyee skaarponee*
clubs	**le mazze** *lay matsay*
equipment	**l'attrezzatura** *lattraytsatooray*
a racket	**la racchetta** *la rakaytta*
I'd like to take lessons.	**Vorrei prendere qualche lezione.** *vorrehee prayndayray kwalkay laytseeonay*
Do you have a fitness room?	**C'è una sala attrezzi?** *cheh oona sala atrayzzee*

YOU MAY SEE

SPOGLIATOI	Locker rooms
PESCA VIETATA	No fishing
RISERVATO AI DETENTORI DI LICENZA	Permit holders only

YOU MAY HEAR

Mi dispiace, è tutto prenotato.	I'm sorry, we're booked.
C'è una caparra/un anticipo di …	There is a deposit of …
Che taglia/che misura ha ?	What size are you?
Deve avere una fotografia formato passaporto.	You need a passport-size photo.

At the beach

Italy abounds in beaches and sea resorts, and it is not too difficult to locate near-deserted coves for a quieter time. Nearly all beaches have private bathing establishments where you can rent cabins, deck chairs and sunbeds. Often the beach boys (**bagnini**) are also lifeguards, distinguished by their red shorts and vests.

A red flag signifies rough sea, a white flag denotes calm.

Is the beach …?	**La spiaggia è …?**	la spee<u>a</u>dja eh
pebbly/sandy	**rocciosa/sabbiosa**	rockee<u>o</u>sa/sabbee<u>o</u>sa
Is there a … here?	**C'è … ?**	cheh …
children's pool	**una piscina per bambini**	
	<u>oo</u>na peesh<u>ee</u>na pehr bamb<u>ee</u>nee	
swimming pool	**una piscina** <u>oo</u>na peesh<u>ee</u>na	
indoor/outdoor	**invernale/all'aperto**	
	eenvayrn<u>aa</u>lay/allap<u>ay</u>rto	
Is it safe to swim/dive here?	**Si può nuotare/tuffare senza pericolo?**	
	see pwo nooot<u>aa</u>ray/too-f<u>ah</u>-ray	
	s<u>ay</u>ntsa payr<u>ee</u>kolo	
Is it safe for children?	**È sicuro per i bambini?**	
	eh seek<u>oo</u>ro pehr i bamb<u>ee</u>nee	
Is there a lifeguard?	**C'è un bagnino?** cheh oon ban<u>yee</u>no	
I want to rent a/some…	**Vorrei noleggiare …**	
	vorr<u>e</u>hee nolaydj<u>aa</u>ray	
deck chair	**una sedia a sdraio**	
	<u>oo</u>na s<u>ay</u>deea ah sdr<u>a</u>eeo	
jet ski	**una moto acquatica**	
	<u>oo</u>na m<u>o</u>to akw<u>a</u>tika	
motorboat	**una barca a motore**	
	<u>oo</u>na b<u>a</u>rka ah mot<u>o</u>ray	
diving equipment	**attrezzature da sub**	
	attraytsat<u>oo</u>ray da soob	
umbrella [sunshade]	**un ombrellone** oon ombrayll<u>o</u>nay	
surfboard	**una tavola da surf** <u>oo</u>na t<u>a</u>vola da surf	
waterskis	**degli sci d'acqua** d<u>a</u>ylye shee d<u>a</u>kwa	
For … hours.	**Per … ore.** pehr … <u>o</u>ray	

Skiing

There is excellent skiing, in the Dolomites and the Italian Alps (Valle D'Aosta); the Apennines and the slopes of Etna also offer skiing.

What's the snow like?	**Com'è la neve?** _komeh la nayvay_
heavy/icy	**spessa/ghiacciata** _spayssa/geeachaata_
powdery/wet	**farinosa/bagnata** _fareenosa/banyaata_
I'd like to rent …	**Vorrei noleggiare …** _vorrehee nolaydjaaray_
poles	**le racchette** _le rachettay_
skates	**i pattini (da ghiaccio)** _ee patteenee (da geeacho)_
ski boots	**gli scarponi (da sci)** _lyee skarponee (da shee)_
skis	**gli sci** _lyee shee_
These are too …	**Questi(-e) sono troppo …** _kwaystee(-ay) sono troppo_
big/small	**grandi/piccoli(e)** _graandee/peekolee(-ay)_
They're uncomfortable.	**sono scomodi(-e).** _sono skomodee(-ay)_
A lift pass for a day/ 5 days, please.	**Uno ski pass per un giorno/cinque giorni, per favore.** _oono ski pass pehr oon jorno/cheengkway jornee pehr favoray_
I'd like to join the ski school.	**Vorrei iscrivermi alla scuola sci.** _vorrehee eeskreevayrmee alla skoola shee._
I'm a beginner.	**Sono un principiante.** _sono oon preencheepeeantay_
I'm experienced.	**Ho esperienza.** _oh ayspayree-ehntsah_

YOU MAY SEE

LA FUNIVIA	cable car/gondola
LA SEGGIOVIA	chair lift
LA SCIOVIA	tow lift

MAKING FRIENDS

INTRODUCTIONS

Greetings vary according to how well you know someone. The following is a guide:

It's polite to shake hands, both when you meet and say good-bye.

Begin any formal conversation, whether with a shop assistant or policeman, with a "**Buongiorno**".

Ciao! is an informal, universal expression, meaning both "hello, hi" and "so long, good-bye."

In Italian, there are two forms for "you" (taking different verb forms):

tu (singular) and **voi** (plural) are used when talking to relatives, close friends and children (and between young people);

Lei (singular) and **Loro** (plural) are used in all other cases (with the 3rd person singular/plural of the verb).

Hello, I don't think we've met.	**Buongiorno, non ci conosciamo.** *bwonjorno non chee konosheeaamo*
My name is …	**Sono …** *sono*
May I introduce …?	**Posso presentarle …?** *posso praysayntaarlay*
Pleased to meet you.	**Piacere/Molto lieto(-a).** *peeachayray/molto leeehto(-a)*
What's your name?	**Come si chiama?** *komay see keeaama*
How are you?	**Come sta?** *komay sta*
Fine, thanks. And you?	**Bene, grazie, e Lei?** *baynay graatseeay ay layee*

AT A RECEPTION

Sono Sheryl. *sono sheryl (My name is Sheryl.)*
Piacere. Sono Franco. *peeachayray sono fraanko*
(Pleased to meet you. My name is Franco.)
Piacere. *peeachayray (Pleased to meet you.)*

Where are you from?

Where do you come from?	**Di dov`è?**	*dee dovay eh*
Where were you born?	**Dove è nato(-a)?**	*dovay eh naato(-a)*
I was born in …	**Sono nato(-a) …**	*sono naato(-a)*
Australia	**in Australia**	*in allowstraaleea*
Britain	**in Gran Bretagna**	*in gran braytanya*
Canada	**in Canada**	*in kanada*
England	**in Inghilterra**	*in eenggeeltayrra*
Ireland	**in Irlanda**	*in eerlanda*
Scotland	**in Scozia**	*in skotseea*
U.S.	**negli Stati Uniti**	*neglee staatee ooneetee*
Wales	**in Galles**	*in gallayss*
Where do you live?	**Dove vive?**	*dovay veevay*
What part of … are you from?	**Da quale parte … viene?**	*da kwalay partay … vee-ehnay*
Italy	**dell'Italia**	*daylleetaaleea*
Sicily	**della Sicilia**	*daylla seecheeleea*
Switzerland	**della Svizzera**	*daylla sveetsayra*
We come here every year.	**Veniamo ogni anno.**	*vayneeaamo onyee anno*
It's my/our first visit.	**È la mia/nostra prima visita.**	*eh la meea/nostra preema veezeeta*
Have you ever been to …?	**È già stato in …?**	*eh ja staato een*
Do you like it here?	**Le piace questo posto?**	*lay peeachay kwaysto posto*
What do you think?	**Cosa pensa?**	*kosa paynsa*
I love the … here.	**Mi piace molto …**	*mee peeachay molto*
I don't really like the … here.	**Non mi piace molto …**	*non mee peeachay molto*
food/people	**la cucina/la gente**	*la koocheena/la jayntay*

Who are you with?/Family

Who are you with?	**Con chi è?**	*kon kee eh*
I'm on my own.	**Sono (da) solo/a.**	*sono (da) solo(-a)*
I'm with a friend.	**Sono con un amico/un'amica.** *sono kon oonameeko/oonameeka*	
I'm with my …	**Sono con …** *sono kon*	
wife	**mia moglie** *meea molyeeay*	
husband	**mio marito** *meeo mareeto*	
family	**la mia famiglia** *la meea fameelya*	
children	**i miei figli** *ee meeayee feelyee*	
parents	**i miei genitori** *ee meeayee jayneetoree*	
boyfriend/girlfriend	**il mio ragazzo/la mia ragazza** *eel meeo ragatso/la meea ragatsa*	
my father/son	**mio padre/figlio** *meeo padray/feelyo*	
my mother/daughter	**mia madre/figlia** *meea madray/feelya*	
my brother/uncle	**mio fratello/mio zio** *meeo fratayllo/meeo dzeeo*	
my sister/aunt	**mia sorella/zia** *meea sorraylla/dzeea*	
What's your son's/ wife's name?	**Come si chiama suo figlio/sua moglie?** *komay see keeama soo-o feelyo/soo molyeeay*	
Are you married?	**È sposato(-a)?** *eh sposaato(-a)*	
I'm …	**Sono …** *sono*	
married/single	**sposato(-a)/single** *sposaato(-a)/single*	
divorced/separated	**divorziato(-a)/separato(-a)** *deevortseeaato(-a)/saypayraato(-a)*	
engaged	**fidanzato(-a)** *feedantsaato(-a)*	
Do you have any children?	**Ha bambini/figli?** *ah bambeenee/feelyee*	
2 boys and a girl	**Due ragazzi e una ragazza** *doo-ay ragatsee ay oona ragatsa*	
How old are they?	**Quanti anni hanno?** *kwantee annee anno*	

What do you do?

What line are you in?	**Che lavoro fa?**	*kay lavooro faa*
What are you studying?	**Che cosa studia?**	*kay kosa stoodeea*
I'm studying …	**Studio …**	*stoodeeo*
I'm in …	**Mi occupo di …**	*mee okoopo dee*
business	**affari**	*afaree*
engineering	**ingegneria**	*eenjaynyayreea*
retail	**commercio**	*kommayrcho*
sales	**vendite**	*vayndeetay*
Who do you work for?	**Per chi lavora?**	*pehr kee lavora*
I work for …	**Lavoro per …**	*lavoro pehr*
I'm a(n) …	**Sono …**	*sono*
accountant	**contabile**	*kontaabeelay*
housewife	**casalinga**	*kazaleengga*
student	**studente(ssa)**	*stoodayntay(ssa)*
retired	**pensionato(a)**	*paynseeonato*
between jobs	**fra un lavoro e l'altro**	*fra oon lavoro ay laltro*
I'm self-employed.	**Lavoro in proprio.**	*lavoro een propreeo*
What are your interests/hobbies?	**Quali sono i suoi interessi/hobby?**	*kwalee sono ee soooee eentayrayssee/hobby*
I like …	**Mi piace…**	*mee peeachay*
music	**la musica**	*la moozeeka*
reading	**leggere**	*laydjayray*
sports	**lo sport**	*lo sport*
I play …	**Gioco …**	*joko*
Would you like to play …	**Le piacerebbe giocare …**	*lay peeachayraybbay jokaaray*
cards	**a carte**	*ah kartay*
chess	**a scacchi**	*ah skaakee*

What weather!

What a lovely day!	**Che bella giornata!** *kay baylla jornaata*
What awful weather!	**Che tempo orribile!** *kay taympo orreebeelay*
Isn't it cold/hot today!	**Che caldo/freddo oggi!** *kay kaldo/frayddo odjee*
Is it usually as warm as this?	**Di solito fa così caldo?** *dee soleeto faa kosee kaldo*
Do you think it's going to … tomorrow?	**Pensa che domani …?** *paynsa kay domaanee*
be a nice day	**sarà una bella giornata** *sara oona baylla jornaata*
rain	**pioverà** *peeovayra*
snow	**nevicherà** *nayveekayra*
What is the weather forecast?	**Che previsioni ci sono?** *kay prayveeseeonay chee sono*
It's …	**È …** *eh*
cloudy	**nuvoloso** *noovoloso*
foggy	**nebbioso** *naybbeeoso*
frosty	**gelato** *jaylaato*
icy	**ghiacciato** *geeachaato*
thundering	**temporalesco** *taymporalaysko*
windy	**ventoso** *vayntoso*
It's raining.	**Piove.** *peeovay*
It's snowing.	**Nevica.** *nayveeka*
It's sunny.	**C'è il sole.** *chay eel solay*
Has the weather been like this for long?	**Il tempo è così da molto tempo?** *eel taympo eh kosee da molto taympo*
What's the pollen count?	**Com'è il conteggio del polline?** *komeh eel kontaydjo dayl polleenay*
high/medium/low	**alto/medio/basso** *alto/maydeeo/basso*
What's the forecast for skiing?	**Che previsioni ci sono per sciare?** *kay prayveeseeonee chee sono pehr sheeaaray*

Enjoying your trip?

I'm here on …	**Sono qui …** _sono kwee_
a business trip	**per affari** _pehr affaaree_
vacation [holiday]	**in vacanza** _een vakantsa_
We came by …	**Siamo venuti(-e) in …** _seeaamo vaynootee(-ay) een_
train/bus/plane	**treno/pullman/aereo** _trayno/pullman/aayreeo_
car/ferry	**auto/traghetto** _owto/tragaytto_
I have a rental car.	**Ho noleggiato una macchina** _o nolaydjaato oona makeena_
We're staying at …	**Alloggiamo …** _allodjaamo_
an apartment	**in un appartamento** _een oon appartamaynto_
a hotel/campsite	**in un albergo/un campeggio** _een oon albayrgo/oon kampaydjo_
with friends	**con amici** _kon ameechee_
Can you suggest …?	**Può consigliare …?** _pwo konseelyaaray_
things to do	**cose da fare** _kosay da faaray_
places to eat	**posti per mangiare** _postee pehr manjaaray_
places to visit	**posti da visitare** _postee da visitaaray_
We're having a great/ an awful time.	**Ci stiamo divertendo/annoiando.** _chee steeaamo deevayrtayndo/annoeeaando_

YOU MAY HEAR

È in vacanza?	Are you on vacation?
Come è arrivato?	How did you travel here?
Dove alloggia?	Where are you staying?
Da quanto tempo è qui?	How long have you been here?
Quanto tempo si trattiene?	How long are you staying?
Dove andrà dopo?	Where are you going next?
Si sta divertendo?	Are you enjoying your vacation?

INVITATIONS

Would you like to have dinner with us on …?	**Vuole venire a cena da noi …?** _vwolay vayneeray a chayna da noee_
May I invite you to lunch?	**Posso invitarla a pranzo?** _posso eenveetaarla ah prandzo_
Can you come for coffee this evening?	**Vuole venire a prendere il caffè da noi questa sera?** _vwolay vayneeray ah prayndayray eel kaffeh da noee kwaysta sayra_
We're having a party. Can you come?	**Facciamo una festa. Vuole venire?** _fachaamo oona faysta. vwolay vayneeray_
May we join you?	**Possiamo venire anche noi?** _passeeaamo vayneeray ankay noee_
Would you like to join us?	**Vuole venire anche Lei?** _vwolay vayneeray ankay layee_

Going out

What are your plans for …?	**Cosa fa …?** _kosa fa_
today/tonight	**oggi/stasera** _odjee/stasayra_
tomorrow	**domani** _domaanee_
Are you free this evening?	**È libero(-a) stasera?** _eh leebayro(-a) stasayra_
Would you like to …?	**Le piacerebbe …?** _lay pee-achayraybbay_
go dancing	**andare a ballare** _andaaray ah ballaaray_
go for a drink/meal	**andare al bar/al ristorante** _andaaray al bar/al reestorantay_
go for a walk	**fare una passeggiata** _faaray oona passaydjaata_
go shopping	**fare acquisti** _faaray akweestee_
I'd like to go to …	**Mi piacerebbe andare …** _mee pee-achayraybbay andaaray_

124

I'd like to see …	**Mi piacerebbe vedere …**
	mee pee-achay<u>rayb</u>bay vay<u>day</u>ray
Do you enjoy …?	**Le piace …?** *lay pee-<u>a</u>chay*

Accepting or declining

Great. I'd love to.	**Sarebbe magnifico.**
	sa<u>rayb</u>bay many<u>ee</u>feeko
Thank you, but I'm busy.	**Grazie, ma ho un altro impegno.**
	<u>graat</u>seeay ma ho oon <u>al</u>tro eempay<u>ny</u>o
May I bring a friend?	**Posso portare un amico/un'amica?**
(male/female)	*<u>pos</u>so por<u>taa</u>ray oon a<u>mee</u>ko(-a)*
Where shall we meet?	**Dove ci incontriamo?**
	<u>do</u>vay chee eenkontree<u>aa</u>mo
I'll meet you …	**Ci vediamo …** *chee vaydee<u>aa</u>mo*
in front of your hotel	**di fronte al suo albergo**
	dee <u>fron</u>tay al <u>soo</u>-o al<u>bay</u>rgo
I'll pick you up at 8 p.m.	**La chiamo alle otto.**
	la kee<u>aa</u>mo <u>al</u>lay <u>o</u>tto
Could we make it a bit	**Facciamo un po' più tardi/prima?**
later/earlier?	*fach<u>aa</u>mo oon po pee<u>oo</u> <u>tar</u>dee/<u>pree</u>ma*
How about another day?	**Facciamo un altro giorno?**
	fach<u>aa</u>mo oon<u>al</u>tro <u>jor</u>no
That will be fine.	**Va bene.** *va <u>bay</u>nay*

Dining out/in

Punctuality varies from region to region in Italy. 15 minutes late may be acceptable in the south, but even 5 minutes would be frowned upon in the north.

Let me buy you a drink.	**Mi permetta di offrirle una bibita.**
	mee payr<u>mee</u>ta dee off<u>reer</u>lay <u>oo</u>na
	bee<u>bee</u>ta
Do you like …?	**Le piace …?** *lay pee<u>a</u>chay*
What are you having?	**Cosa prende?** *<u>ko</u>sa <u>prayn</u>day*
That was a lovely meal.	**E'stato squisito!**
	eh<u>sta</u>to skwee<u>zee</u>to

ENCOUNTERS

Do you mind if I ...?	**Le dispiace se ...?** *lay deespeeachay say*
sit here	**mi siedo qui** *mee see-ehdo kwee*
smoke	**fumo** *foomo*
Can I get you a drink?	**Posso offrirle qualcosa da bere?** *posso offreerlay kwalkosa da bayray*
I'd love to have some company.	**Mi piacerebbe avere un po' di compagnia.** *me pee-achayraybbay avayray oon po dee kompanyeea*
Why are you laughing?	**Perché ride?** *payrkeh reeday*
Is my Italian that bad?	**Parlo così male l'italiano?** *parlo kosee maale leetaleeaano*
Shall we go somewhere quieter?	**Andiamo in un posto più tranquillo?** *andeeaamo een oon posto peeoo trankweello*
Leave me alone, please!	**Mi lasci in pace!** *mee lashee een pachay*
You look great!	**Sei stupendo(-a)!** *sayee stoopayndo(-a)*
Thanks for the evening.	**Grazie per la serata.** *graatseeay pehr la sayraata*
I'm afraid we've got to leave now.	**Penso che sia ora di andare.** *penso che see-a ora dee andaray*
Can I see you again tomorrow?	**Posso rivederla domani?** *posso reevaydayrla domaanee*
See you soon.	**A presto.** *ah praysto*
Can I have your address?	**Posso avere il suo indirizzo?** *posso avayray eel soo-o eendeereetso*

TELEPHONING

Most payphones take phonecards, available in units of €1, €2.5, €5 and €8 from newsstands or tobacco shops. You need to snap off the corner of the card for it to work. You can also often use your credit card for calling home.

To phone home from Italy, dial 00 followed by:

Australia 61	Canada 1	Ireland 353
New Zealand 64	South Africa 27	UK 44 US 1

Note that you will usually have to omit the initial 0 of the area code.

Can I have your telephone number?	**Mi dà il suo numero di telefono?** *mee da eel soo-o noomayro dee taylayfono*
Here's my number.	**Ecco il mio numero.** *ehko eel meeo noomayro*
Please call me.	**Mi chiami, La prego.** *mee keeaamee la praygo*
I'll give you a call.	**La chiamerò.** *la keeamayro*
Where's the nearest telephone booth?	**Dov'è il telefono pubblico più vicino?** *doveh eel taylayfono poobbleeko peeoo veecheeno*
May I use your phone?	**Posso usare il suo telefono?** *posso oozaaray eel soo-o taylayfono*
It's an emergency.	**È un'emergenza.** *eh oon aymayrjayntsa*
I'd like to call someone in England.	**Vorrei fare una chiamata in Inghilterra.** *vorrehee faaray oona keeamaata een eenggeeltayrra*
What's the area [dialling] code for …?	**Qual è il prefisso per …?** *kwaleh eel prayfeesso pehr*
What's the number for Information?	**Qual è il numero del Servizio Informazioni?** *kwaleh eel noomayro del serveezeeoh eenformatseeony*
I'd like the number for …	**Vorrei il numero per …** *vorrehee eel noomayro pehr*
I'd like to call collect [reverse the charges].	**Vorrei telefonare a carico del destinatario.** *vorrehee taylayfonaaray ah kareeko dayl daysteenatareeo*

On the phone

Hello. This is …	**Pronto. Sono …** _pronto. sono_
I'd like to speak to …	**vorrei parlare con …** _vorrehee parlaaray kon_
Extension …	**Interno …** _eentayrno_
Speak louder/ more slowly, please.	**Parli più forte/più lentamente, per piacere.** _parlee peeoo fortay/peeoo layntamayntay pehr peeachayray_
Could you repeat that, please?	**Può ripetere, per piacere?** _pwo reepaytayray pehr peeachayray_
I'm afraid he/she's not in.	**Mi dispiace, non c'è.** _mee deespeeaachay non che_
You have the wrong number.	**Ha sbagliato numero.** _ah zbalyaato noomayro_
Just a moment.	**Un momento.** _oon momaynto_
Hold on, please.	**Resti in linea, per piacere.** _een leeneea pehr peeachayray_
When will he/she be back?	**Quando rientra?** _kwando reeayntra_
Will you tell him/her that I called?	**Per favore, gli/le dica che ho chiamato.** _pehr favoray lyee/lay deeka kay o keeamaato_
My name is …	**Mi chiaimo …** _mee keeamo_
Would you ask him/her to phone me?	**Può dirgli/dirle di richiamarmi?** _pwo deerlyee/deerlay dee reekeeamaarmee_
I must go now.	**Ora devo andare.** _ora dayvo andaaray_
Nice to speak to you.	**È stato un piacere parlare con Lei.** _eh staato oon peeachayray parlaaray kon layee_
I'll be in touch.	**La contatterò.** _la kontattayro_
Bye.	**Arrivederci.** _arreevaydayrchee_

STORES & SERVICES

For a view of what Italians are buying, take a look in the big chain stores **La Rinascente**, **Upim** and **Oviesse**, which have branches in most towns.

Check locally for the location and times of open-air markets, generally held at least once a week in most tourist resorts.

I'd like …	**Vorrei …** _vorrehee_
Do you have …?	**Ha …?** _ah_
How much is that?	**Quanto costa?** _kwanto kosta_
Thank you.	**Grazie.** _graatseeay_

STORES AND SERVICES
Where is …?

Where's the nearest …?	**Dov'è … più vicino(-a)?** _doveh … peeoo veecheeno_
Where's there a good …?	**Dove'è un(a) buon(a) …?** _doveh oon (a) bwon(a)_
Where's the main shopping mall [centre]?	**Dov'è la zona dei negozi?** _doveh la dzona dayee naygotsee_
Is it far from here?	**È lontano da qui?** _eh lontaano da kwee_
How do I get there?	**Come ci arrivo?** _komay chee arreevo_

Stores

antiques shop	**il negozio di antiquariato** _eel naygotseeo dee anteekwareeaato_
bakery	**la panetteria** _la panayttayreea_
bank	**la banca** _la banka_
bookstore	**la libreria** _la leebrayreea_
butcher shop	**la macelleria** _la machayllayreea_
camera shop	**il negozio di ottica/foto** _eel naygotseeo dee otteeka/foto_
pharmacy	**la farmacia** _la farmacheea_
clothing store [clothes shop]	**il negozio di abbigliamento** _eel naygotseeo dee abbeelyamaynto_
delicatessen	**la salumeria** _la saloomayreea_

department store	**il grande magazzino** *eel <u>gran</u>day magats<u>ee</u>no*
drugstore [chemist]	**la farmacia** *la farma<u>chee</u>a*
fish store [fish monger]	**la pescheria** *la payskay<u>ree</u>a*
florist	**il fioraio** *eel feeo<u>ra</u>eeo*
gift shop	**il negozio di articoli da regalo** *eel nay<u>got</u>seeo de ar<u>tee</u>kolee da ray<u>ga</u>lo*
produce store [greengrocer]	**il fruttivendolo** *eel frooteev<u>ay</u>ndolo*
grocery store	**la drogheria** *la drogay<u>ree</u>a*
health food store [shop]	**il negozio di dietetica** *eel nay<u>got</u>seeo dee deeay<u>tay</u>teeka*
jewelry store	**la gioielleria** *la joeeayllay<u>ree</u>a*
liquor store [off licence]	**l'enoteca** *leno<u>te</u>kah*
market	**il mercato** *eel mayr<u>kaa</u>to*
newsstand	**l'edicola** *lay<u>dee</u>kola*
pastry shop	**la pasticceria** *la pasteetchay<u>ree</u>a*
record [music] shop	**il negozio di musica** *eel nay<u>got</u>seeo dee <u>moo</u>zeeka*
shoe store	**il negozio di scarpe** *eel nay<u>got</u>seeo dee <u>skar</u>pay*
shopping mall [centre]	**il centro commerciale** *eel <u>chayn</u>tro kommayr<u>chaa</u>lay*
souvenir store	**il negozio di souvenir** *eel nay<u>got</u>seeo dee souvenir*
sporting goods store	**il negozio di articoli sportivi** *eel nay<u>got</u>seeo dee ar<u>tee</u>kolee spor<u>tee</u>vee*
supermarket	**il supermercato** *eel soopayrmayr<u>kaa</u>to*
cigarette stand	**la tabaccheria** *la tabakkay<u>ree</u>a*
toy store	**il negozio di giocattoli** *eel nay<u>got</u>seeo dee jo<u>kat</u>tolee*

Services

dentist	**il/la dentista** eel/la dayn<u>tee</u>sta
doctor	**il medico/il dottore(-ressa)** eel <u>may</u>deeko/eel dott<u>o</u>ray(-<u>ray</u>ssa)
dry cleaner	**la tintoria/la lavanderia** la teentoreea/la lavandayreea
hairdresser (ladies/men)	**il parrucchiere/la parrucchiera** eel parrookkee<u>ay</u>ray/parrookkee<u>ay</u>ra
hospital	**l'ospedale** lospayd<u>aa</u>lay
launderette	**la lavanderia a gettone** la lavanday<u>ree</u>a ah jayt<u>o</u>nay
library	**la biblioteca** la beebleeoa<u>tay</u>ka
optician	**l'ottico/il negozio di ottica** <u>lo</u>tteeko/eel nay<u>go</u>tseeo dee <u>o</u>tteeka
police station	**il commissariato/la questura** eel kommeessaree<u>a</u>to/la kways<u>too</u>ra

Opening hours

In major cities like Rome, Milan, Bologna and Florence, during the August holidays (**Ferragosto**) you may find very few stores open as most locals have fled to the sea or mountains to escape the humidity.

When does the … open/close?	**Quando apre/chiude …?** <u>kwan</u>do <u>a</u>pray/kee<u>oo</u>day
Are you open in the evening?	**È aperto la sera?** eh a<u>pay</u>rto la <u>say</u>ra
Do you close for lunch?	**Chiude per pranzo?** kee<u>oo</u>day pehr <u>pran</u>dzo
Where is the …?	**Dov'è …?** dov<u>eh</u>
cashier/cash desk	**la cassa** la <u>kas</u>sa
store directory [guide]	**la guida al magazzino** la goo<u>ee</u>da al magats<u>ee</u>no
first floor [ground floor]	**pianterreno** pee<u>a</u>no <u>tay</u>rra
second floor [first floor]	**primo piano** <u>pree</u>mo pee<u>a</u>no

GENERAL TIMES

	Opening	Closing	Lunch break	Closed
stores (winter)	9.30	8	1–3/4	Sun, one half day
(summer)	9.30	8	1–4/5	during the week
some shopping areas	10	7	none	Sun, Mon a.m
post office	8.30	6	none	Sat p.m., Sun
banks (main offices)	8.30	4	1.30–3	weekend

Service

Can you help me?	**Può aiutarmi?** _pwo aeeoo<u>taa</u>rmee_
I'm looking for …	**Cerco …** _<u>chay</u>rko_
I'm just browsing.	**Sto solo dando un'occhiata.** _sto <u>so</u>lo <u>dan</u>do oonokkee<u>aa</u>ta_
Do you have any …?	**Avete …?** _a<u>vay</u>tay_
I'd like to buy …	**Vorrei comprare …** _vor<u>reh</u>ee kom<u>praa</u>ray_
Could you show me …?	**Può farmi vedere …?** _pwo <u>faar</u>mee vay<u>day</u>ray_
How much is this/that?	**Quant'è questo/quello?** _kwan<u>teh</u> <u>kway</u>sto/<u>kwayl</u>lo_
That's all, thanks.	**È tutto, grazie.** _eh <u>toot</u>to <u>graat</u>seeay_

YOU MAY SEE

ORARIO DI APERTURA	business hours
CHIUSO PER LA PAUSA DI MEZZOGIORNO	closed for lunch
ORARIO CONTINUATO	open all day
L'USCITA	exit
L'INGRESSO	entrance
LA SCALA MOBILE	escalator
L'USCITA D'EMERGENZA	emergency/fire exit
L'ASCENSORE	elevator

IN A STORE

Desidera qualcosa? _de<u>see</u>derah kwal<u>ko</u>sa (Can I help you?)_
No grazie. Sto solo dando un'occhiata. _no <u>graat</u>seeay sto <u>so</u>lo <u>dan</u>do oonokee<u>aa</u>ta (No, thanks. I'm just browsing.)_

132

Preference

I want something …	**Voglio qualcosa di …** <u>vo</u>lyo kwal<u>ko</u>sa dee
It must be …	**Deve essere …** <u>day</u>vay <u>ayss</u>ayray
big/small	**grande/piccolo(-a)** <u>gran</u>day/<u>peek</u>kolo(-a)
cheap/expensive	**economico(-a)/caro(-a)** ayko<u>no</u>meeko(-a)/<u>kaa</u>ro(-a)
dark/light	**scuro(-a)/chiaro(-a)** <u>skoo</u>ro(-a)/ kee<u>a</u>ro(-a)
light/heavy	**leggero(-a)/pesante** lay<u>dja</u>yro(-a) pay<u>zan</u>tay
oval/round/square	**ovale/rotondo(-a)/quadrato(-a)** o<u>vaa</u>lay/ ro<u>ton</u>do(-a)/kwa<u>draa</u>to(-a)
genuine/imitation	**autentico(-a)/imitazione** au<u>ten</u>teeko(-a)/ eemeetatsee<u>o</u>nay
I don't want anything too expensive.	**Non voglio niente di troppo caro.** non <u>vo</u>lyo nee<u>ayn</u>tay dee <u>trop</u>po <u>kaa</u>rao
Around … euros.	**Sulle … euro.** <u>sool</u>lay … <u>ay</u>ooro
Do you have anything …?	**Ha qualcosa di …?** ah kwal<u>ko</u>sa dee
larger	**più largo** pee<u>oo</u> <u>lar</u>go
better quality	**di qualità migliore** dee kwalee<u>ta</u> meel<u>yo</u>ray
smaller	**più piccolo** pee<u>oo</u> <u>peek</u>kolo

ESSENTIAL

Che cosa … desidera?	What … would you like?
colore/forma	color/shape
qualità/quantità	quality/quantity
Che tipo preferisce?	What kind would you like?
Su che prezzo vuole rimanere?	What price range are you thinking of?

YOU MAY HEAR

Buongiorno/buonasera, signora/signore.	Good morning/afternoon, madam/sir.
Desidera qualcosa?	Can I help you?
Che cosa desidera?	What would you like?
Glielo(-a) controllo subito.	I'll just check that for you.
È tutto?	Is that everything?
Nient'altro?	Anything else?

cheaper	**più economico/meno caro** *peeoo aykonomeeko/mayno karo*
Can you show me …?	**Può mostrarmi …?** *pwo mostraarmee*
that/this one	**quello/questo** *kwayllo/kwaysto*
these/those	**questi/quelli** *kwaystee/kwayllee*

Conditions of purchase

| Is there a guarantee? | **C'è la garanzia?** *cheh la garantseea* |
| Are there any instructions with it? | **Ci sono anche le istruzioni?** *chee sono ankay leh eestrootseeonee* |

Out of stock

| Can you order it for me? | **Può ordinarmelo(-a)?**
pwo ordeenaarmaylo(-la) |
| How long will it take? | **Quanto tempo ci vuole?**
kwanto taympo chee volay |

Decision

That's not quite what I want.	**Non è esattamente quello che voglio.** *non eh ayssattamayntay kwayllo kay volyo*
No, I don't like it.	**No, non mi piace.** *no non mee peeachay*
That's too expensive.	**È troppo caro.** *eh troppo karo*
I'll take it.	**Lo (La) prendo.** *lo (la) prayndo*

YOU MAY HEAR

Mi dispiace, non ne abbiamo.	I'm sorry, we don't have any.
È esaurito(-a).	We're out of stock.
Posso mostrarle qualcos'altro/ un tipo diverso?	Can I show you something else/ a different kind?
Glielo(-a) ordino?	Shall we order it for you?

IN A STORE

Accetta traveller's cheques? *atchaytta traveller's checks*
(Do you accept traveler's ckecks?)

No, mi dispiace. Ma accettiamo carte di credito. *no mee deespeeachay maa atchayttiamo karteh dee kraydeeto*
(No, I'm sorry. But we accept credit cards.)

Paying

Most stores, restaurants and hotels, and some highway service stations accept major credit cards, traveler's checks and Eurocheques–look for the signs on the door.

Tax can be reclaimed on larger purchases when returning home (outside the EU).

Where do I pay?	**Dove si paga?** _dovay see paga_
How much is that?	**Quant'è/Quanto costa?** _kwanteh/kwanto kosta_
Could you write it down, please?	**Può scrivermelo, per favore?** _pwo skreevayrmaylo pehr favoray_
Do you accept traveler's checks?	**Accetta traveller's cheques?** _atchaytta traveller's checks_
I'll pay ...	**Pago ...** _pago_
by cash	**in contanti** _een kontantee_
by credit card	**con carta di credito** _kon karta dee kraydeeto_
I don't have any small change.	**Non ho spiccioli.** _non o speecholee_
Sorry, I don't have enough money.	**Mi dispiace, non ho abbastanza soldi.** _mee deespeeachay non o abbastantsa soldee_
Could I have a receipt, please?	**Mi dà la ricevuta, per favore?** _mee da la reechayvoota pehr favoray_
I think you've given me the wrong change.	**Credo che si sia sbagliato(-a) nel darmi il resto.** _kraydo kay see see-a zbalyeeaato(-a) nayl daarmee eel raysto_

YOU MAY HEAR

Come paga?	How are you paying?
Questa operazione non è stata approvata/accettata.	This transaction has not been approved/accepted.
Questa carta non è valida.	This card is not valid.
Può mostrarmi un altro documento d'identità?	May I have further identification?

CASSA	cashier
I TACCHEGGIATORI SARANNO	shoplifters will
PUNITI A NORMA DI LEGGE	be prosecuted

Complaints

This doesn't work.	**E' difettoso(-a).** *eh deefayttoso(-a)*
Can you exchange this, please?	**Può cambiarlo, per favore?** *pwo kambeeaarlo pehr favoray*
I'd like a refund.	**Vorrei un rimborso.** *vorrehee oon reemborso*
Here's the receipt.	**Ecco la ricevuta.** *eko la reechayvoota*
I don't have the receipt.	**Non ho la ricevuta.** *non o la reechayvoota*
I'd like to see the manager.	**Vorrei parlare con il direttore.** *vorrehee parlaaray kon eel deerettoray*

Repairs/Cleaning

This is broken. Can you repair it?	**E' rotto(-a). Può ripararlo(-a)?** *eh rotto(-a) pwo reeparaarlo(-la)*
Do you have … for this?	**Ha … per questo?** *ah … pehr kwaysto*
a battery	**una pila** *oona peela*
replacement parts	**dei pezzi di ricambio** *dayee paytsee dee reekambeeo*
There's something wrong with …	**C'è qualcosa che non va …** *cheh kwalkosa kay non va*
Can you ... this ...?	**Può ... questo(-a) ...?** *pwo ... kwaysto(-a)*
clean	**pulire** *pooleeray*
press	**stirare** *steeraaray*
mend	**riparare** *reeparaaray*
Can you alter this?	**Può aggiustarlo(-a)?** *pwo ajeeoostaarlo(-a)*
When will it be ready?	**Quando sarà pronto(-a)?** *kwando sara pronto(-a)*
This isn't mine.	**Questo non è mio.** *kwaysto non eh meeo*
… is missing.	**Manca …** *manka*

BANK/CURRENCY EXCHANGE OFFICE

At some banks, cash can be obtained from ATMs [cash machines] with Visa, Eurocard, American Express and many other international cards. Instructions are often given in English. You can also change money at most hotels, but the rate will not be as good. Main railway stations and airports also have currency exchange offices. Remember your passport when you want to change money.

In 2002 the currency in most EU countries, including Italy, changed to the euro (€), divided into 100 cents (**centesimi**). Switzerland is not in the EU and the currency is the Swiss franc (**franco**), divided into 100 **centesimi**.

Italy
Coins: 1, 2, 5, 10, 20, 50 ct.; €1, 2
Notes: €5, 10, 20, 50, 100, 200, 500

Switzerland
Coins: 5, 10, 20, 50 ct.; 1, 2, 5 SF.
Notes: 10, 20, 50, 100, 500, 1000 SF.

Where's the nearest …?	**Dov'è … più vicino/a?** <u>do</u>vay pee<u>oo</u> vee<u>cee</u>no/aa
bank	**la banca** la <u>ban</u>kaa
currency exchange	**l'ufficio di cambio** loo<u>fee</u>zeeo dee <u>kam</u>beeo

Changing money

Can I exchange foreign currency here?	**Si può cambiare valuta straniera?** see pwo kambee<u>aa</u>ray va<u>loo</u>ta stra<u>nyeh</u>ray
I'd like to change some dollars/pounds into euros.	**Vorrei cambiare alcuni dollari/sterline in euro.** vor<u>rehee</u> kambee<u>aa</u>ray al<u>koo</u>nee <u>dol</u>laree/stayr<u>lee</u>nay en <u>ay</u>ooro
I want to cash some traveler's checks [cheques].	**Voglio incassare dei traveller's cheques/degli Eurocheques.** <u>vol</u>yo eenkas<u>saa</u>ray travellers cheques/deli eurocheques
What's the exchange rate?	**Quant'è il cambio?** kwan<u>teh</u> eel <u>kam</u>beeo
How much commission do you charge?	**Quanto prendete di commissione?** <u>kwan</u>to <u>prayn</u>dayte dee kommeesse<u>eo</u>nay
Could I have some small change, please?	**Posso avere delle banconote di taglio più piccolo?** <u>pos</u>so a<u>vay</u>ray <u>day</u>llay banko<u>no</u>tay dee <u>tal</u>yo pee<u>oo</u> <u>peek</u>kolo
I've lost my traveler's checks. These are the numbers.	**Ho perso i miei traveller's cheques. Ecco i numeri.** oa <u>payr</u>so ee mee<u>ay</u>ee travellers cheques. <u>ek</u>ko ee <u>noo</u>mayree

Security

YOU MAY HEAR	
Posso vedere …?	Could I see …?
il suo passaporto	your passport
un documento d'identità	some identification
la sua carta bancaria	your bank card
Qual è il suo indirizzo?	What's your address?
Dove alloggia?	Where are you staying?
Compili/riempia questo modulo, per favore.	Fill out this form, please.
Per favore firmi qui.	Please sign here.

ATMs [Cash machines]

Can I withdraw money on my credit card here?
Posso fare un prelievo con la mia carta di credito? _posso faaray oon prayleeayvo kon la meea karta dee kraydeeto_

Where are the ATMs [cash machines]?
Dove' è il Bancomat/la cassa automatica? _doveh il bankomat/lay kassa owtomateeka_

Can I use my … card in the ATM [cash machine]?
Posso usare la mia carta … nel Bancomat? _posso oozaaray la meea karta … nayl bankomat_

The ATM [cash machine] has eaten my card.
Il Bancomat si è mangiato la mia carta. _eel bankomat see eh manjaato la meea karta_

YOU MAY SEE	
BANCOMAT/CASSA AUTOMATICA	automated teller [cash machine]
TUTTE LE OPERAZIONI	all transactions
SPINGERE/TIRARE/PREMERE	push/pull/press
APERTO/CHIUSO	open/closed
CASSA	cashiers

PHARMACY

Pharmacies are easily recognized by their sign: a green cross, usually lit up. If you are looking for a pharmacy at night, on Sundays or holidays, you'll find the address of emergency pharmacies (**farmacia di turno**) listed in the newspaper or displayed in all pharmacy windows.

Where's the nearest (all-night) pharmacy?	**Dov'è la farmacia (notturna) più vicina?** _doveh la farmacheea (nottoorna) peeoo veecheena_
What time does the pharmacy open/close?	**A che ora apre/chiude la farmacia?** _ah kay ora apray/keeooday la farmacheea_
Can you make up this prescription for me?	**Può farmi questa ricetta?** _pwo faarmee kwaysta reechaytta_
Shall I wait?	**Devo aspettare?** _dayvo aspayttaaray_
I'll come back for it.	**Passerò a ritirarla.** _passayro ah reeteeraarla_

Dosage instructions

How much should I take?	**Quanto devo prenderne?** _kwanto dayvo prayndayrnay_
How often should I take it?	**Con quale frequenza devo prenderlo(-la)?** _kon kwalay fraykwehntsa dayvo prayndayrlo(-la)_
Is it suitable for children?	**È adatto ai bambini?** _eh adatto ay bambeenee_

YOU MAY SEE

SOLO PER USO ESTERNO	for external use only
NON PER USO INTERNO	not to be taken internally

YOU MAY HEAR

Prenda ... pastiglie/cucchiaini ...	Take ... tablets/teaspoons ...
prima/dopo i pasti	before/after meals
con acqua	with water
intero(-a)	whole
la mattina/la sera	in the morning/at night
per ... giorni	for ... days

Asking advice

What would you recommend for …?	**Che cosa mi consiglia per …?** *kay kosa mee konseelya pehr*
a cold	**un raffreddore** *oon raffraydoray*
a cough	**la tosse** *la tossay*
diarrhea	**la diarrea** *la deearraya*
a hangover	**i postumi di una sbornia** *ee postoomee dee oona zborneea*
hayfever	**la febbre da fieno** *la faybbray da fee-ayno*
insect bites	**le punture d'insetto** *lay poontooray deensaytto*
a sore throat	**il mal di gola** *eel mal dee gola*
sunburn	**una bruciatura di sole** *oona broochatoorah dee soleh*
motion [travel] sickness	**la cinetosi** *la cheenaytozee*
an upset stomach	**mal di stomaco** *mal dee stomako*

Over-the-counter treatment

Can I have …?	**Ha …?** *ah*
an antiseptic cream	**una pomata antisettica** *oona pomaata anteesaytteeka*
(soluble) aspirin	**dell'aspirina (solubile)** *dayllaspeereena (soloobeelay)*
bandage	**delle bende** *dayllay baynday*
condoms	**dei profilattici** *dayee profeelatteechee*
cotton	**del cotone idrofilo** *dayl kotonay eedrofeelo*
an insect repellent/spray	**una pomata contro gli insetti/dello spray insetticida** *oona pomaata kontro lyee eensayttee/dayllo spray eensaytteecheeda*
pain killer	**dell'antinevralgico** *dayllanteenayvraljeeko*
vitamin pills	**delle vitamine** *dayllay veetameenay*

140

Toiletries

I'd like …	**Vorrei …**	*vorrehee*
aftershave	**un dopobarba**	*oon dopobarba*
deodorant	**un deodorante**	*oon deeodorantay*
moisturizing cream	**una crema idratante**	*oona krayma eedratantay*
razor blades	**delle lamette da barba**	
	dayllay lamayttay da barba	
sanitary napkins [towels]	**degli assorbenti**	*daylyee assorbayntee*
soap	**del sapone**	*dayl saponay*
sun block	**un blocco antisolare**	*oon block anteesolaaray*
suntan lotion	**una crema/una lozione abbronzante**	
	oona krayma/oona lotseeonay abbrondzantay	
factor …	**fattore …**	*fattoray*
tampons	**dei tamponi**	*dayee tamponee*
tissues	**dei fazzoletti di carta**	
	dayee fatsolayttee dee karta	
toilet paper	**della carta igienica**	*daylla karta eejayneeka*
toothpaste	**un dentifricio**	*oon daynteefreecho*

For the baby

baby food	**degli alimenti per neonati**	
	daylyee aleemayntee pehr neonaatee	
baby wipes	**dei fazzolettini/delle salviette per neonati**	
	dayee fatzolaytteenee/dayllee salveeayttee pehr neeonaatee	
diapers [nappies]	**dei pannolini**	*dayee pannoleenee*

Haircare

comb	**un pettine**	*oon paytteenay*
conditioner	**del balsamo**	*dayl balsamo*
hair mousse	**della schiuma per capelli**	
	daylla skeeooma per kapellee	
hair spray	**della lacca per capelli**	
	daylla lakka pehr kapayllee	
shampoo	**dello shampoo**	*dayllo shampoo*

CLOTHING

The fashion capital of Italy is Milan, where many of the great designers, such as **Armani**, **Versace**, **Trussardi**, **Ferré**, **Moschino** and **Krizia** have salons.

You'll find that airport boutiques offering tax-free shopping may have cheaper prices but less selection.

General

I'd like …	**Vorrei …** *vor<u>re</u>hee*
Do you have any …?	**Avete ….?** *a<u>vay</u>tay*

YOU MAY SEE

ABBIGLIAMENTO DA DONNA	ladies wear
ABBIGLIAMENTO DA UOMO	menswear
ABBIGLIAMENTO DA BAMBINO	children's wear
SALDI/LIQUIDAZIONI	sale

Color

I'm looking for something in …	**Cerco qualcosa in …** <u>chayr</u>ko kwal<u>ko</u>sa een
beige	**beige** *beige*
black	**nero** *<u>nay</u>ro*
blue	**blu** *bloo*
brown	**marrone** *mar<u>ro</u>nay*
green	**verde** *<u>vayr</u>day*
gray	**grigio** *<u>gree</u>jo*
orange	**arancione** *aran<u>cho</u>nay*
pink	**rosa** *<u>ro</u>sa*
purple	**viola** *vee<u>o</u>la*
red	**rosso** *<u>ro</u>sso*
white	**bianco** *bee<u>an</u>ko*
yellow	**giallo** *<u>jal</u>lo*
light …	**chiaro** *kee<u>aa</u>ro*
dark …	**… scuro** *… <u>skoo</u>ro*
Do you have the same in …?	**Ce l'ha anche in …?** *chay la <u>an</u>kay een*

Clothes and accessories

English	Italian	Pronunciation
belt	**la cintura**	*la cheentoora*
bikini	**il bikini**	*eel beekeenee*
blouse	**la camicetta**	*la kameechaytta*
bra	**il reggiseno**	*eel raydjeesayno*
briefs	**le mutandine**	*lay mootandeenay*
cap	**il berretto**	*eel bayrraytto*
coat	**il cappotto**	*eel kappotto*
dress	**il vestito**	*eel vaysteeto*
handbag	**la borsetta**	*la borsaytta*
hat	**il cappello**	*eel kapayllo*
jacket	**la giacca**	*la jakka*
jeans	**i jeans**	*ee jeans*
jumper	**la maglia**	*la malya*
leggings	**i fuseaux**	*ee fooso*
pants	**i pantaloni**	*ee pantalonee*
pullover	**il maglione**	*eel malyonay*
raincoat	**l'impermeabile**	*leempayrmeeabeelay*
scarf	**la sciarpa/il foulard**	*la sharpa/eel foolar*
shirt	**la camicia**	*la kameecha*
shorts	**gli shorts**	*lyee shorts*
skirt	**la gonna**	*la gonna*
socks	**i calzini**	*ee kaltseenee*
stocking	**le calze**	*lay kaltsay*
suit	**il completo**	*eel komplayto*
sweatshirt	**la felpa**	*la faylpa*
swimming trunks	**i calzoncini da bagno**	*ee kaltsoncheenee da banyo*
swimsuit	**il costume da bagno**	*eel kostoomay da banyo*
T-shirt	**la T-shirt/la maglietta**	*la tee shirt/la malyaytta*
tie	**la cravatta**	*la kravatta*
tights	**il collant**	*eel kollant*
tracksuit	**la tuta da ginnastica**	*la toota da jeennasteeka*
underpants	**le mutande**	*lay mootanday*

Shoes

A pair of ...	**un paio di** *oon pa-yo dee*
boots	**gli scarponi** *lyee skarponay*
flip-flops	**le ciabatte** *lay cheeabattay*
sandals	**i sandali** *ee sandalee*
shoes	**le scarpe** *lay skarpay*
slippers	**le pantofole** *lay pantofolay*
running shoes [trainers]	**le scarpe da ginnastica** *lay skarpay da jeennasteeka*

Walking/hiking gear

windbreaker	**la giacca a vento** *la jakka ah vaynto*
knapsack	**lo zaino** *lo dza-eeno*
walking boots	**gli scarponi** *lyee skarponee*
waterproof jacket	**la giacca a vento** *la jakka ah vaynto*

Fabric

I want something in ...	**Vorrei qualcosa in ...** *vorrehee kwalkosa een*
cotton	**cotone** *kotonay*
denim	**tela jeans** *tayla "jeans"*
lace/leather	**pizzo/pelle** *peetso/ payllay*
linen	**lino** *leeno*
wool	**lana** *lana*
Is this ...?	**È ...?** *eh*
pure cotton	**in puro cotone** *een pooro kotonay*
synthetic	**in fibra sintetica** *een feebra seentayteeka*
Is it hand washable/ machine washable?	**Si può lavare a mano/in lavatrice?** *see pwo lavaaray ah maano/een lavatreechay*

YOU MAY SEE

LAVARE A SECCO	dry clean only
NON STIRARE	do not iron
COLORI SOLIDI	colorfast

Does it fit?

Can I try this on?	**Me lo/la posso provare?**
	may lo/la posso provaaray
Where's the	**Dov'è la cabina di prova?**
fitting room?	*doveh la kabeena dee prova*
It fits well. I'll take it.	**Mi va bene. Lo/La prendo.**
	mee va baynay. lo/la prayndo
It doesn't fit.	**Non mi va bene.** *non mee va baynay*
It's too…	**È troppo …** *eh troppo*
short/long	**corto(-a)/lungo(-a)** *korto(-a)/loonggo(-a)*
tight/loose	**stretto(-a)/largo(-a)** *straytto(-a)/largo(-a)*
Do you have this in	**Ha questo nella taglia/misura …?**
size …?	*ah kwaysto naylla talya/meesoora*
What size is this?	**Che taglia è?** *kay talya eh*
Could you measure me?	**Può prendermi le misure?**
	pwo prendermee leh meesooreh
What size do you take?	**Cha taglia/misura prende?**
	kay talya/meesoora praynday
I don't know Italian sizes.	**Non conosco le misure italiane.**
	non konosko lay meesooray eetaleeaanay

	Dresses/Suits						Women's shoes			
American ⎫	8	10	12	14	16	18	6	7	8	9
British ⎬	10	12	14	16	18	20	4½	5½	6½	7½
Continental	38	40	42	44	46	48	37	38	39	40

	Shirts				Men's shoes							
American ⎫	15	16	17	18	6	7	8	8½	9	9½	10	11
British ⎬												
Continental	38	41	43	45	38	39	41	42	43	43	44	44

YOU MAY SEE

EXTRA GRANDE	extra large (XL)
GRANDE	large (L)
MEDIA	medium (M)
PICCOLA	small (S)

HEALTH AND BEAUTY

I'd like a …	**Vorrei fare…** *vorrehee fare*
facial	**un trattamento per il viso** *oon trattamaynto pehr eel veezo*
manicure	**una manicure** *oona maneekooray*
massage	**un massaggio** *oon massadjo*
waxing	**la ceretta** *la chayraytta*

Hairdresser

Tipping: up to 15% is normal.

I'd like to make an appointment for …	**Vorrei un appuntamento per …** *vorrehee oon appoontamaynto pehr*
Can you make it a bit earlier/later?	**Può un po' prima/più tardi?** *pwo oon po preema/peeoo tardee*
I'd like a …	**Vorrei …** *vorrehee*
cut and blow-dry	**taglio e asciugatura con fon** *talyo ay ashoogatoora kon fon*
shampoo and set	**shampoo e messa in piega** *shampoo ay mayssa een peeayga*
trim	**una spuntatina** *oona spoontateena*
I'd like my hair …	**Vorrei …** *vorrehee*
colored/tinted	**fare il colore** *faaray eel koloray*
permed	**la permanente** *la payrmanayntay*
Don't cut it too short.	**Non li tagli troppo corti.** *non lee talyee troppo kortee*
A little more off the …	**Tagli ancora un po' …** *talyee ankora oon po*
back/front	**dietro/davanti** *deeaytro/davantee*
neck/sides	**sul collo/ai lati** *sool kollo/ay lattee*
top	**sopra** *soprah*
That's fine, thanks.	**Va bene, grazie.** *va baynay graatseeay*

HOUSEHOLD ARTICLES

I'd like a(n)/some …	**Vorrei …** *vorrehee*
adapter	**una presa multipla** *oona praysa moolteepla*
aluminum foil	**della carta stagnola** *daylla karta stanyolay*

bottle opener	**un apribottiglie**	*oon apreebotteelyay*
candles	**delle candele**	*dayllay kandaylay*
clothespins [pegs]	**delle mollette da bucato**	
	dayllay mollayttay da bookaato	
plastic wrap [cling film]	**della pellicola**	*daylla paylleekola*
corkscrew	**un cavatappi**	*oon kavatappee*
lightbulb	**una lampadina**	*oona lampadeena*
matches	**dei fiammiferi**	*dayee feeammeefayree*
paper napkins	**dei tovaglioli di carta**	
	dayee tovalyolee dee karta	
plug *(electrical)*	**una spina elettrica**	
	oona speena aylayttreeka	
scissors	**un paio di forbici**	*oon paeeo dee forbeechee*
screwdriver	**un cacciavite**	*oon katchaveetay*
can [tin] opener	**un apriscatole**	*oon apreeskatolay*

Cleaning products

bleach	**della candeggina**	*daylla kandaydjeena*
dish cloth [tea towel]	**uno strofinaccio per i piatti**	
	oono strofeenatcho pehr ee peeattee	
detergent [washing powder]	**un detersivo per lavatrice**	
	oon daytayrseevo pehr lavatreechay	
dishwashing [washing-up] detergent	**un detersivo per lavastoviglie**	
	oon daytayrseevo pehr lavastoveelyay	
dishwashing [washing-up] liquid	**un detersivo per i piatti**	
	oon daytayrseevo pehr ee peeattee	
garbage [refuse] bags	**dei sacchetti per i rifiuti**	
	dayee sakkayttee pehr ee reeffeeootee	

China/Cutlery

cups	**delle tazze**	*dayllay tatsay*
forks	**delle forchette**	*dayllay forkayttay*
glasses	**dei bicchieri**	*dayee beekkeeehree*
knives	**dei coltelli**	*dayee koltayllee*
mugs	**dei boccali**	*dayee bokkaalee*

JEWELER

Even if you can't afford the wares of **Bulgari** and **Buccellati**, Italy's most famous jewelers, you will find the jewelry is generally beautifully crafted and 18-carat gold is a good buy.

Could I see …?	**Vorrei vedere …** vor*reh*ee vay*day*ray
this/that	**questo/quello** *kweh*sto/*kweh*llo
It's in the window/ display case.	**È in vetrina.** eh eenvay*tree*na
I'd like a(n)/some …	**Vorrei …** vor*reh*ee
alarm clock	**una sveglia** *oo*na *zvay*lya
bracelet	**un braccialetto** oon bratchee*a*laytto
brooch	**una spilla** *oo*na *speel*la
chain	**una catenina** *oo*na katay*nee*na
clock	**un orologio** oon oro*lo*jo
earrings	**degli orecchini** *day*lyee orayk*kee*nee
necklace	**una collana** *oo*na kol*la*na
ring	**un anello** oon a*nayl*lo
watch	**un orologio** oon oro*lo*jo
watch battery	**una pila per orologi** *oo*na *pee*la pehr oro*lo*jee

MATERIALS

Is this real silver/gold?	**È argento/oro vero?** eh ar*jayn*to/*oro vay*ro
Is there a certificate for it?	**C'è il certificato di garanzia?** cheh eel chayrteefeek*aa*to dee garant*see*a
Do you have anything in …?	**Ha qualcosa …?** ah kwal*ko*sa
copper/pewter	**in rame/in peltro** een *ra*may/een *payl*tro
crystal (quartz)	**in cristallo** een krees*tal*lo
cut glass	**in vetro tagliato** een *vay*tro ta*lyaa*to
diamond/pearl	**con diamante/con perle** kon deea*man*tay/ kon *payr*lay
enamel	**in smalto** een *smal*to
gold/silver	**in oro/in argento** een *oro*/een ar*jayn*to
gold-plated	**placcato d'oro** plak*aa*to *do*ro
platinum	**in platino** een *plat*eeno

148

NEWSSTAND/BOOKSTORE

Foreign newspapers can usually be found at rail stations or airports, or on newsstands in major cities.

Tobacco is a state monopoly in Italy. Licensed tobacconists are marked by a large white "**T**" on a black background. Cigarettes are also sold in some cafés and bars with a tobacco license.

Do you sell English-language books/newspapers?	**Avete libri/giornali inglesi?** _avaytay leebree/jornaalee eengglayzee_
I'd like a(n)/some …	**Vorrei …** _vorraiee_
book	**un libro** _oon leebro_
candy [sweets]	**dei dolci** _dayee dolchee_
chewing gum	**della gomma da masticare** _daylla gomma da masteekaaray_
chocolate bar	**una tavoletta di cioccolata** _oona tavolaytta dee chokkolaata_
pack of cigarettes	**un pacchetto di sigarette** _oon pakkaytto dee seegarayttay_
cigars	**dei sigari** _dayee seegaaray_
dictionary	**un dizionario** _oon deetseeonaareeo_
Italian-English	**Italiano-Inglese** _eetaleeano eengglayzay_
envelopes	**delle buste** _dayllay boostay_
guidebook for …	**una guida di …** _oona gooeeda dee_
lighter	**un accendino** _oon atchayndeeno_
magazine	**una rivista** _oona reeveesta_
road map of …	**una carta stradale di …** _oona karta stradaalay_
matches	**dei fiammiferi** _dayee feeaammeefayree_
newspaper	**un giornale** _oon jornaalay_
American/English	**americano/inglese** _amayreekaano/eengglayzay_
paper	**della carta** _daylla karta_
pen	**una penna** _oona paynna_
pencil	**una matita** _oona mateeta_
postcard	**una cartolina** _oona kartoleena_
stamps	**dei francobolli** _dayee frankobollee_
tobacco	**del tabacco** _dayl tabako_

PHOTOGRAPHY

I'm looking for a(n) ... camera.	**Cerco una macchina fotografica ...** _chayrko oona makkeena fotografeeka_
automatic	**automatica** _owtomateeka_
compact	**compact** _kompakt_
disposable	**usa-e-getta** _ooza ay jaytta_
SLR	**SLR** _ayssay ayllay ayrray_
battery	**la pila** _la peela_
camera case	**la custodia della macchina fotografica** _la koostodeea dela makkeena fotografeeka_
flash	**il flash** _eel flash_
filter	**il filtro** _eel feeltro_
lens	**l'obiettivo** _lobeeaytteevo_
lens cap	**il tappo per l'obiettivo** _eel tappo pehr lobyaytteevo_

Film/Processing

I'd like a ... film for this camera.	**Vorrei una pellicola ... per questa macchina (fotografica).** _vorrehee oona paylleekola... pehr kwaysta makkeena (fotografeeka)_
black and white	**in bianco e nero** _een beeanko ay nayro_
color	**a colori** _ah koloree_
24/36 exposures	**da 24/36 pose** _da vaynteekwatro/trayntasay pozay_
I'd like this film developed, please.	**Vorrei fare sviluppare questo film.** _vorrehee faaray zveeloopaaray kwehsto film_
Would you enlarge this, please?	**Può ingrandire questa, per favore?** _pwo eenggrandeeray kwaysta pehr favoreh_
How much do ... exposures cost?	**Quanto costa lo sviluppo ...?** _kwanto kosta lo zveelooppo_
When will the photos be ready?	**Quando saranno pronte le foto?** _kwando saranno prontay lay foto_
I'd like to pick up my photos. Here's the receipt.	**Vorrei ritirare le mie foto. Ecco la ricevuta.** _vorrehee reeteeraaray lay meeay foto. eko la reechayvoota_

POLICE

In Italy, dial ☎ 113 for all emergency services and ☎ 118 for fire. Dial ☎ 7 for the police in Switzerland.

Beware of pickpockets, particularly in crowded places. Report all thefts to the local police within 24 hours for your own insurance purposes.

Where's the nearest …?	**Dov'è … più vicino(-a)?** _doveh … peeoo veecheeno(-a)_
police station	**il commissariato/la questura** _eel kommeessareeaato/la kwehstoora_
Does anyone here speak English?	**C'è qualcuno che parla inglese?** _cheh kwalkoono kay parla eengglayzay_
I want to report a(n) …	**Voglio denunciare …** _volyo daynoonchaaray_
accident/attack	**un incidente/un'aggressione** _oon eencheedayntay/oonaggraysseeonay_
mugging/rape	**un'aggressione per rapina/uno stupro.** _oonaggraysseeonay pehr rapeena/oono stoopro_
My child is missing.	**Il/La mio(-a) bambino(-a) è scomparso(-a).** _eel/la meeo(-a) bambeeno(-a) eh skompaarso(-a)_
Someone's following me.	**Qualcuno mi sta seguendo.** _kwalkoono mee sta saygoo-ayndo_
I've seen a suspicious package.	**Ho visto un pacco sospetto.** _o veesto oon pakko sospaytto_
I need an English-speaking lawyer.	**Vorrei un avvocato che parli inglese.** _vorrehee oon avvokaato kay parlee leengglayzay_
I need to contact the Consulate.	**Devo contattare il consolato.** _dayvo kontataaray eel konsolaato_

YOU MAY HEAR	
Lo/la può descrivere?	Can you describe him/her?
uomo/donna	male/female
biondo(-a)/bruno(-a)	blonde/brunette
con i capelli rossi/grigi	red-headed/gray
con i capelli lunghi/corti/stempiato	long/short hair/balding
altezza approssimativa …	approximate height …
di (circa) … anni	aged (approximately) …
indossava …	He/She was wearing …

Lost property/Theft

I want to report a theft/break-in.	**Voglio denunciare un furto/una rapina.** _volyo daynoonchaaray oon foorto/oona rapeena_
I've been mugged/robbed.	**Sono stato aggredito/derubato.** _sono staato aggraydeto/dayroobaato_
I've lost my …	**Ho perso …** _o payrso_
My … has been stolen.	**Mi hanno rubato …** _mee anno roobaato_
bicycle	**la bicicletta** _la beecheeklaytta_
camera	**la macchina fotografica** _la makeena fotografeeka_
(rental) car	**l'auto (noleggiata)** _lowto (nolaydjaata)_
credit cards	**le carte di credito** _lay kartay dee kraydeeto_
handbag	**la borsetta** _la borsaytta_
money	**i soldi** _ee soldee_
passport	**il passaporto** _eel passaporto_
purse	**il portamonete** _eel poartamonaytay_
ticket	**il biglietto** _eel beelyaytto_
wallet	**il portafoglio** _eel portafolyo_
watch	**l'orologio** _lorolojo_
What shall I do?	**Cosa faccio?** _kosa fatcho_
I need a police report for my insurance claim.	**Devo avere una copia della mia denuncia per la mia assicurazione.** _dayvo avayray oona kopeea daylla meea daynooncha pehr la meea asseekooratseeonay_

YOU MAY HEAR

Cosa manca?	What's missing?
Quando è successo?	When did it happen?
Dove alloggia?	Where are you staying?
Da dove è stato(-a) preso(-a)?	Where was it taken from?
Dov'era lei in quel momento?	Where were you at the time?
Le abbiamo chiamato un interprete.	We're getting an interpreter for you.
Ci occuperemo della faccenda.	We'll look into the matter.
Compili questo modulo, per favore.	Please fill out this form.

POST OFFICE

Italian post offices bear the sign PT. Mail boxes are red in Italy, though some post offices have yellow boxes for express mail.

In major towns, the main post offices are normally open from 8.30 a.m. through to 6 p.m., while smaller branches close at 2 p.m. Stamps can be bought from tobacconists (**tabaccaio**), some hotel desks, as well as from the Post Office.

General queries

Where is the main post office?	**Dov'è l'ufficio postale centrale?** _dovai looffeecho postaalay chentraleh_
What time does the post office open/close?	**A che ora apre/chiude l'ufficio postale?** _ah kay oray apray/keeooday looffeecho postaalay_
Does it close for lunch?	**Chiude per pranzo?** _keeooday pehr prandzo_
Where's the mailbox [postbox]?	**Dov'è la cassetta delle lettere?** _doveh la kassaytta dayllay layttayray_
Where's the general delivery?	**Dov'è il Fermo Posta?** _doveh eel fayrmo posta_

Buying stamps

A stamp for this postcard, please.	**Un francobollo per questa cartolina, per favore.** _oon frankobollo pehr kwaysta kartoleena pehr favoray_
A ...-cent stamp, please.	**Un francobollo da ... centesimi, per favore.** _oon frankobollo da ... chentehseemee pehr favoray_
What's the postage for a letter to ...?	**Quanto costa spedire una lettera a ...?** _kwanto kosta spaydeeray oona layttayra ah_

IN A POST OFFICE

Francobolli per queste cartoline, per favore. _frankobollee pehr kwaysteh kartoleeneh pehr favoray_ (Stamps for these postcards, please.)

Fa tre lire. _faa tray ayooro_ (That's 3 euros.)

Ecco a Lei. _ekko a lay_ (Here you are.)

Sending packages

I want to send this package [parcel] by ...
Voglio spedire questo pacco ...
volyo spaydeeray kwaysto pahkko

airmail
per via aerea *pehr veea aayreea*

express/special delivery
per espresso *pehr ayspraysso*

It contains ...
Contiene ... *konteeaynay*

Telecommunications

I'd like a phonecard, please.
Vorrei una carta telefonica, per favore.
vorraiee oonah kahrtah taylayfoneekah pair fahvoray

5/8 euros.
Da cinque/otto euro.
da cheengkway/otto ayooro

Do you have a photocopier?
Avete il servizio fotocopie?
avaytay eel sayrveetseeo fotokopeeay

I'd like ... copies.
Vorrei ... copie. *vorrehee ... kopee-eh*

I'd like to send a message ...
Vorrei trasmettere un messaggio ...
vorrehee trasmayttayray oon mayssajeeo

by E-mail/fax
per posta elettronica/fax.
pehr posta aylaytroneeka/fax

What's your E-mail address?
Qual è il suo indirizzo di e-mail?
kwalay eel soo-o eendeereetso dee e-mail

Can I access the Internet here?
Posso accedere a Internet?
posso achaydayray a eentayrnet

What are your charges per hour?
Quanto si paga all'ora?
kwanto see paaga allora

How do I log on?
Come ci si collega?
komay chee see kollayga

154

SOUVENIRS

Italy is a shopping wonderland and you'll find no shortage of souvenirs and gifts to take home.

Italian designer clothes for men, women and children are internationally renowned, as well as shoes, accessories and other leather goods (handbags, beauty cases, luggage). You'll also find knitwear, cloth (silk, linen) and lace; or jewelry, including gold and silverware.

Regional crafts include pottery, ceramics, olivewood, glass and crystal work, straw and raffia goods. If you're still stuck for a souvenir, try a bottle of fine Italian wine, liqueur or aperitif or an art book or reproduction.

antiques	**gli oggetti di antiquariato** *lyee ojayttee dee anteekwareeaato*
ceramics	**la ceramica** *la chayraameeka*
doll	**la bambola** *la bambola*
glassware	**gli articoli di vetro** *lyee arteekolee dee vehtro*
jewelry	**i gioielli** *ee joeeehllee*
knitware	**la maglieria** *la malyayreea*
needlework	**il ricamo** *eel reekaamo*
silk	**la seta** *la sehta*
woodwork	**il lavoro in legno** *eel lavoro een lehnyo*

Gifts

bottle of wine	**una bottiglia di vino** *oona botteelya dee veeno*
box of chocolates	**una scatola di cioccolatini** *oona skatola dee chokkolaateenee*
calendar	**un calendario** *oon kalayndaareeo*
key ring	**un portachiavi** *oon portakeeavee*
postcard	**una cartolina** *oona kartoleena*
souvenir guide	**una guida-ricordo** *oona gooeeda reekordo*
ceramic plate	**un piatto di ceramica** *oon peeatto dee cerameekaa*
T-shirt	**una maglietta** *oona malyaytta*

Music

I'd like a …	**Vorrei …** _vorrehee_
cassette	**un nastro/una cassetta** _oon nastro/oona kassaytta_
compact disc	**un compact/un CD** _oon compact/oon cheedee_
record	**un disco** _oon deesko_
videocassette	**una videocassetta** _oona veedeeokassaytta_
Who are the popular Italian singers/bands?	**Chi sono i cantanti/gruppi italiani più famosi?** _chee sono ee kantantee/grooppee eetaleeaanee peeoo famozee_

Toys and games

I'd like a toy/game …	**Vorrei un giocattolo/un gioco …** _vorrehee oon jokattolo/oon joko_
for a boy	**per un bambino** _pehr oon bambeena_
for a 5-year-old girl	**per una bambina di cinque anni** _pehr oona bambeena dee cheenkway annee_
pail and shovel [bucket and spade]	**un secchiello e una paletta** _oon saykeeayllo ay oona palaytto_
chess set	**un gioco degli scacchi** _oon joko daylyee skakee_
doll	**una bambola** _oona bambola_
electronic game	**un gioco elettronico** _oon joko aylayttroneeko_
teddy bear	**un orsacchiotto** _oon orsakkeeotto_

Antiques

How old is this?	**Di che anno è?** _dee kay anno ay_
Do you have anything from the … era?	**Ha qualcosa del periodo … ?** _ah kwalkosa dayl payreeodo_
Can you send it to me?	**Può spedirmelo(-la)?** _pwo spaydeermeelo(-la)_

Will I have problems with customs?	**Avrò problemi con la dogana?** _avro proablaymee kon la dogaana_
Is there a certificate of authenticity?	**C'è il certificato di autenticità?** _cheh eel chayrteefeekato dee owtaynteecheeta_

SUPERMARKET/FOODSTORE

Supermarkets and convenience stores are found in most tourist resorts and all towns; however, Italy is still rich in markets, smaller stores and delicatessens (**salumeria**), where it can be more fun to shop.

At the supermarket

Excuse me. Where can I find …?	**Scusi. Dove posso trovare …?** _skoozee. dovay posso trovaaray_
Do I pay for this here or at the checkout?	**Pago qui o alla cassa?** _pago kwee o alla kassa_
Where are the baskets/ shopping carts [trolleys]?	**Dove sono i cestelli/carrelli?** _dovay sono ee karrayllee/chestayllee_
Is there a … here?	**C'è … ?** _cheh …_
delicatessen	**una salumeria** _oona saloomayreea_
pharmacy	**farmacia** _farmacheea_

YOU MAY SEE

PANE E DOLCI	bread and cakes
PRODOTTI DI PULIZIA	cleaning products
LATTICINI	dairy products
PESCE FRESCO	fresh fish
CARNI FRESCHE	fresh meat
PRODOTTI FRESCHI	fresh produce
PRODOTTI SURGELATI	frozen foods
ARTICOLI CASALINGHI	household goods
POLLAME	poultry
FRUTTA E VERDURA	fruit and vegetables
VINI E LIQUORI	wines and spirits

Food hygiene

AT THE GROCERY STORE

I'd like some of that/these.	**Vorrei un pò di quello/questo.** *vorrehee oon po dee kwayllo/kwaysto*
this one/those	**questo/quelli** *kwaysto/kwayllee*
to the left/right	**a sinistra/destra** *ah seeneestra/daystra*
over there/Here	**lì/qui** *lee/kwee*
Which one/ones?	**Quale/quali** *kwalay/kwalee*
That's all, thanks.	**È tutto, grazie.** *eh tootto graatseeay*
I'd like a(n) ...	**Vorrei ...** *vorrehee*
kilo of apples	**un chilo di mele** *oon keelo dee maylay*
half-kilo of tomatoes	**mezzo chilo di pomodori** *maytso keelo dee pomodoree*
100 grams of cheese	**100 grammi di formaggio** *chaynto grammee dee formadjo*
liter of milk	**un litro di latte** *oon leetro dee lattay*
half-dozen eggs	**mezza dozzina di uova** *maytsa dotseena dee ooova*
... slices of ham	**... fette di prosciutto** *... fehttay dee proshootto*
piece of cake	**un pezzo di torta** *oon paytso de torta*
box of chocolates	**una scatola di cioccolatini** *oona skatola dee chokkolateenee*
bottle of wine	**una bottiglia di vino** *oona botteelya dee veeno*
carton of milk	**una confezione di latte** *oona konfeceeoneh dee lattay*
jar of jam	**un vasetto di marmellata** *oon vasaytto dee marmayllaata*

IN A SUPERMARKET

Scusi. Dove posso trovare lo zucchero? _skoozee_ _dovay posso trovaaray lo tsookkayro_ (Excuse me, where can I find sugar?)
Lì, a sinistra. _lee ah seeneestra_ (Over there, to the left.)
Grazie. _graatseeay_ (Thanks.)

PROVISIONS/PICNIC

beer	**birra** _beerra_
butter	**burro** _boorro_
cheese	**formaggio** _formadjo_
cookies [biscuits]	**biscotti** _beeskottee_
chips	**patatine** _patateenay_
eggs	**uova** _oo-ova_
grapes	**uva** _oova_
ice cream	**gelato** _jaylaato_
instant coffee	**caffè solubile** _kaffeh soloobeelee_
loaf of bread	**pagnotta di pane** _panyotta dee panay_
milk	**latte** _lattay_
rolls (bread)	**i panini** _ee paneenee_
sausages	**salciccie** _salcheechay_
soft drink/soda	**bibita analcolica** _beebeeta analkoleeka_
tea bags	**bustine di tè** _boosteenay dee teh_
bottle of wine	**bottiglia di vino** _botteelyay dee veeno_

del pane _dayl paanay_

Bread; look for **pane all'olio** (olive oil white bread), **pane al latte** (milk bread), **panettone** (Christmas bread enriched with butter and candied fruit, sultanas and raisins), **pandoro** (a large sponge cake topped with powdered vanilla), **pangiallo** and **panforte** (firm nut and honey cake), **panpepato** (spicy nut cake) and **veneziana** (sweet holiday bread with whole almonds).

focaccia _fokatcha_

Savory flatbread; which may be flavored ~ **alla salvia** (sage bread), ~ **alla salsiccia** (sausage bread) or ~ **alle noci** (walnut bread).

CONVERSION CHARTS

The following conversion charts contain the most commonly used measures.

1 grammo (gr)	= 1000 milligrams	= 0.35 oz.
1 etto (hg)	= 100 grams	= .22 lb
1 mezzo chilo	= 500 grams	= 1.1 lb
1 chilo (kg)	= 1000 grams	= 2.2 lb
1 litro (l)	= 1000 milliliters	= 1.06 U.S / 0.88 Brit. quarts
		= 2.11 /1.8 US /Brit. pints
		= 34 /35 US /Brit. fluid oz.
1 centimetro (cm)	= 10 millimeter	= 0.4 inch
1 metro (m)	= 100 centimeters	= 39.37 inches/3.28 ft.
1 chilometro (km)	= 1000 meters	= 0.62 mile
1 metro quadrato (m2)		= 10.8 square feet
1 ettaro (ha)	= 10,000 sq meters	= 2.5 acres
1 chilometro quadrato (km2)		= 247 acres

Not sure whether to put on a bathing suit or a winter coat? Here is a comparison of Fahrenheit and and Celsius/Centigrade degrees.

-40°C	–	-40°F	5° C	–	41°F		Oven Temperatures	
-30°C	–	-22°F	10°C	–	50°F	100° C	–	212° F
-20°C	–	-4° F	15°C	–	59°F	121° C	–	250° F
-10°C	–	14° F	20°C	–	68°F	154° C	–	300° F
-5° C	–	23° F	25°C	–	77°F	177° C	–	350° F
-1° C	–	30° F	30°C	–	86°F	204° C	–	400° F
0° C	–	32° F	35°C	–	95°F	260° C	–	500° F

When you know	Multiply by	To find
ounces	28.3	grams
pounds	0.45	kilograms
inches	2.54	centimeters
feet	0.3	meters
miles	1.61	kilometers
square inches	6.45	sq. centimeters
square feet	0.09	sq. meters
square miles	2.59	sq. kilometers
pints (US/Brit)	0.47 / 0.56	liters
gallons (US/Brit)	3.8 / 4.5	liters
Fahrenheit	5/9, after subtracting 32	Centigrade
Centigrade	9/5, then add 32	Fahrenheit

HEALTH

Before you leave, make sure your health insurance policy covers any illness or accident while on vacation [holiday]. If not, ask your insurance representative, automobile association or travel agent for details of special health insurance. In Italy, EU citizens with a Form E111 are eligible for free medical treatment from the Italian national health system.

Hospital emergency departments (**Pronto Soccorso**) will treat all emergencies. However, it you are a non-EU citizen or without an E111 form, you will later have to sign a declaration that either you or your consulate will pay.

DOCTOR (GENERAL)

Where can I find a doctor/dentist?	**Dove posso trovare un medico/ un dentista?** _dovay posso trovaaray oon maydeeko/oon daynteesta_
Where's there a doctor who speaks English?	**C'è un medico che parla inglese?** _cheh oon maydeeko kay paarla eengglayzay_
What are the office hours?	**Quando apre l'ambulatorio?** _kwando apray lamboolatoreeo_
Could the doctor come to see me here?	**Posso avere una visita domiciliare?** _posso avayray oona veeseeta domeecheelyaaray_
Can I make an appointment ...?	**Vorrei (fissare) un appuntamento ...?** _vorrehee (feessaaray) oon appoontamaynto_
for tomorrow	**per domani** _pehr domaanee_
for as soon as possible	**al più presto** _al peeoo praysto_
It's urgent.	**È urgente.** _eh oorjayntay_
I've got an appointment with Doctor ...	**Ho un appuntamento con il dottor/ la dottoressa ...** _oh oon apoontamaynto kon eel dottor/la dottorayssa_

Accident and injury

My … is hurt/injured.	**… si è fatto(-a) male/è ferito(-a).**
	see eh fatto(-a) malay/eh fayreeto(-a)
husband/wife	**Mio marito/Mia moglie**
	meeo mareeto/meea molyeeay
son/daughter	**Mio figlio/Mia figlia** *meeo feelyo/meea feelya*
friend	**Il mio amico/La mia amica**
	eel meeo ameeko/la meea ameeka
He/She is unconscious.	**Ha perso conoscenza.** *ah payrso konoshayntsa*
He/She is bleeding . (heavily)	**Perde (molto) sangue.** *payrday (molto) sanggway*
He/She is injured	**È ferito(-a).** *eh fayreeto(-a)*
I've got a/an …	**Ho … o**
burn	**una scottatura** *oona skottatoora*
cut	**un taglio** *oon talyo*
insect bite	**una puntura d'insetto**
	oona poontoora deensaytto
rash	**un'eruzione sulla pelle** *oonayrootseeonay*
	soollah payllay
swelling	**un gonfiore** *oon gonfeeoray*

Short-term symptoms

I've been feeling sick [ill] for … days.	**Mi sento male da … giorni.** *mee saynto* *malay da … jornee*
I feel faint.	**Mi sento svenire.** *mee saynto svayneeray*
I feel feverish.	**Mi sento la febbre.** *mee saynto la faybbray*
I've been vomiting.	**Ho vomitato.** *o vomeetaatao*
I have diarrhea.	**Ho la diarrea.** *o la deeaarraya*
I have a/an…	**Ho … o**
cold	**il raffreddore** *eel raffrayddoray*
cramps	**i crampi** *ee krampee*
headache	**mal di testa** *mal dee taysta*
sore throat	**mal di gola** *mal dee gola*
stiff neck	**il collo rigido** *eel kollo reejeedo*
stomachache	**mal di stomaco** *mal dee stomako*

Health conditions

I have arthritis.	**Ho l'artrite**	*o lartreetay*
I have asthma.	**Ho l'asma**	*o lasma*
I am …	**Sono …**	*sono*
diabetic	**diabetico(-a)**	*deeabayteeko(-a)*
epileptic	**epilettico(-a)**	*aypeelaytteeko(-a)*
handicapped	**disabile**	*deesabeelay*
(… months) pregnant	**incinta di … mesi**	*eencheenta dee … maysee*
I have a heart condition.	**Ho disturbi cardiaci.**	*o deestoorbee kardeeachee*
I have high blood pressure.	**Ho la pressione alta.**	*o la praysseeonay alta*
I had a heart attack … years ago.	**Ho avuto un infarto … anni fa.**	*o avooto oon eenfaarto … annee fa*

Parts of the body

appendix	**l'appendice** *lappayndeechay*		kidney	**il rene** *eel raynay*	
arm	**il braccio** *eel bratcho*		knee	**il ginocchio** *eel jeenokkeeo*	
back	**il dorso/la schiena** *eel dorso/la skeeehna*		leg	**la gamba** *la gamba*	
			lip	**il labbro** *eel labbro*	
bladder	**la vescica** *la vaysheeka*		liver	**il fegato** *eel faygato*	
bone	**l'osso** *losso*		mouth	**la bocca** *la bokka*	
breast	**il petto/il seno** *eel paytto/eel sayno*		muscle	**il muscolo** *eel mooskolo*	
			neck	**il collo** *eel kollo*	
chest	**il torace** *eel toraachay*		nose	**il naso** *eel naaso*	
ear	**l'orecchio** *loraykkeeo*		rib	**la costola** *la kostola*	
eye	**l'occhio** *lokkeeo*		shoulder	**la spalla** *la spalla*	
face	**la faccia/il viso** *la fatcha/eel veezo*		skin	**la pelle** *la payllay*	
			stomach	**lo stomaco** *lo stomako*	
finger	**il dito** *eel deeto*		thigh	**la coscia** *la kosha*	
foot	**il piede** *eel peeehday*		throat	**la gola** *la gola*	
gland	**la ghiandola** *la geeandola*		thumb	**il pollice** *eel polleechay*	
hand	**la mano** *la mano*		toe	**il dito del piede** *eel deeto dayl peeehday*	
head	**la testa** *la taysta*				
heart	**il cuore** *eel koooray*		tongue	**la lingua** *la leenggooy*	
jaw	**la mascella** *la mashehlla*		tonsils	**le tonsille** *lay tonseellay*	
joint	**l'articolazione** *larteekolatseeonay*		vein	**la vena** *la vayna*	

Doctor's Inquiries

Da quanto tempo si sente così?	How long have you been feeling like this?
È la prima volta che ha questo disturbo?	Is this the first time you've had this?
Prende altre medicine?	Are you taking any other medicines?
È allergico(-a) a qualcosa?	Are you allergic to anything?
È vaccinato(-a) contro il tetano?	Have you been vaccinated against tetanus?
Ha perso l'appetito?	Have you lost your appetite?

Examination

Le misuro la temperatura/ la pressione del sangue.	I'll take your temperature/ blood pressure.
Arrotoli/tiri sù la manica.	Roll up your sleeve.
Si spogli fino alla vita.	Undress to the waist.
Si sdrai, per favore.	Please lie down.
Apra la bocca.	Open your mouth.
Respiri profondamente.	Breathe deeply.
Tossisca, per favore.	Cough please.
Dove le fa male?	Where does it hurt?
Fa male qui?	Does it hurt here?

Diagnosis

Deve fare una radiografia.	I want you to have an x-ray.
Voglio un campione di sangue/feci/urina.	I want a specimen of your blood/stool/urine.
Deve farsi visitare da uno specialista.	I want you to see a specialist.
Deve andare in ospedale.	I want you to go to the hospital.
È rotto(-a)/slogato(-a).	It's broken/sprained.
È lussato(-a)/strappato(-a).	It's dislocated/torn.
Ha ...	You've got (a/an) ...
l'appendicite	appendicitis
la cistite	cystitis

la febbre	temperature
l'influenza	flu
un'avvelenamento alimentare	food poisoning
una frattura	fracture
la gastrite	gastritis
l'ernia	hernia
un'infiammazione al/alla ...	inflammation of ...
il morbillo	measles
la polmonite	pneumonia
la sciatica	sciatica
la tonsillite	tonsilitis
un tumore	tumor
una malattia venerea	venereal disease
È infetto(-a).	It's infected.
È contagioso(-a)	It's contagious.

Treatment

Le do ...	I'll give you ...
un antisettico	an antiseptic
un analgesico	a pain killer
Le prescrivo ...	I'm going to prescribe ...
una cura di antibiotici	a course of antibiotics
delle supposte	some suppositories
È allergico(-a) a qualche medicina?	Are you allergic to any medicines?
Prenda una pillola ...	Take one pill ...
ogni ... ore/... volte al giorno	every ... hours/... times a day
prima dei/dopo i pasti	before/after meals
in caso di dolore	if there is any pain
per ... giorni	for ... days
Ritorni fra ... giorni.	I'd like you to come back in ... days.
Consulti un medico quando ritorna a casa.	Consult a doctor when you get home.

GYNECOLOGIST

I have …	**Ho …** *o*
abdominal pains	**dolori addominali** *doloree addomeenaalee*
period pains	**mestruazioni dolorose** *maystrooatseeonay dolorosay*
a vaginal infection	**un'infezione vaginale** *ooneenfaytseeonay vajeenaalay*
I haven't had my period for … months.	**Non ho le mestruazioni da … mesi.** *non o lay maystrootseeonay da … maysee*
I'm on the Pill.	**Prendo la pillola (anticoncezionale).** *prayndo la peellola (anteekonchaytseeonaalay)*

HOSPITAL

Please notify my family.	**Per favore informi la mia famiglia.** *pehr favoray eenformee la meea fameelya*
I'm in pain.	**Ho dolori.** *o doloree*
I can't eat/sleep.	**Non posso mangiare/dormire.** *non posso manjaaray/dormeeray*
When will the doctor come?	**Quando verrà il dottore?** *kwando vayrra eel dottoray*
Which section [ward] is … in?	**In che reparto/corsia è …?** *een kay raypaarto/korseea eh*
I'm visiting …	**Visito …** *veeseeto*

OPTICIAN

I'm nearsighted/farsighted [shortsighted/longsighted].	**Sono miope/presbite.** *sono meeopay/praysbeetay*
I've lost …	**Ho perso …** *o payrso*
one of my contact lenses	**una lente a contatto** *oona laynte ah kontatto*
my glasses	**gli occhiali** *lee okeeaalee*
a lens	**una lente** *oona layntay*
Could you give me a replacement?	**Può sostituirmelo(-la)?** *pwo sosteetooeermaylo(-la)*

DENTIST

If you need to see a dentist, you'll probably have to pay the bill on the spot; save all receipts for reimbursement.

I have a toothache.	**Ho mal di denti.** *o mal dee dayntee*
This tooth hurts.	**Questo dente mi fa male.** *kwaysto dayntay mee fa malay*
I don't want it extracted.	**Non voglio un'estrazione.** *non volyo oon aystratseeonay*
I've lost a filling/a tooth.	**Ho perso un'otturazione/un dente.** *o pehrso oonottooratseeonay/oon dayntay*

YOU MAY HEAR

Le faccio un'iniezione/ un'anestesia locale.	I'm going to give you an injection/ a local anesthetic.
Ci vuole un'otturazione/ una capsula/una corona.	You need a filling/cap [crown].
Devo fare un'estrazione.	I'll have to take it out.
Posso fissarlo solo temporaneamente.	I can only fix it temporarily.
Non mangi niente per ... ore.	Don't eat anything for ... hours.

PAYMENT/INSURANCE

How much do I owe you?	**Quanto Le devo?** *kwanto lay dayvo*
I have insurance.	**Sono assicurato.** *sono asseekooraato*
Can I have a receipt for my health insurance?	**Vorrei una ricevuta per la mia assicurazione medica.** *vorrehee oona reechayvoota pehr la meea asseekooratseeonay maydeeka*
Would you fill out this health insurance form, please?	**Compili questo modulo di assicurazione medica, per favore.** *koampeelee kwehsto modoolo dee asseekooratseetseeonay maydeeka pehr favoray*
Do you have... ?	**Ha ...?** *ha*
Form E111/health insurance	**il modulo E111/l'assicurazione medica** *eel modoolo ay-chento-oondeechee/ lasseekooratseeonay*

DICTIONARY ENGLISH-ITALIAN

A

a few alcuni(e)
a little un poco
a lot molto(-a)
a.m. di mattina
abbey abbazia f
able, to be potere
about *(approximately)* circa
above *(place)* sopra
abroad all'estero
abscess ascesso
accept, to accettare
access accesso m
accessories accessori mpl
accident incidente; *(road)* incidente stradale m
accidentally accidentalmente
accommodations sistemazione f
accompaniments condimenti mpl, salse f
accompany, to accompagnare
accountant contabile m/f
ace *(cards)* asso m
activities le attività fpl
acne acne f
across attraverso
action film film m d'azione
actor/actress attore m/attrice f
adaptor presa f multipla
address indirizzo m
adhesive bandage bende fpl adesive
adjoining room camera f adiacente
admission charge prezzo m d'entrata
adult adulto m
advance, in in anticipo
aerial *(car/tv)* antenna f
aerobics aerobica f
after *(time)* dopo; *(place)*
aftershave dopobarba m
after-sun lotion lozione f doposole
afternoon, in the nel pomeriggio
age: what age? età: quanti anni?
aged, to be avere … anni

ago fa
agree: I agree sono d'accordo
air conditioning aria f condizionata
air mattress materasso m di gomma
air pump pompa f per l'aria
air-freshener deodorante m per ambienti
airline linea f aerea
airmail via f aerea
airplane aeroplano m
airport aeroporto m
air steward/hostess assistente m/f di volo
aisle seat posto m nel corridoio
alarm clock sveglia f
alcoholic *(drink)* alcolico(-a)
all tutto(-a)
all-night bar bar m aperto tutta la notte
all-night pharmacy farmacia f notturna
allergic, to be essere allergico(-a) a
allergy allergia f
allowed: is it allowed? è permesso?
almost quasi
alone solo(-a)
alphabet alfabeto m
already già
also anche
alter, to ritoccare
aluminum foil carta f stagnola
always sempre
am: I am sono
amazing meraviglioso(-a)
ambassador ambasciatore m
amber ambra f
ambulance ambulanza f
American *(person/adj)* americano(-a) m/f
American football calcio m americano
amethyst ametista m
amount ammontare m, cifra (f)
and e
anesthetic anestetico m
angling pesca f con la lenza
animal animale m
announcement: what was that announcement? cos'era quell'annuncio?
another un altro/un'altra
another time un'altra volta

antacid antiacido m
antibiotics antibiotici mpl
antifreeze antigelo m
antique oggetti mpl di antiquariato
antiques shop negozio m di antiquariato
antiseptic antisettico m; ~ cream pomata f antisettica
any qualsiasi
anyone: does anyone speak English? c'è qualcuno che parla inglese?
anyone else altre persone
anything cheaper qualcosa di più economico
anything else? nient'altro?
apartment appartamento m
apologies scuse fpl
apologize: I apologize chiedo scusa
appendicitis appendicite f
apples mele fpl
appointment appuntamento m
approximately circa/approssimativamente
architect architetto m/f
architecture architettura f
area regione f; ~ code codice m, prefisso m
arm braccio m
armbands (swimming) bracciali mpl salvagente
around (place) attorno, intorno; (time) circa
arrange: can you arrange it? può organizzarlo(-a)?
arrest, to be under essere in arresto
arrive, to arrivare
art arte f
art gallery galleria d'arte f, pinacoteca f
artery arteria f
arthritic, to be essere artritico(-a)
artificial sweetener dolcificante m
artist artista m/f
ashtray posacenere m
asked for ... ho ordinato ...
asking the way chiedere la strada
asleep, to be essere addormentato(-a)
aspirin aspirina f
asthmatic, to be essere asmatico(-a)

astringent astringente m/f
at (place) a; (time) a/alle
at least almeno, minimo
ATM (cash machine) Bancomat m
attack (crime) aggressione f; (medical) attacco m
attendant guardiano m
attractive attraente m/f
aunt zia f
Australian (n) australiano(-a) m/f
Austrian (person) austriaco(-a) m/f
authentic: is it ? è autentico(-a)?
automatic (car) auto f con cambio automatico
automatic camera macchina f fotografica automatica
autumn autunno m
avalanche valanga f
away via
awful orribile

baby bambino m/bambina f; neonato(-a) m/f
baby food alimenti per neonati
baby seat seggiolino m
baby wipes fazzolettini mpl/salviette fpl per neonati
baby's bottle biberon f
babysitter babysitter f
back dorso m, schiena f
backache mal m di schiena
backpack zaino m
backpacking girare il mondo con lo zaino
bad cattivo(-a)
baked al forno
bakery panetteria f
ball palla f
ballet balletto m
ballroom sala f da ballo
bandage bende fpl
bank banca f
bank account conto m bancario
bank card carta bancaria f
bank loan prestito m bancario
bar (hotel) bar m
barber shop barbiere m

barge *(long boat)* lancia f
basic expressions espressioni comuni
basin catino m
basket cestello m
basketball pallacanestro f
bath towel asciugamano m
bath: to take a fare il bagno
bathroom bagno m; sala f da bagno
battery batteria f; pila f
be able, to potere
be, to essere
beach spiaggia f
beard barba f
beautiful bello(-a); stupendo(-a)
because perché
because of a causa di
bed letto m
bed: I'm going to vado a letto
bedding biancheria f da letto
bee ape f
beer birra f
before *(time)* prima di
begin, to *(see also to start)* iniziare
beginner principiante m/f
beginning inizio m
belong: this belongs to me questo
è mio
below °C sotto i °C
belt cintura f
beneath sotto
berth cuccetta f
best migliore m/f
better migliore
between fra, tra
bib bavaglino m
bicycle bicicletta f
bicycle parts parti della bicicletta
bicycle rental noleggio *(m bicyclette)*
big grande
bill conto m; **put it on the ~** lo metta
sul conto
bin liner sacco m di plastica per
bidoni di spazzatura
binoculars binocolo m
bird uccello m
birthday compleanno m
biscuits biscotti m
bite *(insect)* puntura f

bitten: I've been bitten by a dog
sono stato morso da un cane
bitter amaro(-a)
bizarre bizzarro(-a)
black nero(-a)
black and white film *(camera)*
bianco e nero
black coffee *(weak)* caffè m (lungo)
bladder vescica f
blanket coperta f
bleach candeggina f
bleeding, to be perdere sangue
blind tapparella f
blister vescica f
blocked bloccato(-a); **the drain is ~**
le fognature sono bloccate; **the road is
~** la strada è bloccata
blood sangue m
blood group gruppo m sanguigno
blood pressure pressione f (del
sangue)
blouse camicetta f
blow-dry asciugatura f a fon
blue blu
blush *(rouge)* fard m
board, on a bordo
boarding pass carta f d'imbarco
body: parts of the body parti fpl del
corpo
boiled bollito
bone osso m
book libro m
book of tickets blocchetto m di
biglietti
book, to prenotare
booked up, to be essere prenotato(-a)
booking prenotazione f
booking office ufficio m prenotazioni
bookstore libreria f
boots stivali mpl; *(for sport)*
scarponi mpl
border *(country)* frontiera f
boring noioso(-a)
born: I was born in sono nato a/nel
borrow: may I borrow your …?
posso prendere in prestito il suo…?
bottle bottiglia f
bottle-opener apribottiglie m
bowel intestino m

box of chocolates scatola f di cioccolatini
box office biglietteria f
boxing pugilato m
boy bambino m; ragazzo m
boyfriend ragazzo m
bra reggiseno m
bracelet braccialetto m
brass ottone m
bread pane m
break, to rompere; ~ **the journey** interrompere il viaggio
break-in rapina f
breakage rottura f
breakdown guasto m
breakfast (prima) colazione f
breast petto m, seno m
breathe, to respirare
breathtaking mozzafiato
bridge ponte m; (cards) bridge m
briefcase valigetta f portadocumenti
briefs mutandine fpl
brilliant splendido(-a)
bring, to portare
Britain Gran Bretagna f
British (person/adj) britannico(-a) m/f
brochure opuscolo m
broken rotto(-a)
bronchitis bronchite f
bronze (adj) bronzeo(-a)
brooch spilla f
broom scopa f
brother fratello m
brown marrone m
browse, to dare un'occhiata
bruise contusione f
brush spazzola f
bubble bath schiuma f da bagno
bucket secchio m
buffet car vagone m ristorante
build, to costruire
building edificio m
built costruito(-a)
buoy boa f
burger hamburger m
burger stand chiosco m degli hamburger
burn bruciatura f
burn: it's burned è bruciato(-a)

bus autobus m
bus route percorso m d'autobus
bus station stazione f d'autobus
bus stop fermata f d'autobus
business trip viaggio m d'affari
business, on per lavoro
businessman uomo m d'affari
businesswoman donna f d'affari
busy, to be (occupied) occupato(-a)
but ma
butane gas butano m, gas m
butcher shop macelleria f
butter burro m
button bottone m
buy, to comprare
bye! arrivederci
bypass circonvallazione f / bypass (medicine)

C

cabaret cabaret m
cable car funivia f
café bar m
cake torta f
cake shop pasticceria f
calendar calendario m
call, to chiamare; (phone) telefonare; ~ **call the police!** chiami la polizia!
camcorder videocamera f
camera macchina f fotografica
camera case custodia f per macchina fotografica
camera store [shop] negozio m di ottica/foto
campbed lettino m da campeggio
camping campeggio m
camping equipment attrezzatura f da campeggio
campsite campeggio m
can I posso
can opener apriscatole m
cancel, to annullare
cancer (disease) cancro m
candles candele fpl
candy caramella f
cap berretto m
cap (dental) capsula f corona f
capital city capitale f

car auto(mobile) f, macchina f; **by ~** in auto/macchina

car alarm antifurto m per auto

car rental noleggio auto m, autonoleggio m

car pound deposito auto m

car repairs meccanico m

car wash lavaggio auto m

cardphone telefono m a scheda

cards carte

careful: be careful! faccia attenzione!

carpet *(fitted)* moquette f; *(rug)* tappeto m

carrier bag sacchetto m

carry-cot portabebè m

carton scatola f (di cartone); **~ of milk** confezione f di latte

cartoon cartoni mpl animati

cash contanti mpl, soldi mpl

cash card carta f bancaria

cash desk cassa f

cash machine Bancomat m

cash, to incassare

cassette cassetta f, nastro m

castle castello m

cat gatto m

catch, to *(bus)* prendere (l'autobus)

cathedral cattedrale f

cave caverna m, grotta f

CD compact m, CD m

CD-player lettore m di compact

cent centesimo m

central heating riscaldamento m centralizzato

center of town centro m città

ceramics ceramica f

certificate certificato m

certification certificato m

chain catenina f

chair sedia f

chair-lift seggiovia f

change *(coins)* moneta f; resto m, spiccioli mpl

change lanes, to cambiare corsia

change, to cambiare

change: keep the change tenga il resto

chapel cappella f

charcoal carbone m

charter flight volo m charter

cheap a buon prezzo, economico

cheaper più economico(-a); meno caro(-a)

check conto m

check in, to registrare

check out, to *(hotel)* saldare il conto

checkbook libretto m degli assegni

checkers *(draughts)* gioco m della dama

checkout cassa f

check guarantee card carta f bancaria

cheek quancia f

cheers! salute!

cheese formaggio m

chemist farmacia f

chess scacchi

chess set gioco m degli scacchi

chest torace m

chewing gum gomma f da masticare

chickenpox varicella f

child bambino m/bambina f; figlio m/figlia f

child seat *(in car)* seggiolino m

children bambini mpl; figli mpl

children's meals piatti mpl per bambini

chin mento m

Chinese (cuisine) *(cucina)* cinese

chips patatine fpl

choc-ice cremino m

chocolate cioccolata f; **box of ~** scatola f di cioccolatini

chocolate bar tavoletta f di cioccolata

chop *(meat)* braciola f

Christian *(adj)* cristiano(-a)

Christmas Natale m

church chiesa f

cigarette machine distributore m automatico di sigarette

cigarettes, pack of pacchetto m di sigarette fpl

clamps (car) i ceppi bloccaruote fpl

class: first class prima classe f

clean *(adj)* pulito(-a)

clean, to pulire

cleaning person cameriera f

cliff scogliera f/rupe f

cling film pellicola f trasparente

cloakroom guardaroba m

clock orologio m
close *(near)* vicino(-a)
close, to chiudere
clothes abbigliamento m, vestiti
clothes dryer asciugatore m elettrico
clothes line corda f per il bucato
clothing store *(clothing store)* negozio
m di abbigliamento
cloudy, to be essere nuvoloso
clown clown, pagliaccio m
clubs *(golf)* mazze fpl
coach corriera f, pullman m; *(train
compartment)* carrozza f
coat cappotto m
code *(area/dialling)* codice m telefonico
coffee caffè m
coin moneta f
cold freddo(-a)
cold *(flu)* raffreddore m
cold meats affettati mpl
collapse: he's collapsed ha avuto un
collasso
collect, to ritirare
color colore m; *(film)* a colori
comb pettine m
come back, to *(return)* ritornare; *(for
collection)* passare a ritirare
communication difficulties difficoltà
di comunicazione
compact camera macchina f
compact
company *(business)* azienda f;
(companionship) compagnia f
compartment *(train)* scompartimento m
complaints reclami mpl; **to make a ~**
fare un reclamo
computer computer m, ordinatore m
concert hall sala f concerti
concession tariffa f speciale
concussion, to have a avere la
commozione cerebrale
condoms profilattici mpl
conductor direttore m d'orchestra
conference conferenza f
confirm, to *(reservation)* confermare
confirmation conferma f
congratulations! congratulazioni!
connection *(transport)* coincidenza f

conscious, to be *(medical)* riprendere
conoscenza
Consulate consolato m
consult, to consultare
consultant *(medical)* specialista m/f
contact lens lenti fpl a contatto
contact, to contattare
contact lens fluid fluido m per lenti
a contatto
contagious, to be essere contagioso(-a)
contain, to contenere
contraceptive contraccettivo m
convenience store negozio m di
alimentari
convenient conveniente
convertible *(car)* auto f decappottabile
cook cuoco m, cuoca f
cook, to cucinare
cooker cucina f a gas/elettrica
cookies biscotti mpl
cooking *(cuisine)* cucina f
copper rame m
copy copia f
corkscrew cavatappi m
corn pad callifugo m
corner angolo m
correct *(also right)* giusto
cosmetics cosmetici mpl
cottage villa f, cottage m
cotton cotone m
cotton wool *(absorbent cotton)*
cotone m idrofilo
cough tosse f
cough syrup sciroppo m per la tosse
cough, to tossire
counter *(shop)* bancone m *(post office,
bank)* sportello m
country *(nation)* paese m
countryside campagna f
couple *(pair)* paio m
courier *(guide)* guida m/f,
l'accompagnatore m
course *(meal)* portata f
courthouse palazzo m di giustizia
cousin cugino m, cugina f
cover *(lid)* coperchio m
cover charge coperto m
craft shop negozio m di artigianato
cramps crampi mpl

crash: I've had a crash ho avuto un incidente d'auto
creche asilo-nido m
credit card carta f di credito
credit status posizione f finanziaria
credit credito m
crib culla f
crisps chips fpl
crockery stoviglie fpl
cross, to (road) attraversare
cross-country skiing trail pista f per sci di fondo
crossroads incrocio m
crowded affollato(-a)
crown (dental) corona f
cruise crociera f
crutches stampelle f
cup tazza f
cupboard credenza f, l'armadio m
currency valuta f
currency exchange office ufficio m cambio
curtains tende fpl
cushion cuscino m
customs dogana f
customs declaration dichiarazione f doganale
cut taglio m
cut and blow-dry taglio m e asciugatura a fon
cutlery posate fpl
cycle helmet casco m da ciclista
cycle path pista f ciclabile
cycling ciclismo m
cyclist ciclista m/f
cystitis cistite f

daily giornalmente
damaged, to be essere danneggiato(-a)
damp (n) umidità f; (adj) umido(-a)
dance (performance) danza f
dancing, to go andare a ballare
dangerous pericoloso(-a)
dark scuro(-a); buio(-a)
daughter figlia f
daughter-in-law nuora f
day giorno m; (ticket) giornaliero

day trip gita f di un giorno
dead morto(-a); (battery) scarico(-a)
deaf, to be essere sordo(-a)
dear (greeting) caro(-a)
decide: we haven't decided yet non abbiamo ancora deciso
deck (ship) ponte m
deck chair sedia f a sdraio
declare, to dichiarare
deduct, to (money) detrarre
deep profondo(-a)
deep frozen surgelato(-a)
defrost, to scongelare
degrees (temperature) gradi mpl
delay ritardo m
delicatessen salumeria f
delicious (food) squisito(-a); delizioso(-a)
deliver, to consegnare
dental floss filo m interdentale
dentist dentista m/f
dentures dentiera fsing
deodorant deodorante m
depart, to (train, bus) partire
department store grande magazzino m
departure (train) partenza f
departure lounge sala f partenze
depend: it depends on dipende da
deposit caparra f; anticipo m
describe, to descrivere
design (dress) disegno m
designer stilista m/f
desk scrivania f
dessert dolce m
destination destinazione f
details dettagli mpl
detergent detersivo m
develop, to (photos) sviluppare
diabetes diabete m
diabetic diabetico(-a)
dialing (area) code codice m, prefisso m
diamond diamante m; (cards) quadri mpl
diapers pannolini mpl
diarrhea diarrea f; to have ~ avere la diarrea
dice dadi mpl
dictionary dizionario m

diesel diesel m
diet: I'm on a diet sono a dieta
difficult difficile
digital digitale
dine, to mangiare
dining car carrozza ristorante f
dining room sala f da pranzo
dinner jacket smoking m
dinner, to have cenare
direct diretto
direct, to indicare la via
direct-dial telephone telefono m a linea diretta
direction direzione f; **in the ~ of** in direzione
director *(of company)* direttore m; *(film)* regista m/f
directory *(telephone)* elenco m telefonico
Directory Inquiries Informazioni Elenco Abbonati
dirty sporco(-a)
disabled disabili m/fpl
discount sconto m; **can you offer me a ~?** può farmi uno sconto?
disgusting disgustoso(-a)
dish *(meal)* piatto m
dish cloth strofinaccio m per i piatti
dishes posate fpl
dishwashing detergent detersivo m per lavastoviglie
dislocated, to be essere lussato(-a)
display cabinet armadietto m vetrina
display case astuccio m
disposable camera macchina f usa-e-getta
distilled water acqua f distillata
district zona f
disturb: don't non disturbare
dive, to tuffarsi
diversion deviazione f
divorced, to be essere divorziato(-a)
dizzy, to feel avere il capogiro
do: things to do cose fpl da fare
doctor dottore(ssa) m/f, medico m
dog cane m
doll bambola f
door porta f
dosage dose f

double bed letto m matrimoniale
double room camera f doppia
down giù
downstairs al piano inferiore
downtown area centro m
dozen dozzina f
drain fognatura f
draught *(wind)* corrente f d'aria
dress vestito m
drink bibita f
drinking water acqua f potabile
drinks bevande f
drip: the faucet [tap] drips rubinetto perde
drive, to guidare
driver conducente m; *(bus, etc)* autista m/f
driver's [driving] license patente di guida f
drop someone off, to fare scendere
drowning: someone is ~ qualcuno sta annegando
drugstore farmacia f
drunk ubriaco(-a)
dry-clean, to lavare a secco
dry cleaner lavanderia f
dry clothes, to asciugare i vestiti
dubbed, to be essere doppiato
during durante
dusty polveroso(-a)
duty: to pay duty pagare il dazio
duvet piumone m

E

each: how much each? quant'è ciascuno?
ear orecchio m; **~ache** mal d'orecchio m; **~drops** le gocce fpl per le orecchie; **~rings** orecchini mpl
earlier più presto/prima
early di buon'ora, presto
east est m
Easter Pasqua f
easy facile
eat, to mangiare; **places ~** posti mpl per mangiare
eaten: have you ~? ha già mangiato?; **we've already ~** abbiamo già mangiato

economical economico(-a)
economy class in classe turistica
eggs uova fpl
either ... or ... o ... o ...
elastic *(adj)* elastico(-a)
electric: ~ meter contatore m dell'elettricità; **~ shaver** rasoio m elettrico
electrical items articoli mpl elettrici
electrician elettricista m
electricity elettricità f
electronic: ~ flash flash m elettronico; **~ game** gioco m elettronico
elevator ascensore m
else: something ~ qualcos'altro
embark, to *(boat)* imbarcarsi
embassy ambasciata f
emerald smeraldo m
emergency emergenza f; **it's an ~** è un'emergenza; **~ room** pronto soccorso m
emergency exit uscita f d'emergenza
empty vuoto(-a)
enamel smalto m
end, to finire
end: at the end in fondo
engaged, to be essere fidanzato(-a)
engine motore m
engineer ingegnere m/f
England Inghilterra f
English *(language)* inglese m
enjoy, to piacere
enlarge, to *(photos)* ingrandire
enough abbastanza
entertainment: what ~ is there? che divertimenti/spettacoli ci sono?
entertainment guide guida degli spettacoli
entirely completamente
entrance fee tariffa f d'ingresso
entry visa visto m d'entrata
envelope busta f
epileptic epilettico(-a); **to be ~** essere epilettico(-a)
equally equamente
equipment *(sports)* attrezzatura f
error errore m
escalator scala mobile f
essential essenziale
estate agent agente m/f immobiliare

EU Unione f Europea, UE
euro (€) euro m
evening dress abito m da sera
events manifestazioni fpl
every day ogni giorno
every week ogni settimana
examination *(medical)* visita f medica
example, for per esempio
excellent *(adj)* eccellente
except eccetto
excess baggage eccedenza bagaglio f
exchange rate tasso m di cambio
exchange, to cambiare
excluding meals pasti m esclusi
excursion escursione f, gita f
excuse me *(apology. attention)* scusi
exhausted, to be essere esausto(-a)
exhibition mostra f
exit uscita f; **at the ~** all'uscita
expensive caro(-a)
expiration date data f di scadenza
expire, to: when does it expire? quando scade?
exposure *(photos)* posa f
expressway autostrada f
extension interno
extension cord prolunga f
extra *(additional)* supplementare
extracted, to be *(tooth)* avere un'estrazione
extremely estremamente
eye occhio m

fabric *(material)* stoffa f
face faccia f, viso m
facial trattamento per il viso m
facilities servizi mpl; attrezzature f
factor *(sun protection)* fattore m
factory outlet vendita diretta in fabbrica
faint, to feel sentirsi svenire
fall *(season)* autunno m
fall: he's had a fall è caduto
family famiglia f
famous famoso(-a)
fan *(air)* ventaglio m
far lontano(-a); **how ~ is it?** quanto dista?; **is it ~?** è lontano?

farsighted presbite
fare tariffa f
fashionable, to be essere alla moda
fast-food restaurant tavola calda f, self-service m
fast, to be *(clock)* anticipare
fat grasso m
father padre m
fault: it's my/your fault è colpa mia/sua
faulty difettoso(-a)
faulty, to be essere difettoso(-a)
favorite favorito(-a)
fax facilities servizio m fax
fax, to spedire un fax
feeding bottle biberon m
feel ill, to sentirsi male
feel sick, to sentirsi male/vomitare
female donna f; femmina f
festival festival m
fetch help! chiami aiuto!
feverish, to feel sentirsi la febbre
few pochi (e)
fiancé(e) fidanzato(-a) m/f
field campo m
fight *(brawl)* rissa f
fill out, to compilare/riempire
filling *(dental)* otturazione f; *(in sandwich)* ripieno m
filling station stazione f di servizio
film *(camera)* pellicola f; film m
film speed velocità f della pellicola
filter filtro m; **~ paper** *(for coffee)* filtro m del caffè
find out: could you find that out? può informarsi?
fine *(penalty)* multa f; *(well)* bene
finger dito m
fire alarm allarme m antincendio
fire department pompieri (pl)
fire escape uscita f di sicurezza
fire extinguisher estintore m
fire: there's a fire! al fuoco!
fireplace caminetto m
first primo(-a)
first class in prima classe; di prima classe
first course primo (piatto) m
first floor *(UK)* primo piano m

first floor *(US)* pianterreno m
first name nome m
first-aid kit astuccio m di pronto soccorso
fish store pescheria f
fishing rod canna f da pesca
fishing, to go andare a pesca
fit, to *(clothes)* andare bene
fitting room cabina di prova f
fix, to: can you fix it? può ripararlo(-a)?
flag bandiera f
flash *(photography)* flash m elettronico
flashlight *(torch)* pila f
flat *(tire)* pneumatico m scoppiato
flavor: what flavors do you have? che gusti avete?
flea pulce f
flea market mercato m delle pulci
flight volo m: **~ number** numero m del volo; **~ attendant** assistente m/f di volo
flip-flops ciabatte fpl
flood inondazione f
floor *(level)* piano m
floor mop mocho m; Vileda (trademark)
floor show spettacolo m di varietà
florist fiorista m
flour farina f
flower fiore m
flu influenza f
fluent: to speak fluent Italian parlare italiano correntemente
fly *(insect)* mosca f
fly, to volare
foggy, to be essere nebbioso(-a)
folding chair/table sedia/tavola f pieghevole
folk art arte f popolare
folk music musica f folk
follow, to seguire
food poisoning avvelenamento m alimentare
foot piede m
football *(soccer)* calcio m
footpath sentiero m
for a week per una settimana
forecast previsioni fpl
foreign straniero(-a)
foreign currency valuta f straniera
forest foresta f

forget, to dimenticare
fork forchetta f; *(in the road)* incrocio m
form modulo m
formal dress tenuta f da sera
forms moduli mpl
fortunately fortunatamente
forward: please forward my mail per favore faccia proseguire la mia posta
foundation *(make-up)* crema f base
fountain fontana f
four-door car auto f a quattro porte
four-wheel drive auto fuoristrada f
foyer *(hotel/theater)* atrio m
frame *(glasses)* montatura f
France Francia f
free *(available, not busy)* libero(-a); *(of charge)* gratuito(-a)
French *(cuisine)* (cucina) Francese
French *(language)* francese m
frequent: how frequent? con che frequenza?
frequently frequentemente
fresh fresco(-a)
freshly squeezed fruit juice spremuta f di frutta
fridge frigorifero m
fried fritto(-a)
friend amico m/amica f
friendly amichevole, simpatico(-a)
fries patate f fritte
frightened, to be essere spaventato(-a)
fringe frangia f
from da; ~ ... to *(time)* da ... a
front door porta f d'ingresso; ~ **key** chiave f della porta d' ingresso
frosty, to be *(weather)* essere gelato(-a)
frozen congelato(-a)
fruit juice succo m di frutta
fuel *(gasoline/petrol)* carburante (benzina) m
full pieno(-a)
full board *(A.P.)* pensione f completa
full insurance polizza f di assicurazione completa
fun, to have divertirsi

funny *(amusing/odd)* buffo/divertente
furniture i mobili mpl
fuse fusibile m
fuse box fusibili mpl
fuse wire filo m a piombo

gallon gallone m
gambling giocare d'azzardo
game *(toy)* gioco m
garage garage m, autorimessa f
garden giardino m
gardener giardiniere m
gardening giardinaggio m
gas bottle bombola f del gas
gas: I smell gas! c'è odore di gas!
gasoline benzina f
gastritis gastrite f
gate *(airport)* uscita f
gay club locale m gay
generous: that's very ... è molto generoso
genuine autentico(-a)
get, to *(find)* cercare
get by: may I get by? permesso?
get off, to *(transport)* scendere
get out, to *(of vehicle)* scendere
get to, to arrivare a; **how do I get to ...?** come si arriva a ...?
gift regalo m
gift shop negozio m di articoli da regalo
girl ragazza f; bambina f
girlfriend ragazza f
give way, to *(on the road)* dare la precedenza
give, to dare
glacier ghiacciaio m
gland ghiandola f
glass bicchiere m
glasses *(optical)* occhiali mpl
gliding volare con il deltapiano
gloomy tetro(-a)
glossy finish *(photos)* smaltato(-a)
glove guanto m
go, to andare; **let's go!** andiamo!; **where does this bus go?** dove va questo autobus?
go away! vada via!

go back, to *(turn around)* ritornare
go for a walk, to fare una passeggiata
go out, to *(in evening)* uscire
go shopping, to fare acquisti
goggles occhialini per il nuoto
gold oro m
goldplate placcato d'oro
good buono(-a)
good afternoon buonasera *(from pm)*
good evening buonasera
good morning buongiorno
good night buonanotte
good-bye arrivederci
gorge gola f
got: have you got any ...? avete pl de... ?
grade *(fuel)* grado del carburante m
gram grammo m
grandparents nonni mpl
grapes uva f
grass erba f
gratuity mancia f
gray grigio
graze escoriazione f
greasy *(hair)* grasso(-a)
great fun molto divertente
Greek (cuisine) (cucina) Greca
green verde
greengrocer fruttivendolo m
greetings saluti
greyhound racing corsa f di levrieri
grilled alla griglia
grocer *(grocery)* drogheria f
ground: camping ~ terreno m del campeggio
ground floor pianterreno
groundsheet telo m per il terreno
group gruppo m
guarantee garanzia f
guarantee: is it guaranteed? è garantito(-a)?
guide *(tour)* guida m/f
guidebook guida f/m turistica
guided tour visita f guidata
guitar chitarra f
gum *(mouth)* gengiva f
gynecologist ginecologo m/f

H

hair capelli mpl
hair brush spazzola f dei capelli
hair dryer asciugacapelli m, fon m
hair gel gel m dei capelli
hair spray lacca f
haircare prodotti per i capelli
haircut taglio di capelli m
hairdresser's parrucchiera f, parrucchiere m
half, a mezzo
half board *(M.A.P.)* mezza pensione f
half fare metà prezzo
half past e mezza/... e trenta
hammer martello m
hand mano f
hand cream crema f per le mani
hand luggage bagaglio a mano m
hand towel asciugamano m
hand washable lavaggio a mano
handbag borsetta f
handicapped, to be essere disabile
handicrafts artigianato m
handkerchief fazzoletto m
handle maniglia f
hang-gliding fare il deltapiano
hanger gruccia f
hangover postumi mpl della sbornia
happen: what happened? che cosa è successo?
happy: I'm not happy with the service non sono soddisfatto(-a) del servizio
harbor porto m
hard shoulder *(road)* corsia f d'emergenza
hardware store negozio m di ferramenta
hat cappello m
hatchback auto f a cinque porte
have, to avere
have to, to *(must)* dovere
hayfever febbre f da fieno
head testa f
head waiter capocameriere m
headache mal di testa m
heading, to be *(in a direction)* andare in direzione di

health food store [shop] negozio *m* di dietetica
health insurance assicurazione *f* medica
hear, to sentire
hearing aid protesi *f* per udito
heart cuore *m*
heart attack infarto *m*
heart condition condizione *f* del cuore
hearts *(cards)* cuori *mpl*
heating riscaldamento *m*
heavy pesante
height altezza *f*
helicopter elicottero *m*
hello buongiorno; salve
help aiuto *m*
help, to aiutare; **help me!** aiuto!
helper assistente *m/f*
hemorrhoids emorroidi *fpl*
her lei; suo(-a)
here qui
hernia ernia *f*
hers suo(-a)
hi! ciao!
high alto(-a)
high/main street via principale *f*
high tide alta marea *f*
hike *(walk)* escursione *f* a piedi
hiking fare escursioni a piedi
hill collina *f*
him lui
hire out, to *(rent out, to)* noleggiare
hire, for libero
hire, to noleggiare
his suo(-a)
history storia *f*
hitchhike, to fare l'autostop
HIV-positive sieropositivo(-a)
hobby *(pastime)* hobby
hockey field campo *m* di hockey
hold, to *(contain)* contenere
hold on, to restare in linea
hole *(in clothes)* buco *m*
holiday resort posto *m* di villeggiatura
holiday, on per/in vacanza
home casa *f*; **to go ~** rientrare
homeopathic remedy rimedio *m* omeopatico

homosexual *(adj)* omosessuale
honeymoon, to be on essere in luna di miele
hopefully speriamo!
horse cavallo *m*
horseracing ippica
horseback trip escursione *f* a cavallo
hospital ospedale *m*, policlinico *m*
hot caldo(-a); *(weather)* caldissimo(-a)
hot chocolate cioccolata *f* calda
hot dog hot dog
hot spring sorgente *f* calda
hot water acqua *f* calda; **~ bottle** bottiglia *f* dell'acqua calda
hotel albergo *m*
hour ora *f*; **in an ~** fra un'ora
hours *(opening)* orario *m* di apertura
house casa *f*
household articles casalinghi *mpl*
housewife casalinga *f*
how? come?
how are you? come sta?
how far? quanto dista?
how long? quanto (tempo)?
how many? quanti?
how much? quanto?; quanto costa?
how often? con che frequenza?; ogni quanto?
how old? quanti anni?
however comunque
hungry, to be avere fame
hurry, to be in a avere fretta
hurt, to be essere ferito(-a); farsi male; **it hurts** fa male
husband marito *m*,

I

I'd like vorrei
I'll have prendo
I've lost ho perso
ice ghiaccio *m*
ice cream gelato *m*
ice cream parlor gelateria *f*
ice dispenser distributore *m* di ghiaccio
ice lolly ghiacciolo *m*
ice pack borsa *f* da ghiaccio
ice rink pista *f* di pattinaggio su ghiaccio, palazzo *m* del ghiaccio
ice-hockey hockey *m* su ghiaccio

icy, to be essere ghiacciato(-a)
identification documento m d'identità
ill, to be stare male
illegal, to be essere illegale
illness malattia f
imitation imitazione f
immediately immediatamente
impressive di grande effetto
in *(place)* in; *(time)* fra
in-law: father/mother-in-law
suocero(-a)
included: is it included? è
incluso/compreso?
inconvenient scomodo(-a)
Indian (cuisine) (cucina) indiana
indicate, to indicare
indigestion indigestione f
indoor al caperto
indoor pool piscina f invernale
inexpensive economico(-a)
infection infezione f
inflammation infiammazione f
informal *(dress)* abbigliamento m
casual
information informazione f
information desk banco m
informazioni
information office ufficio m
informazioni
injection iniezione f
injured, to be essere ferito(-a)
innocent innocente
inquiry desk banco m informazioni
insect insetto m
insect bite puntura f d'insetto
insect repellent [spray] pomata f
contro gli insetti/ dello spray insetticida
inside dentro
inside lane corsia f interna
insist: I insist insisto
insomnia insonnia f
instant coffee caffè m solubile
instead of invece di
instructions istruzioni fpl
instructor istruttore m
insulin insulina f
insurance assicurazione f
insurance certificate polizza f
d'assicurazione

insurance claim richiesta f di
rimborso assicurazione
insurance company compagnia f
d'assicurazione
interest *(hobby)* gli interessi
interest rate tasso m d'interesse
interesting interessante
international internazionale
International Student Card Carta f
Internazionale dello studente
interpreter interprete m/f
intersection intersezione f
interval intervallo m
into dentro, in
introduce oneself, to presentarsi
introductions presentazioni
invitation invito m
invite, to invitare
involved, to be essere coinvolto(-a)
iodine iodio m
Ireland Irlanda f
Irish *(n)* irlandese m/f
iron *(for clothing)* ferro m da stiro
iron, to stirare
is there ...? c'è...?
island isola f
it is è
Italian *(language)* italiano m; *(person)*
italiano(-a) m/f
itch: it itches prude
itemized bill conto m dettagliato

J

jack *(cards)* fante m
jacket giacca f
jam marmellata f/conserva f di frutta
jammed: it's jammed è bloccato(-a)
jar vasetto m
jaw mascella f
jellyfish medusa f
jet lag: I have soffro il cambiamento
di fuso orario
jewelry store/jeweler's gioielleria f
Jewish *(adj)* ebreo(-a)
job: what's your job? che lavoro fa?
join: may we join you possiamo
venire anche noi?
joint *(body)* articolazione f; *(meat)*
pezzo m (di carne)

joke scherzo m barzelletta f
joker *(cards)* jolly m
journalist giornalista m/f
journey viaggio m
jug *(of water)* brocca f
jumper maglia f
junction *(exit)* uscita f autostrada; *(intersection)* intersezione f autostrada

K

kerosene cherosene m
ketchup ketchup m
kettle bollitore m
key chiave f
key ring portachiavi m
kidney rene m
kilo(gram) chilo(grammo) m
kilometer chilometro m
kind *(pleasant)* gentile
kind: what kind of ...? che tipo di ...?
king *(cards, chess)* re m
kiosk chiosco m
kiss, to baciare
kitchen paper carta f da cucina
kitchenette zona cottura f
knee ginocchio m
knife coltello m
knight *(chess)* cavallo m
knocked down, to be essere buttato a terra
know: I don't know non lo so
kosher puro(-a)

L

label etichetta f
lace pizzo m
ladder scala f
ladies room *(toilet)* toilette f signore
lake lago m
lamp lampada f
land, to atterrare
landing *(house)* pianerottolo m
landlord/landlady padrone m, padrona f di casa
lane corsìa f
language course corso m di lingua
large grande

last ultimo(-a)
last, to *(time)* durare
late *(delayed)* in ritardo; tardi
later più tardi
laugh, to ridere
launderette lavanderia f a gettone
lavatory bagno m
lawn prato m coltivato
lawyer avvocato m
laxative lassativo m
lead, to *(road)* portare
lead-free *(gas/petrol)* benzina verde f
leader *(of group)* capogruppo m/f
leaflet opuscolo m
leak, to *(roof/pipe)* perdere; *(car)*
learn, to *(language/sport)* imparare
learner studente m, studentessa f
least expensive meno caro m, meno cara f
leather pelle f
leave, to *(exit)* partire; *(abandon)* lasciare; **leave me alone!** mi lasci in pace!
lecturer docente, insegnante m/f
left-hand side dal lato sinistro
left, on the a sinistra
left-handed mancino(-a)
left-luggage office *(baggage check)* deposito m bagagli
leg gamba f
legal matters *(car accident)* questioni legali
legal, to be essere legale
lemon limone m
lemonade limonata f
lend: could you lend me ...? può prestarmi ...?
length lunghezza f
lens obiettivo m; lenti fpl
lens cap tappo m per obiettivo
lesbian club club m per lesbiche
less (di) meno
lesson lezione f
letter lettera f; **by ~** per lettera
letterbox cassetta f per lettere
level *(ground)* livellato, piano
library biblioteca f
license plate number numero di targa m

lie down, to sdraiarsi
lifebelt cintura f di salvataggio
lifeboat scialuppa f di salvataggio
lifeguard bagnino m
lifejacket giubba f di salvataggio
lift pass ski pass f
light *(color)* chiaro(-a); *(weight)* leggero(-a)
light bulb lampadina f
lighter accendino m
lighthouse faro m
lightning fulmine m
like, to piacere; **I'd like …** vorrei …; **I don't like it** non mi piace
like this *(similar)* come questo(-a)
limousine berlina f
line *(subway [metro])* linea f; *(profession)* professione f, lavoro m
line: an outside line, please una linea esterna, per favore
linen lino m
lip(s) labbro m, labbra fpl
lipsalve balsamo m per le labbra
lipstick rossetto m
liqueur liquore m
liter/litre litro m
little piccolo(-a)
live, to vivere; **~ together** abitare insieme
liver fegato m
loaf of bread pagnotta f di pane
lobby *(theater/hotel)* atrio m
local regionale, locale
local anesthetic anestesia f locale
local road strada f comunale
lock *(key)* serratura f; *(canal)* chiusa f
lock oneself out, to chiudersi fuori
locked, to be essere chiuso(-a); **it's locked** è chiuso a chiave
locker armadietto m
locker rooms spogliatoi mpl
lollipop leccalecca m
long *(clothing)* lungo(-a)
long *(time)* molto; **how long?** quanto tempo?; **how much longer?** per quanto tempo?
long-distance call telefonata f interurbana

look: I'm just looking sto solo guardando
look for, to cercare
loose *(clothing)* largo(-a)
lose, to perdere; **I've lost …** ho smarrito …; ho perso
lost, to be essere smarrito
lost-and-found/lost property office ufficio m oggetti smarriti
lotion lozione f
lots molti (e)
loud, it's too è troppo rumoroso(-a)
louder più forte
love: I love Italian food amo la cucina italiana;
I love you ti amo
low-fat magro(-a)
lower berth cuccetta f in basso
lubricant lubrificante m
luck: good luck buona fortuna
luggage *(baggage)* bagaglio m
luggage allowance peso m consentito
luggage locker deposito m bagagli automatico
luggage tag etichetta f per bagaglio
luggage ticket biglietto m per i bagagli
luggage carts *(trolleys)* carrelli mpl
lumpy *(mattress)* pieno di protuberanze
lunch pranzo m
lung polmone m

machine washable lavabile in lavatrice
madam signora
made: what is it made of? di che cosa è fatto(-a)?
magazine rivista f
magician mago m
magnetic north nord m magnetico
magnificent magnifico
maid cameriera f
maiden name nome m da nubile
mail, to imbucare
mail *(post)* posta f
mailbox cassetta f postale
main principale

main course secondo (piatto) m
main train station stazione f ferroviaria principale
main street via f principale
mains conduttura f principale
make (brand) marca f
makeup cosmetici mpl trucco m
male uomo, maschio m
mallet maglio m
man uomo m
manager direttore m, direttrice f; gestore m/f
manicure manicure f
manual (car) manuale m
many molti (e)
map carta f, cartina
margarine margarina f
market mercato m; ~ **day** giorno m di mercato
married, to be essere sposato(-a)
mascara mascara m
mask (diving) maschera f subacquea
mass messa f
massage massaggio m
match (game) partita f
matches fiammiferi mpl
material (fabric) stoffa f
matinée spettacolo m del pomeriggio
matter: what's the matter? cosa succede?; **it doesn't matter** non importa
mattress materasso m
may I ...? posso ... ?
maybe forse
me me
meal pasto m;
mean, to significare
measles morbillo m
measure, to misurare
measurement le misure fpl
meat carne f
medical certificate certificato m medico
medicine medicina f
medium (regular) medio(-a); (steak) cottura media
meet, to incontrare; **pleased to meet you** piacere/molto lieto(-a)

meeting place luogo m d'incontro
member (of club) socio m
memorial monumento m commemorativo
men (toilets) bagno m, signori mpl
mend, to riparare
mention: don't mention it prego
menu menu m
message messaggio m
metal metallo m
meter (taxi) tassametro m
methylated spirits alcol denaturato
microwave (oven) forno m a microonde
midday mezzogiorno
midnight mezzanotte
migraine emicrania f
mileage chilometraggio m
milk latte m; **with ~** con latte
milk of magnesia latte m di magnesia
million un milione
mince carne f tritata
mine mio(-a)
mineral water acqua f minerale
minibar minibar m
minibus minibus m
minimum (n) minimo m
minister ministro m
minor road strada f secondaria
minute minuto m
mirror specchio m
miss, to passare, mancare; **have I missed the bus to ...?** ho perso l'autobus per ...?
missing, to be mancare; scomparire
mistake errore m
misunderstanding: there's been a ~ c'è stato un malinteso
mittens guantoni mpl
mobile home camper m
modern art arte f moderna
moisturizing cream crema f idratante
monastery monastero m
money soldi mpl
money order vaglia m postale
money-belt cintura f portasoldi
month mese m
monthly (ticket) mensile
monument monumento m

moped motorino m
more (di) più; **I'd like some more …**
vorrei ancora un po' di …
morning, in the al mattino; di mattina
moslem *(adj)* mussulmano(-a)
mosquito zanzara f
mosquito bite puntura f di zanzara
mother madre f
motorbike motocicletta f
motorboat barca f a motore
motorcycle motocicletta f
motorcycle parts
motorway autostrada f
mountain montagna f
mountain pass passo m di montagna
mountaineering alpinismo m
mousetrap trappola f per topi
moustache baffi mpl
mouth bocca f
move, to cambiare; *(car)* spostare la
macchina; *(house)* traslocare; **don't**
move him! non lo muova!
Mr. signor m
Mrs. signora f
much molto
mugged, to be essere aggredito(-a)
mugging aggressione per rapina f
mugs boccali mpl
multiple trip *(ticket)* biglietto m
multiplo
mumps gli orecchioni mpl
muscle muscolo m
museum museo m
music musica f
music box carillon m
musician musicista m/f
must: I must devo
mustard senape f
my mio
myself: I'll do it myself lo faccio io

N

nail polish lo smalto m per unghie
nail scissors le forbicine f da unghie
name cognome m
name *(first name)* nome m; **what's**
your name? come si chiama?
napkin tovagliolo m
narrow stretto(-a)

national health servizio m sanitario
nationality nazionalità f
natural history storia f naturale
nature reserve riserva f naturale
nature trail percorso m naturalistico
nausea nausea f
navy blue blu m marino
near vicino
nearsighted miope
nearest più vicino(-a)
neck collo m; *(clothes)*
necklace collana f
need: I need to … ho bisogno di …
needle ago m
negative *(photo)* negativo m
neighbor vicino(-a) m/f
nephew nipote m
nerve nervo m
nervous system sistema m nervoso
never mai
never mind non importa
new nuovo(-a)
New Year Anno m Nuovo
New Zealand Nuova Zelanda f
newsagent giornalaio m
newsdealer giornalaio m
newspaper giornale m
newsstand edicola f
next prossimo(-a); **next stop!**
prossima fermata!
next to accanto(-a) a; vicino(-a) a
niece nipote f
night, at di notte; **per night** per notte
night porter portiere m di notte
nightdress camicia f da notte
nobody else nessun altro
noisy rumoroso(-a)
non-alcoholic analcolico(-a)
non-smoking area zona non fumatori f
none nessuno(-a)
noon mezzogiorno
no one nessuno(-a)
normal normale
north nord m
Northern Ireland Irlanda f del nord
nose naso m
nosebleed emoraggia nasale f
not yet non ancora
note banconota f

notebook taccuino m
nothing else nient'altro
nothing to declare niente da dichiarare
notice board bacheca f
notify, to informare
now subito; ora, adesso
nudist beach spiaggia f nudista
number numero m; *(telephone)*
numero (di telefono) m
number plate *(registration plate)*
numero di targa m
nurse infermiere(-a) m/f
nut *(for bolt)* dado m per bullone
nylon nylon m

o'clock, it's ... è .../sono le ...
observatory osservatorio m
occasionally occasionalmente
occupations occupazioni mpl
occupied occupato(-a)
of di, da
of course naturalmente, certamente
off-peak bassa stagione f
office ufficio m
often sovente/spesso
oil olio m
oil lamp lampada f a olio
oily *(hair)* grasso(-a)
okay d'accordo./va bene
old vecchio(-a)
old town città f vecchia; città f storica
old-fashioned antiquato(-a)
olive oil olio m d'oliva
omelet frittata f
on *(day, date)* il
on *(place)* in
on the left a sinistra
on the other side all'altro lato
on the right a destra
on/off switch interruttore m
once una volta; **~ a week** una volta
alla settimana
open aperto(-a); **~ to the public**
aperto(-a) al pubblico **~ to traffic**
aperto(-a) al traffico
open, to aprire
opening hours orario m d'apertura
opera house teatro m dell'opera

operation operazione f
operator operatore m
opposite di fronte
optician ottico m; negozio m di ottica
or o/oppure
orange arancione
oranges arance fpl
orchestra orchestra f
order, to ordinare; *(taxi)* chiamare
our nostro
out: he's out è fuori/non c'è
outdoor all'esterno; **~ pool** piscina f
all'aperto
outside fuori
outside lane corsia f di sorpasso
oval ovale
oven forno m
over sopra
over there laggiù
overcharged: I've been prezzo è
eccesivo
overdone *(adj)* troppo cotto(-a)
overdraft scoperto m
overdrawn, to be avere uno scoperto
bancario
overheat, to surriscaldare
overnight una notte f
overnight service servizio m
ventiquattro ore
owe: how much do I owe you?
quanto le devo?
own: on my own da solo(-a)
owner proprietario

pacifier tettarella f
pack, to fare i bagagli
pack of cards mazzo m di carte
pack of cigarettes pacchetto m di
sigarette
package pacco m
packed lunch pranzo m al sacco
pack [packet] pacco m, pacchetto m
padlock lucchetto m
pail secchiello m
pain, to be in stare male
painkillers antinevralgico m;
analgesico m, antidolorifico m
paint, to dipingere

painted dipinto(-a)
painter pittore m, pittrice f
painting quadro m
pair of, a un paio di
pajamas pigiama m
palace palazzo m
palpitations palpitazioni fpl
panorama panorama m/vista f
pantomime pantomima f
pants pantaloni mpl
pantyhose collant m
paper carta f
paper napkins tovaglioli mpl di carta
paraffin paraffina f
paralysis paralisi f
parcel (package) pacco m
pardon? prego?
parents genitori mpl
park parco m, giardini mpl
park ranger guardia f forestale
park, to parcheggiare
parking parcheggio m
parking disk disco m orario
parking lot parcheggio m
parking meter parchimetro m
parliament building palazzo m del
Parlamento
partner (boyfriend/girlfriend)
compagno m, compagna f
parts (components) pezzi mpl di
ricambio
party (social) festa f
pass passo m
pass, to passare
passenger passeggero m, passeggera f
passport passaporto m
passport control controllo m passaporti
pastry shop pasticceria f
patch, to rattoppare
path sentiero m
patient paziente m/f
pavement, on the sul marciapiede m
pay, to pagare; ~ a fine pagare
un'ammenda/una multa; ~ by credit
card pagare con carta di credito
pay phone telefono m a scheda
payment pagamento m
peak picco m/cima f
pebbly (beach) pietroso(-a)

pedalo pedalò m
pedestrian crossing attraversamento
m pedonale
pedestrian zone/precinct isola
f/zona f pedonale
pedicure pedicure f
pen penna f
pencil matita f
penicillin penicillina f
penknife coltellino m
penpal il, corrispondente m/f
people gente f
people carrier (minivan) furgoncino m
pepper (condiment) pepe m; (vegetable)
peperone m
per day al giorno; per giorno
per hour all'ora; per ora
per night per notte
per week alla settimana
performance spettacolo m
perhaps forse
period periodo m; (menstrual)
mestruazioni fpl
period pains dolori mpl mestruali
perm (hair) permanente f
perm, to fare la permanente
permit permesso m, licenza f
personal stereo stereo m personale
pet (animal) animale m domestico
pharmacy farmacia f
phone telefono m
phone call telefonata f
phonecard carta f telefonica
photo, to take a fare una fotografia
photo: passport-size photo
fotografia f formato passaporto
photocopy fotocopia f
photographer fotografo m/negozio m
di ottica
photography fotografia f
phrase frase f
phrase book frasario m
piano pianoforte m
pick up, to passare a prendere; (ticket)
ritirare
pick-up truck autocarro m
picnic picnic m, scampagnata f; ~
area area f per pic nic

piece articolo di bagaglio m; pezzo m;
a ~ of ... un pezzo di ...
Pill (*contraceptive*), **to take the**
prendere la pillola (contraccettiva)
pillow cuscino m
pillowcase federa f
pilot light luce f-spia
pink rosa
pint pinta f
pipe (*smoking*) pipa f
pipe cleaners puliscipipa m
pipe tobacco tabacco m da pipa
piste map carta f delle piste
pitch (*for camping*) posto m tenda
pity: it's a pity è un peccato
place (*space*) posto m
place a bet, to scommettere
plain pianura f; (*not patterned*) in
tinta unita
plane volo m
plans, to have fare dei progetti
plant pianta f
plastic bags sacchetti mpl di plastica
plate piatto m
platform binario m
platinum platino m
play, to (*drama*) rappresentare
(*music*) suonare
playground parco m giochi
playgroup club m per bambini
playing cards carte fpl da gioco
playing field campo m da gioco
pleasant gradevole
please per piacere./per favore
pliers le pinze fpl
plug (*bath*) presa f; (*electric*) spina f
elettrica
plumber idraulico m
p.m. di pomeriggio, di sera
pneumonia polmonite f
point of interest luoghi mpl d'interesse
point to, to indicare
poison veleno m
poisonous velenoso(-a)
police polizia f, carabinieri (pl)
police report denuncia f
police station commissariato m,
questura f
pollen count conteggio m del polline

polyclinic policlinico m
pond stagno m
pony ride passeggiata f in pony
pop music musica f pop
popcorn popcorn m
port (*harbor*) porto m
porter portiere m; facchino m
portion porzione f
possible: as soon as possible
appena possibile
possibly possibilmente
post, to (*mail, to*) imbucare
post (*mail*) posta f
post office ufficio m postale
postbox (*mailbox*) cassetta f
delle lettere
postcard cartolina f
poster manifesto m
postman postino m
potato patata f
pottery ceramica f
pound (*sterling*) lira f sterlina
power failure interruzione f della
corrente
power point presa f di corrente
practice: to practice speaking Italian
praticare l'italiano parlato
pregnant, to be esser incinta
prescribe, to prescrivere
prescription ricetta f
present (*gift*) regalo m
press, to stirare
pretty carino(-a)
priest prete m
primus stove fornello m da campeggio
prison carcere m
private bathroom bagno f privato
probably probabilmente
program programma m; **~ of events**
programma m delle manifestazioni
prohibited: is it prohibited? è
proibito?
promenade deck ponte m di coperta
pronounce, to pronunciare
properly correttamente
Protestant protestante
pub osteria f
public building edifici pubblici mpl
public holidays giorni mpl festivi

pullover maglione m
pump *(gas/petrol)* pompa f
puncture *(flat)* foratura f
pure *(material)* puro(-a)
purple viola
purpose motivo m scopo m
purse portamonete m
push-chair passeggino m
put: where can I put ...? dove posso mettere ..?
put aside, to *(in shop)* mettere da parte
put up: can you put me up for the night? può ospitarmi per una notte?
putting course terreno m da golf

Q

quality qualità f
quantity quantità f
quarantine quarantina f
quarter, a un quarto
quarter past *(after)* e un quarto
quarter to *(before)* meno un quarto
quay molo m
queen *(cards, chess)* regina f
question domanda f
quick veloce
quickest: what's the quickest way to ... qual è la via più breve per ...?
quickly presto!
quiet silenzioso(-a)
quieter più tranquillo(-a)

R

rabbi rabbino m
race *(cars)* gara f automobilistica; *(horses)* corsa f di cavalli
racetrack ippodromo m
racing bike bicicletta f da corsa
racket *(tennis, squash)* racchetta f
rail station stazione f ferroviaria
railroad ferrovia f
rain, to piovere
raincoat impermeabile m
rape stupro m
rapids rapide fpl
rare *(unusual)* raro(-a); *(steak)* poco cotta

rarely raramente
rash eruzione f della pelle
rather piuttosto; **~ noisy** piuttosto rumoroso(-a)
ravine burrone m
razor rasoio m
razor blades lamette fpl da barba
re-enter, to rientrare
reading *(interest)* lettura f
reading glasses gli occhiali mpl da lettura
ready, to be essere pronto(-a); **are you ready?** è pronto(-a)?
real *(genuine)* vero/autentico
real estate agent agente m/f immobiliare
receipt ricevuta f
reception *(desk)* ricezione f
receptionist ricezionista m/f
reclaim tag talloncino m
reclaim, to ottenere il rimborso m
recommend, to consigliare; raccomandare; **can you recommend?** può consigliare?
record *(lp)* *(disco)* LP m
red rosso(-a)
red wine vino m rosso
reduction sconto m, riduzione f
refreshments rinfreschi (pl)
refrigerator frigorifero m
refund rimborso m
regards to ... saluti a ...
region regione f
register receipt ricevuta f di cassa
registered mail posta f raccomandata
registration form modulo m di registrazione
registration number numero di targa m
regular *(gas/petrol)* normale; *(size of drink)* medio(-a)
regulations: I didn't know the regulations non conoscevo il regolamento
religion religione f
remember: I don't remember non ricordo
removed, to be essere rimossa
rent, to noleggiare
rent: for rent affittasi

rental car auto f noleggiata
repair, to riparare
repairs riparazioni fpl
repeat, to ripetere; **please repeat that** per piacere può ripetere
replacement *(n)* sostituzione f
replacement part pezzo di ricambio m
report, to denunciare
representative rappresentante m/f
required necessario(-a)
reservation prenotazione f
reservation desk botteghino m
reserve, to prenotare
rest, to riposare
retired, to be essere in pensione
return ticket biglietto di andata e ritorno m; biglietto circolare m
return, to *(travel)* ritornare; *(surrender)* restituire
reverse the charges, to *(call collect, to)* telefonare a carico del destinatario
revolting disgustoso(-a)
rheumatism reumatismo m
rib costola f
right *(correct)* giusto(-a)
right, on the a destra
right of way diritto m di passaggio; precedenza f
right-handed che usa la mano destra
ring anello m
rip-off bidonata f
river fiume m
road strada f
road accident incidente m stradale
road assistance soccorso m stradale
road map carta f stradale
road signs segnaletica f, lindicazioni fpl stradali
roasted arrosto(-a)
robbed, to be essere derubato(-a)
robbery rapina f
rock climbing alpinismo m di roccia
rock concert concerto m rock
rocks rocce fpl
roller blades roller blades mpl
rolls panini mpl
romance *(film/play)* romanzo m
romantic romantico(-a)

roof *(house/car)* tetto m
roof-rack portabagagli m esterno
rook *(chess)* torre f
room camera f
room service servizio m in camera
rope corda f
round *(shape)* rotondo(-a); *(of golf)* giro m; **it's my ~** è il mio turno
roundabout rotatoria f
roundtrip ticket biglietto di andata e ritorno m; biglietto circolare m
route strada f, percorso m
row remare
rowboat barca f a remi
rude, to be essere maleducato(-a)
rugby rugby m
ruins rovine fpl
run into, to *(crash)* venire addosso
run out, to *(fuel)* finire
run over, to *(people)* investire
rush hour ora f di punta

safe *(lock-up)* cassaforte f
safe *(not dangerous)* sicuro(-a); **to feel ~** sentirsi sicuro(-a)
safety sicurezza f
safety pins spille fpl di sicurezza
sailboat barca f a vela
salad insalata f
sales rep agente m/f di vendita
salt sale m
same day lo stesso giorno
same: the same again please lo stesso, per favore
sand sabbia f
sandals sandali mpl
sandwich panino m
sandwich bar paninoteca f
sandy sabbioso(-a)
sanitary napkins assorbenti mpl
satellite TV televisione f satellitare
satisfied: I'm not satisfied with this non sono soddisfatto(-a) di
sauce salsa f
saucepan pentola f
sausages salcicce fpl
saw *(tool)* sega f

say: how do you say ...? come si dice ..?; what did he say? cosa ha detto?
scarf sciarpa f
scenic route strada f panoramica
scheduled flight volo m di linea
school scuola f
sciatica sciatica f
scientist scienziato m, scienziata f
scissors un paio di forbici fpl
scooter motoretta f
Scotland Scozia f
Scottish (person/adj.) scozzese m/f
screw vite f
screwdriver cacciavite m
scrub brush spazzola f dura
sculptor scultore m, scultrice f
sea mare m
seafront lungomare m
seasick, I feel ho il mal di mare
season ticket tessera f
seasoning condimenti mpl
seat posto m
second secondo(-a)
second class di seconda classe
second floor (US) primo piano m
secondhand di seconda mano
secretary segretaria f
security guard guardia f di sicurezza
sedative sedativo m
see, to (inspect, witness) vedere; ~ someone again rivedere
self-catering in affitto
sell, to vendere
send, to mandare; spedire
senior citizens anziani (pl)
separated, to be essere separato(-a)
separately (adv) separatamente
septic tank fognatura f
serious serio
served, to be (meal) essere servito; sevire
service servizio m: ~ charge servizio m; is service included? è compreso il servizio?
service station stazione f di servizio
serviette tovagliolo m
set menu menù m fisso
sex (act) sesso m

shade sfumatura f
shady ombreggiato
shallow basso(-a)
shampoo shampoo m
shampoo and set shampoo e messa in piega
shampoo for dry/oily hair shampoo m per capelli secchi/grassi
shape forma f
sharp tagliente
shatter, to (glass) rompere
shaver rasoio m elettrico
shaver socket presa f per rasoio
shaving brush pennello m da barba
shaving cream crema f da barba
she lei
sheet (bedding) le lenzuola fpl
shelf scaffale m
ship nave f
shirt camicia f
shiver, to sentirsi i brividi
shock (electric) scossa f elettrica
shoelaces lacci mpl delle scarpe
shoepolish lucido m da scarpe
shoe repair riparatura f delle scarpe
shoe-cleaning service servizio m pulizia scarpe
shoemaker calzolaio m
shoes scarpe fpl
shop (store) grande magazzino m
shop assistant commesso(-a) m/f
shop/storekeeper negoziante m/f
shopping area zona f dei negozi
shopping basket (bag) cesto f della spesa; cestello m
shopping mall [centre] centro m commerciale
shopping list lista f della spesa
shopping cart [trolley] carrello m
shopping, to go (food) andare a fare la spesa; (other items) andare a fare acquisti
shore (sea/lake) riva f del mare/lago
short corto(-a)
shorts shorts mpl
shoulder spalla f
show spettacolo m
show, to indicare, mostrare; can you show me? può indicarmi?

shower gel gel m per doccia

shower room sala f docce (pl)

showers docce f

shutter persiana f

shy timido(-a)

sick, to feel sentirsi male; **I'm going to be ~** mi viene da vomitare

side (of road) lato m

side order contorno m

side street strada f laterale

sidewalk marciapiede m

sights luoghi mpl d'interesse

sightseeing tour giro m turistico

sightseeing, to go visitare luoghi d'interesse

sign (road) segnali (pl), indicazioni stradali fpl

signpost indicatore m stradale

silk seta f

silver argento m

silverplate placcato d'argento

similar, to be essere simile a

since (time) da

singer cantante m/f

single, to be essere single

single (one-way) **ticket** biglietto di andata m; biglietto di corsa semplice m

single room camera f singola

sink lavandino m

sister sorella f

sit, to sedersi; sedere

sit down, please si accomodi, prego

six-pack of beer confezione f di sei lattine di birra

size misura f, taglia f

skates pattini mpl da ghiaccio

skating rink palazzo m del ghiaccio

ski bindings gli attacchi mpl per sci

ski boots scarponi mpl da sci

ski instructor istruttore m di sci

ski lift sciovia f ski lift m

ski pants pantaloni mpl da sci

ski poles racchette fpl da sci

ski school scuola f di sci

ski suit tutta f da sci

ski wax cera f per sci

skid: we skidded abbiamo slittato

skiing sci m

skin pelle f, epidermide f

skin-diving equipment attrezzatura f per l'immersione subacquea

skirt gonna f

skis sci mpl

sledge slitta f

sledge run pista f per slitte

sleep, to dormire

sleeping bag sacco m a pelo

sleeping car vagone m letto

sleeping pill sonnifero m

sleeve manica f

slice fetta f

slide film le diapositive fpl

slip (undergarment) sottoveste f

slippers pantofole fpl

slope (ski) discesa f

slow lento(-a)

slow down! rallenti!

slow, to be (clock) ritardare

slowly lentamente

small piccolo(-a); basso(-a)

small change moneta f; spiccioli mpl

small spoon cucchiaino m

smell: there's a bad smell c'è cattivo odore

smoke, to fumare

smoke: I don't smoke non fumo

smoking area zona fumatori f

snacks spuntini mpl

sneakers scarpe fpl da tennis

snorkel maschera f da subacqueo

snow neve f

snow, to nevicare

snowed in, to be essere bloccato dalla neve

snowplow spazzaneve m

soaking solution (contact lenses) soluzione f per lenti a contatto

soap sapone m

soap powder detersivo m in polvere

socket presa f

socks calzini mpl

sofa divano m

sofa-bed divano-letto m

soft drink (soda) bibita f frizzante; bibita f analcolica

sold out tutto esaurito(-a)

sole (shoes) suola f

soluble aspirin aspirina f solubile

some alcuni, del/dei/dell'/della/delle
someone qualcuno
sometimes qualche volta
son figlio m
soon presto; **as ~ as possible** al più presto
sore throat mal m di gola
sore: it's sore fa male
sorry! sono spiacente
sort tipo m
sound-and-light show spettacolo m di suoni e luci
sour acido(-a), aspro(-a)
south sud m
souvenir ricordo m, souvenir m; **~ guide** guida f ricordo
spa stazione f termale
space spazio m
spade (shovel) paletta f (cards) carta f di picche
speak, to parlare; **~ to someone** parlare con qualcuno; **do you speak English?** parla inglese?
special rate condizioni fpl speciali; tariffa speciale f
special requirements richieste f particolari
specialist specialista m/f
specimen campione m
spectacles occhiali mpl
speed limit limite di velocità m
spell, to sillabare
spend, to spendere
spicy speziato(-a)
spin-dryer asciugatore m elettrico
spine spina f dorsale
sponge spugna f
spoon cucchiaio m
sports club palestra f/associazione f sportiva
sports ground campo m sportivo
sprained, to be essere slogato(-a)
sprained muscle strappo m muscolare
spring (season) primavera f; (water) fonte f
square (shape) quadrato(-a); (street) piazza f
stain macchia f
stainless steel acciaio m inossidabile

stairs scale fpl
stale non fresco(-a)
stall: the engine stalls motore s'inceppa
stalls (orchestra) platea f
stamp francobollo m; **~ machine** distributore m automatico di francobolli
stand in line, to aspettare, fare la coda
standby ticket biglietto m non prenotato
start inizio m
start, to cominciare **starter** antipasto m
stately home palazzina f
statement (legal) dichiarazione f, denuncia f
station stazione f
stay, to fermarsi, rimanere
sterilizing solution soluzione f sterilizzante
stiff neck torcicollo m
still: I'm still waiting sto ancora aspettando
sting puntura f
stocking calze fpl
stolen, to be essere rubato(-a)
stomach stomaco m; **~ ache** dolore m allo stomaco; **~ cramps** crampi mpl allo stomaco
stool (feces) feci fpl
stop (bus, tram, metro) fermata f
stop, to fermarsi; **please stop here** si fermi qui, per favore
stopover sosta f
store detective personale m di sicurezza
store guide guida f al magazzino
stove stufa f
straight ahead (sempre) dritto
strange strano(-a)
straw (drinking) cannuccia f
strawberry (flavor) fragola f
stream ruscello m, torrente m
string cordino m
stroller passeggino m
strong (potent) forte
stuck: the key's stuck la chiave è bloccata

students studenti pl
study, to studiare
stunning magnifico(-a)
stupid: how stupid! che stupidaggine!
style stile m
styling mousse schiuma f per capelli
subtitled, to be avere i sottotitoli
subway metropolitana
subway station stazione f (della) metropolitana
suede pelle f scamosciata
sugar zucchero m
suggest, to suggerire
suit completo m
suitable for adatto(-a) per la
summer estate f
sun block blocco m antisolare
sun lounger sedia f a sdraio
sunbathe, to prendere il sole
sunburn scottatura f solare
suncare prodotti solari
Sunday domenica f
sundeck *(ship)* ponte m superiore
sunglasses occhiali mpl da sole
sunshade *(umbrella)* ombrellone m
suntan lotion crema f/lozione f abbronzante
sunstroke colpo di sole m
super *(gas/petrol)* super
superb stupendo(-a)
supermarket supermercato m
supervision sorveglianza f
supplement supplemento m
suppositories supposte fpl
sure: are you sure? è sicuro(-a)?
surfboard tavola f da surf
surname cognome m
suspicious sospettoso(-a)
swallow, to inghiottire
sweatshirt felpa f
sweet *(taste)* dolce
sweets *(dessert)* dolci mpl; *(candy)* caramelle f
swelling gonfiore m
swim, to nuotare
swimming *(activity)* nuoto
swimming pool piscina f
swimming trunks calzoncini mpl da bagno

swimsuit costume m da bagno
Swiss *(person)* svizzero(-a) m/f
switch interruttore m
switch on/off, to accendere/spegnere
Switzerland Svizzera f
swollen, to be essere gonfio(-a)
symptoms sintomi m
synagogue sinagoga f
synthetic in fibra sintetica

T

T-shirt maglietta f
table tavolo m
tablecloth tovaglia f
table tennis tennis m da tavolo
tablet pastiglia f
take away, to da asporto
take photographs/pictures, to fare fotografie
take someone home, to riaccompagnare
take, to *(room, bus, medicine)* prendere *(carry)* portare;
taken *(occupied)* occupato(-a)
talcum powder borotalco m
talk, to parlare
tall alto(-a)
tampons tamponi mpl
tan abbronzatura f
tap *(faucet)* rubinetto m
tape measure metro m a nastro
tarpaulin telo m per il terreno
taste gusto m
taxi tassì m
taxi driver autista m/f di tassì
taxi stand posteggio m di tassì
tea tè m
tea bags bustine fpl di tè
teacher insegnante m/f
team squadra f
teaspoon cucchiaino m
teat *(for baby)* tettarella f
teddy bear orsacchiotto m
teenager adolescente m/f
telephone telefono m
telephone bill *(in hotel)* conto m del telefono
telephone booth cabina f telefonica, telefono m pubblico

telephone directory elenco m telefonico

telephone kiosk cabina f telefonica

telephone number numero m di telefono

telephone token gettone m telefonico

telephone, to telefonare

television televisione f

telex telex m

tell, to dire; **tell me** dimmi

temperature temperatura f

temporary provvisorio(-a)

tendon tendine m

tennis ball palla f da tennis

tennis court campo m da tennis

tent tenda f

tent pegs picchetti mpl

tent pole palo m della tenda

terrible terribile

tetanus tetano m

thank you grazie

that quello(-a)

that one quello(-a)

that's all è tutto

thawing snow neve f fondente

theater [theatre] teatro m

theft furto m

their loro

theirs loro m/f

them loro

theme park parco m a tema

then *(time)* poi

there là

there is ... c'è

thermometer termometro m

thermos bottle [flask] termos m

these questi

they loro

thick spesso(-a)

thief ladro m

thigh coscia f

thin sottile

think, to credere; **I think** penso

think about it, to pensarci

third terzo(-a); **a ~** un terzo

thirsty assetato(-a)

this one questo(-a)

those quelli

thread filo m

throat gola f

throat lozenges pastiglie fpl per la gola

thrombosis trombosi f

through per, attraverso

thumb pollice m

ticket biglietto m

ticket agency/office biglietteria f

tie cravatta f

tie pin spilla f da cravatta

tight *(clothing)* stretto(-a)

tights collant m

till receipt scontrino m di cassa

time *(of day)* ora f; **on ~** in orario; **free ~** tempo m libero; **at what ~?** a che ora?

timetable orario m

tin (can) lattina f; **~ opener** apriscatole m

tin foil carta f stagnola

tint, to fare il colore

tinted *(glass/lens)* colorati (e)

tip mancia f

tipping dare la mancia

tire pneumatico m

tired, to be essere stanco(-a)

tissues fazzoletti mpl di carta

to *(place)* a

toaster tostapane m

tobogganing andare in toboga

today oggi

toe dito m del piede

toilet toilette f

toilet paper carta f igienica

toilets toilettes fpl/bagni mpl

tomorrow domani

tongue lingua f

tonic water acqua f tonica

tonight stasera; **for ~** per questa sera

tonsillitis tonsillite f

tonsils tonsille fpl

too *(also)* anche; *(extreme)* troppo

too much troppo

tooth dente m

toothache mal m di denti

toothbrush spazzolino m da denti

toothpaste dentifricio m

top cima f

top floor ultimo piano m

torch torcia f

totally totalmente
tough *(food)* duro(-a)
tour giro m, gita f
tour guide guida m/f turistica
tour operator agente m di viaggio
tour representative rappresentante m/f dell'agenzia di viaggi
tourist turista m/f
tourist office Ufficio del Turismo m/ Ente del Turismo m
tow, to trainare
tow rope fune f da traino
towards verso
towel asciugamano m
towelling tela f per asciugamani
tower torre f
town città f
town hall Municipio m
town plans cartine f
toy giocattolo m
track sentiero m
tracksuit tuta f da ginnastica
traditional tradizionale
traffic traffico m
traffic jam ingorgo stradale m
traffic light semaforo m
traffic offense/violation infrazione f stradale
tragedy tragedia f
trail sentiero m
trailer roulotte f
trailer park parco m roulotte
train treno m
train times orario m ferroviario
training shoes scarpe fpl da ginnastica
tram tram m
transfer *(transport)* trasferta f
transfer, to trasferire
transit, in durante il viaggio
translate, to tradurre
translation traduzione f
translator traduttore m, traduttrice f
trash rifiuti m
trash bags sacchetti mpl per i rifiuti
trash cans bidoni mpl per i rifiuti
travel agency agenzia f di viaggio
travel sickness *(car/air/sea)* mal d'auto/d'aria/di mare
travel, to viaggiare, partire

traveler's checks traveller's cheques mpl
tray vassoio m
tree albero m
tremendous straordinario(-a)
trim *(hair)* spuntatina f
trip gita f
trolley carrello m
trouble: I'm having trouble with … ho difficoltà con …
trouser press stirapantaloni m
trousers pantaloni mpl
truck camion m
true: that's not true non è vero
try on, to provare
tube tubo m
tumor tumore m
tunnel tunnel m
turn, to girare
turn down (volume, heat), to abbassare (volume, riscaldamento)
turn off, to spegnere
turn on, to accendere
turn up, to *(volume, heat)* alzare
turn(ing) svolta f
TV room sala f televisione
tweezers le pinzette fpl
twice due volte
twin bed due letti mpl
two-door car auto a due porte f
type: what type? che tipo?
typical tipico(-a)
tyre pneumatico m

ugly brutto(-a)
UK Regno m Unito
ulcer ulcera f
umbrella ombrello m
uncle zio m
unconscious, to be perdere conoscenza
under *(place)* sotto
underdone *(adj)* non abbastanza cotto(-a)
underpants mutande fpl
underpass sottopassaggio m
understand, to capire; **do you understand?** capisce?; **I don't understand** non capisco

undress, to spogliarsi
uneven *(ground)* in dislivello
unfortunately sfortunatamente
uniform uniforme m/f
United States gli Stati Uniti mpl
university università f
unleaded gasoline benzina f senza piombo
unlimited mileage chilometraggio m illimitato
unlock, to aprire a chiave, sbloccare
unpleasant sgradevole
unscrew, to svitare
until fino a
up to fino a
upmarket elegante m/f
upper berth cuccetta superiore f
upset stomach mal m di stomaco
upstairs al piano superiore
urgent urgente
us: for/with ~ per/con noi
U.S. Stati fpl Uniti, USA
use, to usare
use: for my personal use per mio uso personale
useful utile m/f
utensils stoviglie fpl

V

vacancy camere libere
vacant libero(-a)
vacate, to lasciare lbero(-a)
vacation vacanza f
vaccinated against, to be essere vaccinato(-a) contro
vaccination vaccinazione f
vaginal infection infezione f vaginale
valet service servizio m di pulizia
valid valido
validate, to *(ticket)* convalidare
valley valle f
valuable prezioso(-a)
value valore m
vanilla *(flavor)* vaniglia f
VAT *(sales tax)* I.V.A. (Imposta Valore Aggiunto) f
VAT receipt Ricevuta f Fiscale
vegan, to be seguire una dieta macrobiotica

vegan: suitable for vegans adatto(-a) per chi non consuma prodotti derivati da animali
vegetables le verdure fpl
vegetarian vegetariano(-a)
vehicle veicolo m
vehicle registration (document) documenti del veicolo
vein vena f
velvet velluto m
vending machine distributore m automatico
venereal disease malattia f venerea
ventilator ventilatore m
very molto
vet veterinario m
video arcade sala f giochi
video game videogioco m
video recorder videoregistratore m
view: with a view of the sea con vista sul mare
viewing point punto m panoramico
village paese m
vineyard vigne fpl
visa visto m
visit visita f
visit, to visitare
visiting hours ore fpl di visita
vitamin pills vitamine fpl
voice voce f
volleyball pallavolo
voltage voltaggio m
vomit, to vomitare

W

wading pool piscina per bambini
waist vita f **~ pouch** borsello m da cintura
wait attesa f
wait for, to aspettare; **wait!** aspetti!
waiter/waitress cameriere(-a) m/f
waiting room sala f d'aspetto
wake, to *(self)* svegliarsi
wake someone, to svegliare qualcuno
wake-up call sveglia f telefonica
Wales Galles m
walk: to go for a walk andare a fare una passeggiata
walk home, to rientrare a piedi

walking passeggiare, camminare
walking boots scarponi mpl
walking distance, within raggiungibile a piedi
walking route percorso m a piedi
walking gear abbigliamento m escursionismo
wall muro m
wallet portafoglio m
want, to volere
ward *(hospital)* reparto m, corsia f
warm *(weather)* caldo(-a)
warm, to riscaldare
warmer più caldo(-a)
wash basin lavello *(kitchen)* m, lavandino *(bathroom)* m
wash, to lavare
washing, to do fare il bucato
washing instructions istruzioni di lavaggio
wasp vespa f
watch orologio m
watch band cinturino m dell'orologio
watch battery pila f per orologi
watch maker orologeria f
watch TV, to guardare la televisione
water acqua f
water carrier bidone m dell'acqua
water heater boiler m
waterfall cascata f
waterproof impermeabile m/f
waterskiing sci m d'acqua
waterskis sci mpl d'acqua
wave onda f
way *(direction)* strada f; **I've lost my ~** mi sono smarrito; **it's in the ~** blocca il passaggio; **on the ~ to** sulla strada di
we noi
weak coffee caffè m lungo
weak: I feel weak mi sento debole
wear, to indossare
weather tempo m
weather forecast previsioni fpl del tempo
wedding matrimonio m
wedding ring fede f nuziale
week settimana f

weekend fine f settimana; **on [at] the ~** al fine settimana
weekend rate tariffa f per fine settimana
weekly *(ticket)* settimanale
weight: my weight is … peso …
welcome to … benvenuto(-a) a
well-done *(steak)* ben cotta
Welsh *(person/adj)* gallese m/f
west ovest m
wetsuit tuta f per immersione
what? cosa?
what kind of …? che tipo di … ?
what time …? a che ora …?
what's the time? che ora è?
wheelchair carrozzella f
when? quando?
where? dove?; **~ is …?** dov'è …?
where are you from? da dove viene?/di dov'è?
where else? dove?
which? quale?; **~ stop?** quale fermata?
while mentre
whist *(cards)* gioco m del whist
white bianco
who? chi?
whole: the whole day tutto il giorno
whose di chi
why? perchè?
wide largo(-a)
wife moglie f
wildlife fauna f
windbreaker giace f a vento
window finestra f; finestrino m; *(shop)* vetrina f
window seat posto m accanto al finestrino
windshield [windscreen] parabrezza m
windy, to be essere ventoso(-a)
wine vino m; **~ bottle** bottiglia f di vino
winery vigne fpl
wine list lista f dei vini
winter inverno m
wishes: best wishes to … tanti auguri mpl a …
with con
withdraw, to fare un prelievo
without senza

witness testimone m/f
wood *(forest)* bosco m; *(material)*
legno m
wool lana f
work, to lavorare; *(operate)*
funzionare; **it doesn't work** non
funziona
worry: I'm worried sono
preoccupato(-a)
worse peggiore; **it's gotten [got] ~** è
peggiorato(-a)
worst *(adv./adj.)* peggio, peggiore m/f
worth: is it worth seeing? vale la
pena vederlo?
wound ferita f
wrap up, to impacchettare
write-off *(car)* inservibile
write: write soon! scriva presto!
writing pad carta f da lettere
wrong sbagliato(-a); *(not right)* non
funziona; **~ number** numero m
sbagliato; **there's something ~ with ...**
c'è qualcosa che non va con ...; **what's**
~? che guasto ha?

XYZ

x-ray radiografia f
yacht yacht m
year anno m
yellow giallo
yes sì
yesterday ieri
yield *(give way)* dare la precedenza
yogurt yogurt m
you *(sing/plur/formal)* tu/voi/Lei
young giovane
your(s) *(formal)* Suo(-a), *(familiar)*
tuo(-a)
youth hostel ostello m della gioventù
zero zero
zip(per) cerniera f
zone zona f
zoo zoo m
zoology zoologia f

DICTIONARY ITALIAN-ENGLISH

This Italian-English Dictionary covers all the areas where you may need to decode written Italian: hotels, public buildings, restaurants, shops, ticket offices and transportation. It will also help with understanding forms, maps, product labels, road signs and operating instuctions (for telephones, parking meters etc.). If you can't locate the exact sign, you may find key words or terms listed separately.

A

a passo d'uomo dead slow
a proprio rischio at the owner's risk
a scelta at your choice ...
a stomaco vuoto on an empty stomach
abbazia abbey
abbigliamento da bambino children's wear
abbigliamento da donna ladies wear
abbigliamento da uomo menswear
abbigliamento sportivo sportswear
abiti per uomo menswear
accendere i fari/luci switch on headlights
accettazione admissions
acciaio steel
accostarsi a sinistra/destra keep to the left/right
aceto vinegar
acqua non potabile do not drink water
acqua potabile drinking water
aereo plane
affitasi camere rooms to rent
affitasi appartamento apartment to let
agenzia di assicurazioni insurance agency
agenzia di viaggi travel agency

agenzia immobiliare real estate agency
aggiornato updated
agitare prima dell'uso shake well before use
ai binari to the platforms
al coperto indoor
albergo hotel
alianti gliding
alimentari grocer's
alimenti surgelati frozen foods
aliscafo hydrofoil
all'aperto outdoor/open-air
allacciare le cinture fasten your seatbelt
alle cabine cabin decks
alotto lounge
alpinismo mountaineering, abseiling
alpinismo da roccia rock climbing
alt stop
alta tensione high voltage
altezza height
altezza massima ... metri headroom
altitudine altitude
alzare il ricevitore lift receiver
ambasciata embassy
ambulatorio oculistico eye infirmary
ancora meglio improved
andata one-way/single
andata e ritorno round trip
andata semplice one-way
anti-urto shock-proof
antiquario antiques store/shop
aperto open
aperto tutti i giorni anche la domenica open every day including Sundays
aprire qui open here
area di ristoro rest area
area di servizio service area
argenteria silver shop
argento silver
aria condizionata air conditioning
aromi (naturali) (natural) flavoring
arredi per arredamento furnishings
arrivi arrivals

articoli di bellezza e profumeria
makeup and perfume
articoli per cucina kitchen equipment
articoli per il bagno bathroom
accessories
articoli per la camera di letto
bedroom accessories
ascensore elevator
aspettare il proprio turno please
wait your turn
aspettare il tono wait for tone
attendere prego please wait
attenti ai ladri beware of pickpockets
attenti al cane beware of the dog
attenzione ghiaia loose gravel
**attenzione non scendere il gradino
prima dell'apertura della porta** do
not descend steps before doors open
(on buses)
attenzione, prego please be careful
**attenzione, questa macchina non da
resto** this machine does not give
change
attenzione, ... avviso/avvertimento
warning
attesa di ... minuti circa wait approx
... minutes
attrezzatura per pesca subacquea
underwater fishing equipment
attrezzatura per scuba scuba diving
equipment
autonoleggio car rental
autostrada expressway
autunno fall/autumn
avanti cross now

B

bagno restroom/toilets
bagno schiuma foambath
baia bay
balconata balcony, dress circle
balcone balcony
ballo dance
bambini children
bambini solo se accompagnati no
unaccompanied children

banca bank
banco di pesce fishstall *(at market)*
bancomat cash dispenser
barca a remi rowboat
barca a vela sailboat, yacht
batelli di salvataggio lifeboats
batello a vapore steamer
belvedere view point
benvenuti! welcome
benzina gas
bevande analcoliche soft drinks
bevande extra drinks
not included
bevande incluse drinks included
bibite fresche e snacks refreshments
available
biblioteca library
biglietteria ticket office
biglietti tickets
biglietti per oggi tickets for today
biglietto di andata e ritorno return
ticket
biglietto ordinario day ticket
biglietto settimanale weekly ticket
binario platform
biodegradabile disposable
birra beer
borse handbags
bracciole waterwings
bretella expressway junction
burrone profondo canyon

C

cabina bathing cabana/hut
cabina di ponte deck cabin
caduta massi falling rocks
caduta slavine avalanche danger
calcio soccer
calle street *(in Venice)*
calzolaio shoe repairs/cobbler's
cambiare a change at
cambiare per change *(to other
metro lines)*
cambio exchange rate
cambio valute bureau de change

Camera dei Deputati parliament building

camere libere vacancies/accommodations available

camerini fitting rooms

camion truck

campeggio campsite

campi di tennis tennis courts

campo field

campo di battaglia battle site

campo giochi/sportivo sports ground

cancellato cancelled

cancello gate

canna da pesca fishing rod

canoa canoe

canottaggio canoeing, rowing

cantante singer

cantante lirica opera singer

canto Gregoriano Gregorian chant

capella chapel

Capodanno New Year's Day

capolinea terminal

capsule capsules

carne meat

carozza coach

carozza non fumatori (non)smokers compartment

carozza/vagone ristorante dining-car

carrelli carts/trolleys

carta d'imbarco embarkation card

carta riciclata recycled paper

cartelle cliniche medical records

cartoleria stationer's

casa house

casa di cura privata health clinic

casa patrizia stately home

cascata waterfall

casco crash helmet

cassa cashier, checkout

cassa di risparmio savings bank

cassa rapida express checkout

cassette luggage lockers; cassettes

cassieri cashiers

castello castle

catena di montagne mountain range

cavalcavia road bridge

centralino/centralinista operator

centesimo cent

centrifuga dry spin

centro città downtown area

centro commerciale shopping area

centro congressi convention hall

centro direzionale business district

centro sportivo sports center

ceriali cereals

check-in check-in counter

chiamare ... per il ricevimento dial ... for reception

chiamare ... per una linea esterna dial ... for an outside line

chiesa church

chilometro kilometer

chirurgia surgery

chiudere il cancello keep gate shut

chiudere la porta please shut the door

chiuso (per restauro) closed (for restoration)

chiuso al traffico closed to traffic

chiuso fino a ... closed until ...

chiuso per ferie closed for holiday

chiuso per pranzo closed for lunch

chiuso per rinnovo locali closed for repairs

chiusura festiva closed for holidays

chiusura settimanale closed/day off

ciambella rubber ring

ciclismo cycling

ciniglia chenille

cinte belts

cintura di salvataggio lifebelt

cioccolateria confectioner's

circo circus

circonvallazione ring road

città city

città universitaria university

città vecchia old town

cittadini extracomunitari non-EU citizens

cognome surname

collina/colle hill

colonna sonora soundtrack

colori resistenti colorfast

comando polizia/comando Carabinieri police station
comincia alle ore ... begins at ...
commissioni bank charges
completo full
compreso inclusive
compreso nel prezzo included in the price
compresse tablets
compri due paghi uno buy 2 get 1 free
compriamo a ... currency bought at ...
compro e vendo ... we buy and sell ...
comunicazioni interurbane/ internazionali/intercontinentali (con operatore) long distance calls (with operator): intercity/ international/intercontinental
con bagno with private bathroom
con sottotitoli subtitled
con vista sul mare with sea view
concerto concert
conservanti preservatives
consiglio per la consumazione serving suggestion
consultare il proprio medico prima dell'uso consult your doctor before use
consumare entro il ... best before ...
contatore della luce electric meter
contenitore per batterie/vetro/aluminio/latta/plastica container for battery/bottle/ aluminum/tin/plastic/ paper recycling
conto account
conto corrente current account
contorni vari choice of vegetables
contro la forfora against dandruff
controcoperta upper deck
controllo please show your bags before leaving *(in shop)*; check/control
controllo valuta currency control
convalidare il biglietto (prima della prossima fermata/prima di salire sul treno) validate your ticket (before next bus stop/before getting on train)
coperto cloudy
corsia d'emergenza emergency lane

corsa di levrieri greyhound racing
corsi di cavallo horseracing
corsia lane
corsia ciclabile cycle track
corsia di sorpasso passing lane
corsia preferenziale do not walk
corso semplice one-way
costa coast
costo per chilo (Kg)/etto/litro/metro price per kilo/330 grams/liter/meter
cotone cotton
crema per le mani hand cream
crociere cruises
cucina cookery
cuffie obbligatorie bathing caps must be worn
cuoio leather
cura intensiva intensive care
curva pericolosa dangerous bend
curve per ... Km bends for ...km

D

da consumarsi entro il ... best before ...
da non prendere per via orale not to be taken orally
da ... a .../dalle ore... alle ore ... from ... to ...
danza dance
danza classica ballet
danza folcloristica folk dancing
dare la precedenza yield/give way
darsena docks
data di nascita date of birth
degustazione vini winetasting
della casa homemade
della stagione in season
deltaplano hang gliding
depositi deposits
deposito ambulanze ambulance station
deposito bagagli left-luggage office
deviazione alternative route, detour/diversion
deviazione per camions/TIR truck route/alternative lorry
di giornata fresh daily

diagnosi e cura treatment room
diapositive slides
diga dam
diocesi diocese
diretto direct
direttore manager
disco orario parking disk
dissolvere in acqua dissolve in water
divieto d'attracco no anchorage
divieto di balneazione no swimming/
bathing
divieto di campeggio no camping
**divieto di ingresso esclusi i mezzi
degli handicappati** access for
disabled person vehicles only
**divieto di ingresso escluso veicoli
autorizzati** authorized vehicles only
divieto di scarico no dumping
divieto di sorpasso no passing
divieto di sosta no stopping
docce showers
dogana customs con.trol
domani tomorrow
domenica Sunday
Domenica delle Palme Palm Sunday
domicilio home address
donne women only, women (toilets)
dopo i pasti after meals
dopobarba aftershave
doposole aftersun
doppiato dubbed
doppio senso two-way traffic
durante i pasti with meals

E

€ euro
edicola newsagent's
edificio pubblico public building
elenco telefonico telephone directory
elicottero helicopter
emergenza emergency
emergenza sanitaria medical
(health) emergency
entrata entrance
Epifania Epiphany (January 6)
equitazione horseback riding

esaurito sold out
**esibire documenti/carta d'identità/
passaporto** proof of identity required
esibire la ricevuta sul paravento
place ticket on windshield
espresso made to order
estate summer
estero foreign
estintore fire extinguisher
estuario estuary
etto 330 grams
extra extra charge/supplement

F

fabbrica factory
fantascienza science fiction
farina wheat flour
farina integrale fermenti lattici vivi
whole wheat flour
farmacia drugstore
faro marina lighthouse
fatto su misura made to measure
fattore 8 factor 8 (sunlotion)
fattoria farm
febbraio February
fermata bus stop
fermata a richiesta request stop
fermata del tram tram stop
fermata service stopping
Ferragosto Assumption Day (August 15)
ferro iron
ferrovia railroad
Festa del Lavoro Labor Day (May 1)
Festa dell'Assunzione Assumption
Day (August 15)
**Festa dell'Immacolata Concezione (8
dicembre)** Immaculate Conception
(December 8)
Festa della liberazione (25 aprile)
Liberation Day (April 25)
festa nazionale national holiday
fibre alimentari fibre (food)
fiera fair
fila row
film d'orrore horror film

film per famiglia universal *(film classification)*
filobus trolleybus
filosofia philosophy
fine autostrada/superstrada end of expressway/motorway
fine deviazione end of detour/diversion
fine lavori stradali end of roadworks
finestrino window seat
finire la cura/il trattamento finish the course
fino a ... until ...
fioraio florist's
Firenze Florence
firma signature
fiume river
fon hairdryer
Fondamenta canal-side *(Venice)*
fontana fountain
formaggio cheese
fortezza fortress
fotottico photographic store
fragile – vetro fragile – glass
frana landslide
francobolli stamps
franchigia bagagli luggage allowance
freno d'emergenza emergency brake
fresco fresh
frontiera border crossing
frutta fruit
fruttivendolo greengrocer's
fumetti comics
funivia cable car/gondola
funzione religiosa church service
fuochi d'artificio fireworks
fuori servizio out of order

<hr>

G

gabinetti restrooms [toilets]
gabinetti pubblici public restrooms
galleria shopping mall (dress) circle; gallery
galleria chiusa (mountain) tunnel closed
galleria d'arte art gallery
gara contest

gas per campeggio camping gas
gennaio January
Genova Genoa
genuino genuine
ghiaccio icy snow
ghiaccio nero black ice
giardini pubblici park
giardino garden
giardino botanico botanical garden
gift omaggio free gift
ginocologo gynecologist
gioaccatoli toystore
giornalaio newsagent's
giorni feriali weekdays
giovedì Thursday
giugno June
gocce drops
goielleria jeweler's
gola gorge
gomma rubber
grassi fat content
grassi vegetali vegetable fats
grotta cave
gruppi groups welcome
guanti, cinte e sciarpe gloves, belts and scarves
guardaroba cloakroom
guida ai piani store guide

<hr>

H

hockey su ghiaccio ice hockey

<hr>

I

il cuoco suggerisce ... the chef suggests ...
il migliore del mondo world's best
imbarco ad uscita n° ... boarding at gate no. ...
imbarco immediato boarding now
immigrazione immigration control
in casi di guasti telefonare al numero ... in case of breakdown, phone/contact ...
in funzione sistema di vigilanza/allarme surveillance/alarm system in operation

incrocio crossing
indirizzo address
indirizzo di casa home address
industria cinematografica
movies/cinema
informazioni information desk,
reception
informazioni elenco abbonati
enquiries
informazioni nutirizionali nutritional
information
ingoiare intere swallow whole
ingrandimento enlargement service
ingresso access only, entrance
ingresso libero admission free
ingresso per gli handicappati
entrance for disabled persons
ingresso per soli residenti access to
residents only
inizia alle ore ... commencing ...
inizio autostrada freeway entrance
inizio spettacolo curtain up
**innestare la prima marcia prima di
lasciare la macchina** leave your car
in first gear
inserire monete insert coin
inserire carta di credito insert
credit card
**inserire il denaro nella macchina e
ritirare il biglietto** insert money in
machine and remove ticket
inverno winter
inversione di marcia change
direction
irritante per gli occhi e la pelle
harmful for eyes and skin
isola pedonale pedestrians only/
pedestrian zone
istituto di credito bank
istruzioni per l'uso instructions for use
itinerario naturale nature trail
itinerario panoramico scenic route
itinerario turistico tourist route
IVA VAT/sales tax
IVA compreso/incluso VAT included

l'originale the original
La Befana (6 gennaio) Epiphany
(January 6)
la merce non può essere cambiata
goods cannot be exchanged
lago (artificiale) (artificial) lake
lana wool
lastri x-ray
latte e latticini dairy products
latteria dairy
lavaggio macchine car wash
lavanderia laundry, washing facilities
lavare a mano hand wash only
lavare in acqua fredda/tiepida
wash in cold/warm water
lavori in corso (a ... metri)
construction (... m) ahead
**leggere attentamente le istruzioni
prima dell'uso** read instructions
carefully before use
legno wood
lettino sun lounger
lettura di poesie poetry reading
levate alle ore ... times of collection
libero vacant, for rent
libreria bookstore
libretto di circolazione/documenti
registration papers
lino linen
liquidazione clearance sale
liquori liqueurs
lista menu
Livorno Leghorn
lo chef suggerisce ... the chef
suggests ...
locanda guest house
luna park amusement park
lunedì Monday
Lunedì dell'Angelo Easter Monday
luogo di nascita place of birth

macchina car
macelleria butcher's

magazzino department store
maggio May
mare sea
mare mosso rough sea
marionette puppets
marmellate e conserve preserves
martedì Tuesday
marzo March
maternità maternity
mattina a.m.
medico doctor
meglio se servito fresco best served chilled
meno di 8 articoli 8 items or less
menù fisso set menu
menù turistico tourist menu
mercato market
mercato coperto covered market
merce da dichiarare goods to declare
mercoledì Wednesday
messa mass
messa vespertina Evensong
metallo metal
metropolitana/metro subway
mezza pensione half board
mimo mime
miniera mine
misura unica one size fits all
mittente sender
mobili ed arredamenti furniture
mobilificio furniture warehouse
molo dock (boarding)
molta neve heavy (snow)
monastero monastery
monsignore monseignor
montagna mountain
monumenti antichi ruins
monumento (ai caduti) (war) memorial
monumento di interesse turistico tourist feature
monumento storico ancient monument
mulino mill
mulino a vento windmill
multicine multiplex cinema
municipio town hall

muro wall
museo museum
musica music
musica da camera chamber music
musica dal vivo live music
musica lirica opera

N

Napoli Naples
Natale Christmas
nave ship
nazionalità nationality
nebbia fog
negozio di musica music store/shop
neve snow
neve artificiale artificial snow
neve bagnata wet snow
neve fresca fresh snow
neve ghiacciato icy snow
neve leggera powdery snow
niente flash no flash
niente resto exact change/no change given
niente rimborsi no refunds
nocivo harmful
noleggio for rent
noleggio abiti/vestiti dress rental
nome name
nome dei figli name of children
nome del coniuge name of spouse
nome di famiglia surname
nome di ragazza maiden name
non allacciato disconnected
non appoggiarsi alla porta do not lean against door
non asciugare al sole do not dry in direct sunlight
non avvicinarsi keep clear
non bruciare do not burn
non calpestare il prato/l'erba keep off the grass
non compreso exclusive
non danneggia le pellicole film safe
non esporre a fonti di calore do not expose to heat
non gettare rifiuti do not litter

non incluso not included
non lasciare bagagli incustoditi do not leave baggage unattended
non lasciare oggetti di valore nel-l'automobile do not leave valuables in your car
non parlare al conducente do not talk to the driver
non più di 4 persone no more than 4 persons
non scongelare prima di cucinare do not defrost before cooking
non si accetta nessuna responsabil-ità per danni o furto the owners can accept no responsibility for any damage or theft
non si accettano assegni no checks
non si accettano carte di credito no credit cards
non stirare do not iron
non superare 375 kg do not exceed 375 kilos (in elevators)
non toccare do not touch
non usare candeggia do not bleach
nulla da dichiarare nothing to declare
numero di targa license plate number
numero verde toll free number
numeri di emergenza emergency telephone numbers
numeri utili useful numbers
numero del passaporto passport number
numero della carta di credito credit card number
numero di soccorso pubblico di emergenza general emergency number
numero di volo flight number
nuoto swimming

O

occupato occupied/engaged
offerta speciale special offer
officina meccanica car repairs
oggetti elettrici electrical shop/store/appliances
oggetti smarriti lost property

oggi today
ogni ... ore every ... hours
Ognissanti All Saints' Day (November 1)
olio oil; sauces
ombrellone sun umbrella [sunshade]
omeopatico homeopath
ommaggio ...% se spendi più di ... % discount if you spend more than ...
operatore operator
orari timetables
orario opening/business/visiting hours
orario continuato open all day
orario di visite visiting hours
orchestra sinfonica symphony orchestra
24 ore su 24 24-hour service
oreficeria jeweler's
oro gold
ospedale hospital
ospizio hospice
osservatoria observatory
ostello della gioventù youth hostel
ottico optician
ottobre October
ottone brass

P

pacchi packages
padiglione pavilion
padre Father
pagare alla cassa please pay at cash desk
pagare qui please pay here
pagato (grazie) paid (with thanks)
pagine gialle yellow pages
palco (pl. **palchi**) box
palude marsh, swamp
pane bread
panificio bakery/baker's
paracadutismo parachuting
parcheggio parking (permitted); parking lot
parcheggio libero free parking
parcheggio per biciclette parking for bicycles

parcheggio per soli residenti parking for residents only
parcheggio riservato ai clienti customer parking lot
parcheggio sotterraneo underground garage
parcheggio vietato/divieto di sosta no parking
parrucchiere hairdresser's/hairstylist's
partenze departures
partita match
Pasqua Easter Sunday
passaggio a livello railroad/level crossing
passaggio sotteraneo underground passage
passo carrabile do not block entrance
pasticceria pastry shop
pattini skates
pedaggio toll
pedoni pedestrians
pelle leather
pellicola film
pendenza incline [gradient]
penisola peninsula
pensione completa full board
pensione guest house
per vegetariani suitable for vegetarians
per ... giorni for ... days
percorso del traghetto ferry route
percorso per autobus/pullmans bus route
pericolo danger
pericolo di bufere storm warning
pericolo di burrasche gale warning
pericolo di ghiaccio icy road
pericolo di slavine danger of avalanches
pericoloso dangerous
personale staff only
pesce fish; angling
pesce fresco fresh fish
pesce surgelato frozen fish
pescheria fish store
pesistica weight-lifting
piatti pronti oven to table

piatto del giorno dish of the day
piazza square
picco peak
piccola colazione breakfast
piccoli prezzi grande qualità low prices, top quality
pillole pills
pinacoteca art gallery
pioggia rain
piscina swimming pool
piscina per tuffi diving pool
pista bianca (ski trail)for beginners
pista blu e pista rossa for intermediates *(ski trail)*
pista chiusa closed
pista ciclabile cycle lane/track
pista nera for advanced skiers
pista per principianti for beginners *(ski trail)*
pista pericolosa dangerous trail
platea stalls
polizia police
polizia stradale highway/traffic police
pollame poultry
poltrona n° seat no.
pomata ointment
pomeriggio p.m.
pompa pump
ponte bridge
ponte bassa (altezza ... m.) low bridge (height ... m.)
ponte di coperta upper deck
ponte di passeggiate promenade deck
ponte levatoio drawbridge
porta gate (to town/city); door
porta antincendio fire door
porta automatica automatic door
portiere notturno night porter
porto harbor
posta post office
posto corridoio aisle seat
posto fumatore smoking
posto non fumatore no smoking
posto n° seat no.
posto riservato agli invalidi please give up this seat to the disabled

pozzo well

PP.TT. post office

prato (campeggio) grass (camping site)

prefisso area code

preghiera prayers

prelievi withdrawals

prelievi di sangue blood tests

prendere il biglietto take ticket

prendere la ricevuta dalla cassa automatica pay at the meter

prenotazione biglietti ticket reservation

prenotazioni reservations, advance bookings

prezzi fissi no discounts

prezzi speciali per gruppi special price for groups

prezzo rate

prezzo al litro price per liter/litre

prezzo per chilo (Kg)/etto price per kilo/330 grams

prima classe first class

prima dei pasti before meals

prima di coricarsi before going to bed (medicine dose)

primavera spring

primo piano first floor

prodotti antiallergici antiallergic products

prodotti di bellezza beauty products

proibito circolare nella chiesa durante le funzioni liturgiche/durante la santa messa no entry during services

pronto intervento emergency services

pronto soccorso accident and emergency; medicine box

proprietà privato private property

prossima levata alle ore ... next collection at ...

prossima visita guidata alle ore ... next tour at ...

punto d'imbarco embarkation point

punto d'incontro meeting point

punto di raduno muster station

Q

questa macchina non da resto this machine does not give change

questa sera/stasera this evening

qui si vendono carte telefoniche phone cards on sale here

R

racchetta racket/raquet; ski poles/sticks

raccordo anulare ring-road

rallentare slow down

rallentare, scuola/bambini caution, school/children

reclamo bagagli baggage claim

referti test results

regali gifts

reggersi ai corrimano hold on to the side (escalator)

resto massimo (€2) maximum change given (€.2)

ricambi per auto car accessory/spares shop/store

ricevimento reception

riduzioni reductions

rifugio ski shelter

rilasciato il ... da ... issued on ... by ...

rimozione forzata unauthorized vehicles will be towed away

rio stream

riparazioni repairs

riserva d'acqua reservoir

riserva naturale nature reserve

riservato reserved

ritardo delayed

rocca castle, fortress

roccia (campeggio) stone (camping site)

romanzi novels

rompere il vetro in caso di pericolo break glass in case of emergency

rotatoria (a ... metri) roundabout/circle (... m. ahead)

roulotte trailer/caravan

rubinetto water tap

rupe cliff

sabato Saturday
sabbia mobile quicksand
sala banchetti reception facilities
sala congressi/conferenze
conference room
sala d'attesa waiting room
sala da pranzo dining room
sala giochi games room
sala operatoria operating theater
sala passeggeri passenger lounge
sala TV television room
saldi clearance sale
sale salt
salita entrance (get on)
salotto lounge
salvagenti lifejackets
San Gennaro St. Januarius
(September 19, Naples)
San Giovanni Battista St. John The
Baptist (June 24, Florence)
San Marco Saint Mark's Day (April
25, Venice)
San Pietro e Paolo Saint Paul's and
Peter's Day (June 29, Rome)
San Silvestro New Year's Eve
Sant'Ambrogio Saint Ambrose's Day
(December 7, Milan)
Santo Stefano Boxing Day
(December 26)
sanzioni per i trasgressori tres-
passers will be prosecuted
**sanzioni per i viaggiatori senza
biglietto** penalty for traveling without
a ticket
sanzioni se viaggiate senza biglietto
penalty for traveling without ticket
saporito tasty
scadenza della carta di credito
credit card expiration date
scala d'emergenza emergency stairs
scala mobile escalator
scarico merci deliveries only
scarpata escarpment

scarponi da sci ski boots
schiuma per la barba shaving cream
sci skis, skiing
sci di fondo cross-country skiing
sci nautico waterskiing
sciovia tow (ski) lift
sconto di …% se spendi più di …
… % discount if you spend more than …
scuola school
scuola rallentare slow, school
sdraia deck-chair
**se i sintomi persistono consultare il
proprio medico** if symptoms persist,
consult your doctor
seconda scelta sale
secondo piano second floor
segale rye
seggiovia chairlift
selezionare destinazione/zona
select destination/zone
semaforo provvisorio temporary
traffic light
senso unico one-way street
sentiero footpath, track
senza grassi fat-free
senza intervallo no intermission
senza piombo unleaded
senza zucchero sugar-free
sereno sunny weather
servizio service charge
servizio compreso/incluso service
included
servizio di camera room service
servizio diretto direct service
servizio immediato while you wait
servizio non incluso service not
included
servizio notturno night service
seta silk
si accettano gruppi parties welcome
si accettano carte di credito we
accept credit cards
si prega consegnare le borse please
leave your bags here
si prega controllare il resto please
check your change

si prega di aspettare dietro la linea please wait behind barrier

si prega di non consumare cibo nella camera no food in the room please

si prega fare un contributo please make a contribution

si prega mantere il silenzio durante le funzioni religiose quiet, service in progress

si prega pulire la camera make up this room please

si prega rispettare questo luogo sacro please respect this place of worship

si prega tenere il biglietto please retain your ticket

sicurezza security

signore women only; ladies (toilets)

signori gentlemen (toilets)

slittino sledge

soccorso stradale breakdown services

solista soloist

solo ciclisti cyclists only

solo contanti cash only

solo giorni feriali weekdays only

solo giorni festivi Sundays only

solo per gli abbonati season ticket holders only

solo per uso esterno not for internal consumption

solo rasoi shavers only

solo residenti residents only

solo stasera/una serata for 1 night only

solo uso esterno for external use only

sono previste sanzioni per chi non può esibire lo scontrino fiscale/il biglietto you are liable to be fined if you don't keep your receipt/ticket

sopra il livello del mare above sea level

sopraelevata flyover

sorgente spring

spegnere il motore turn off engine

spettacolo spectacular

spettacolo serale evening performance

spettatori spectators

spiaggia beach

spiaggia per nudisti nudist beach

spingere push

spogliatoi changing rooms

SQ subject to availability

squisito delicious

staccare la corrente prima di (togliere) disconnect from electric mains before (removing)

stampa e sviluppo photographic store

stampe prints

stazione degli autobus bus station/terminal

stazione di pedaggio toll booth

stazione di servizio service/filling station

stazione ferroviario train station

stirare a temperatura bassa cool iron

storia history

storia dell'arte art history

strada road

strada a doppia corsia dual highway

strada a doppio senso traffic from the opposite direction

strada a senso unico one-way street

strada bianca gravel/unpaved road

strada chiusa road closed

strada dissestata uneven road surface

strada in costruzione road under construction

strada nazionale main road/highway

strada principale main street

strada senza uscita cul-de-sac; no through traffic

strada stretta narrow road

straniero(-a) foreign

strappare qui tear here

strisce pedonali pedestrian crossing

studio medico doctor's office [surgery]

succhi di frutta fruit juices

suonare la campanella ring the bell

super four-star (gas)

superstrada expressway

supplemento (notturno, aeroporto, bagagli, festivo) supplement (night-time, airport, baggage, Sunday, holiday)
surgelato frozen
sviluppo developing
svincolo junction/interchange

T

tagliare qui cut here
tangenziale bypass
tavola da sci snowboard
tavola da surf surfboard
tavoli al piano superiore seats upstairs
tassì taxi
teatro per ragazzi children's theater
telefono per solo carte card phone
telefono SOS/di emergenza emergency telephone
teleselezione direct dialing
tenere in frigo keep refrigerated
tenere in un ambiente fresco keep in a cool place
tenere lontano dagli occhi keep away from eyes
tenere lontano dai bambini keep out of reach of children
tenere lontano dal sole do not expose to sunlight
tennis da tavola table tennis
terme baths
tessera season ticket
tessera mensile monthly ticket
tessuti per arredamento upholstered [soft] furnishings
tier tribuna stand/grandstand
tintoria dry cleaner's
tintura per capelli hair dye
tipografia printing & copying
tirare pull
tiro all'arco archery
tomba grave, tomb
Torino Turin
torre tower
tossico poisonous, toxic
traffico intenso delays likely

traffico lento slow traffic
traghetto passenger ferry
transito con catene chains required
transito con catene o pneumatici da neve use chains or snow tires
treno train
trotta harness racing
tuffo deep water diving
tutte le operazioni all transactions

U

ufficio cambi exchange office
ufficio informazioni information office
ufficio postale post office
ufficio prenotazioni ticket reservations
ultima novità brand new
ultima stazione di servizio per … chilometri last gas station for … kilometers
ultima vista alle ore … last entry at …
una bibita inclusa includes 1 complimentary drink
uomini men only; men (toilets)
usare con cautela take care when using
uscita exit, way out; gate
uscita autostrada freeway/motorway exit
uscita camions truck/lorry exit
uscita d'emergenza emergency/fire exit
uso della cucina cooking facilities

V

vaccinazioni ecografie vaccinations
vaglia postali/telegrafici postal money order and electronic transfers
vagone letto sleeper (train)
validità del passaporto passport expiration date
validità della carta di credito credit card expiration date

valido per (75 minuti) valid for (75 minutes)

valido per le fasce ... valid for zones ...

veicoli lenti slow vehicles

veicoli pesanti heavy vehicles

vela sailing

veleno(so) poison(ous)

velocità massima ... km/ora maximum speed

vendere entro il ... sell by ...

vendiamo a ... currency sold at...

venerdì Friday

venti forti strong winds

venti moderati light winds

verdura vegetables

vernice fresco wet paint

vero genuine

vetro glass

vetro riciclato recycled glass

via street

viaggi/viaggiare travel

viale avenue, boulevard

vicino al mare within easy reach of the sea

vicolo alley

vicolo cieco dead end

videogiochi video games

vietato forbidden

vietato a veicoli con peso superiore a closed to heavy vehicles

vietato accendere il fuoco no fires

vietato ai minori di ... anni no children under ...

vietato ai pedoni no pedestrians

vietato avvicinarsi alle macchine durante la traversata no access to car decks during crossing

vietato di sosta no waiting

vietato fermarsi fino a ... no stopping (between ... and ...)

vietato fotografare no photography

vietato fumare no smoking

vietato gettare rifiuti don't dump rubbish

vietato giocare con la palla no ball games

vietato l'ingresso no entry

vietato l'ingresso dopo l'inizio dello spettacolo no entry once the performance has begun

vietato pescare no fishing

vietato pescare senza autorizzazione fishing by permit only

vietato salire no entry

vietato scendere no exit

vietato sporgersi dalla finestra do not lean out of windows

vietato suonare il clacson use of horn prohibited

vigili del fuoco fire brigade

vigneti vineyards

visite guidate guided tours

vivaio garden center

voi siete qui you are here

voli internazionali international flights

voli nazionali domestic flights

volo numero ... flight number ...

... volte al giorno ... times a day

Z

zona a parcheggio limitato giorni feriali limited parking zone on weekdays

zona fumatore smoking area

zona non fumatori no smoking area

zona pedonale pedestrian zone/precinct

zona riservata a carico e scarico loading bay

zucchero sugar

REFERENCE

Regular verbs and their tenses

There are three verb types which follow a regular pattern, their infinitives ending in **-are**, **-ere**, and **-ire**, e.g. *to speak* **parlare**, *to sell* **vendere**, *to finish* **finire**. Here are the most common present, past and future forms:

	PRESENT	PAST	FUTURE
io *I*	parl<u>o</u>	ho parlato	parler<u>ò</u>
tu *you* (informal)	parl<u>i</u>	hai parlato	parler<u>ai</u>
lui/lei/Lei *he/she/you* (form.)	parl<u>a</u>	ha parlato	parler<u>à</u>
noi *we*	parl<u>iamo</u>	abbiamo parlato	parler<u>emo</u>
voi *you* (pl. inform.)	parl<u>ate</u>	avete parlato	parler<u>ete</u>
loro/Loro *they/you* (form.)	parl<u>ano</u>	hanno parlato	parler<u>anno</u>
io *I*	vend<u>o</u>	ho venduto	vender<u>ò</u>
tu *you* (informal)	vend<u>i</u>	hai venduto	vender<u>ai</u>
lui/lei/Lei *he/she/you* (form.)	vend<u>e</u>	ha venduto	vender<u>à</u>
noi *we*	vend<u>iamo</u>	abbiamo venduto	vender<u>emo</u>
voi *you* (pl. inform.)	vend<u>ete</u>	avete venduto	vender<u>ete</u>
loro/Loro *they/you* (form.)	vend<u>ono</u>	hanno venduto	vender<u>anno</u>
io *I*	fin<u>isco</u>	ho finito	finir<u>ò</u>
tu *you* (informal)	fin<u>isci</u>	hai finito	finir<u>ai</u>
lui/lei/Lei *he/she/you* (form.)	fin<u>isce</u>	ha finito	finir<u>à</u>
noi *we*	fin<u>iamo</u>	abbiamo finito	finir<u>emo</u>
voi *you* (pl. inform.)	fin<u>ite</u>	avete finito	finir<u>ete</u>
loro/Loro *they/you* (form.)	fin<u>iscono</u>	hanno finito	finir<u>anno</u>

Very often, people ommit the pronoun, using only the verb form.

Examples: **Vivo a Roma.** *I live in Rome.*
                 Parla italiano? *Do you speak Italian?*

There are many irregular verbs whose forms differ considerably.

The most common way to express the past is by using the conjugated form of *to have* **avere** and the past participle of the verb as demonstrated on the previous page. Many verbs, especially verbs related to movement are conjugated with *to be* **essere**. In that case the participle agrees with number and gender of the subject.

avere *to have*	**essere** *to be*
io ho *I have*	**io sono** *I am*
tu hai *you have*	**tu sei** *you are*
lui/lei/Lei ha *he/she/you have*	**lui/lei/Lei è** *he/she/you is*
noi abbiamo *we have*	**noi siamo** *we are*
voi avete *you have*	**voi siete** *you are*
loro/Loro hanno *they/youhave*	**loro/Loro sono** *they/you are*

Examples: **Ho** lavorato. *I worked.*

Lei è andata a Palermo. *She went to Palermo.*

Siamo andate in autobus *We (fem.) went by bus.*

Nouns and articles

Generally nouns ending in **-o** are masculine, their plural ending changing to **-i**. Those ending in **-a** are usualli feminine, their plural ending changing to **-e**. Nouns ending in **-e** can be either gender.

The definite articles are **il** (masc) and **la** (fem). The plural form is **i** (masc) and **le** (fem). When a masculine noun begins with a vowel, **z-, sc-, sp-, st-**, or **gn-** , the singular article changes to **lo**, the plural to **gli**.

Examples: SINGULAR   PLURAL

il treno *the train*   **i** treni *the trains*

lo studio *the studio*   **gli** studi *the studios*

la casa *the house*   **le** case *the houses*

The indefinite articles also indicate their gender: **un** (masc.) and **uno** when a masculine noun begins with a **z-, sc-, sp-, st-,** or **gn-** or **s-.** The feminine form takes **una** or **un'** when the noun begins with a vowel.

Examples: SINGULAR   PLURAL

un treno *a train*   treni *trains*

uno studio *a studio*   studi *studios*

una casa *a house*   case *houses*

un' ora *a n hour*   ore *hours*

Possessive determiners

Possessives are used to show that the noun belongs to something or someone. They relate to gender and number of the noun that follows:

	SINGULAR		PLURAL	
	MASC.	FEM.	MASC.	FEM.
my	il mio	la mia	i miei	le mie
your (inf.)	il tuo	la tua	i tuoi	le tue
your (form.)	il Suo	la Sua	i Suoi	le Sue
his/her/its	il suo	la sua	i suoi	le sue
our	il nostro	la nostra	i nostri	le nostre
your (pl, inf.)	il vostro	la vostra	i vostri	le vostre
your (pl., form)	il Loro	la Loro	i Loro	le Loro
their/	il loro	la loro	i loro	le loro

Examples: **Dov'è il Suo biglietto?** *Where is your ticket?*

La vostra corriera parte alle 8. *Your bus leaves at 8.*

La tua casa è bella. *Your (singular) house is pretty.*

Wordorder

The conjugated verb generally comes after the subject.

Example: **Vorrei una birra.** *I'd like a beer.*

Questions are formed by simply raising your voice at the end of the sentence or by reversing the order of subject and verb when using key question words like *how* **come**.

Examples: **Avete cartine?** *Do you have maps?*

Come ci arrivo? *How do I get there?*

Hai visto Carlo? *You saw Carlo?*

Negations

Negative sentences are generally formed by putting *not* **non** before the verb which is to be negated.

Examples: **Non fumiamo.** *We don't smoke.*

Non capisco. *I don't understand.*

Il treno non arriva. *The train doesn't arrive.*

Adjectives

Adjectives describe nouns and agree with them in gender and number. Singular forms end in **-o** (masc), **-a** (fem) or **-e** (masc/fem). Plural forms end in **-i** (masc), **-e** (fem) and **-i** (masc/fem).

Examples: **un ristorante grande** *a large restaurant*
                    una camicia bianca *a white shirt*
                    le scarpe italiane *the Italian shoes*

A few common adjectives normally precede the noun:

Examples: **un bel giardino** *a beautiful garden*
                    la piccola casa *the little house*
                    una larga strata *a wide street*

Adjectives linked to the subject with a verb also agree in number and gender with the noun they relate to.

Examples: **Il clima è mite.** *The climate is mild*.
                    Il nostro capo è simpatico . *Our boss is nice*.
                    Ho visitato molti musei. *I visited many museums*.

Comperatives and superlatives

ADJECTIVE	COMPARATIVE	SUPERLATIVE
ricco	**il più ricco**	**ricchissimo**
rich	*richer*	*the richest*
vecchio	**meno vecchio**	**il meno vecchio**
old	*less old*	*the least old*

Example: **Ha qualcosa di meno caro?** *Do you have anything cheaper?*

Adverbs and adverbial expressions

Adverbs describe verbs. In Italian, the majority are formed by adding **-mente** to the feminine form of the adjective.

ADJECTIVE	FEMININE	ADVERB
lento *slow*	**lenta** *slow*	**lenta**mente *slow<u>ly</u>*

Adjectives ending in **-re** or **-le** drop the final **-e** before adding **-mente**. Like in English, there are a number of exceptions to the rule, e.g. *good* **buono** / *well* **bene**.

Examples: **Maria guida lentamente.** *Maria drives slowly.*
                    Roberto guida normalmente. *Robert drives normally.*
                    Parlo bene italiano. *I speak Italian well.*

Some common adverbial time expressions:

attualmente *presently*
non ancora *not yet*
ancora *still*
finalmente *finally*

NUMBERS

Larger numbers are built up using the components below: e.g.

3 456 789   **tremilioniquattrocentocinquantaseimila
e settecentoottantanove**

Mille, **milione** and **miliardo** have plural forms (**mila**, **milioni**, **miliardi**).
Note that **e** can be used to break larger numbers up.

0	**zero** *dzehro*		40	**quaranta** *kwaranta*
1	**uno** *oono*		50	**cinquanta** *cheengkwanta*
2	**due** *doo-ay*		60	**sessanta** *sayssanta*
3	**tre** *tray*		70	**settanta** *sayttantta*
4	**quattro** *kwattro*		80	**ottanta** *ottanta*
5	**cinque** *cheengkweh*		90	**novanta** *novanta*
6	**sei** *sayee*		100	**cento** *chaynto*
7	**sette** *sehttay*		101	**centouno** *chaynto-oono*
8	**otto** *otto*		200	**duecento** *doo-aychaynto*
9	**nove** *novay*		500	**cinquecento**
10	**dieci** *dee-ehchee*			*cheenkwehchaynto*
11	**undici** *oondeechee*		1000	**mille** *meellay*
12	**dodici** *dodeechee*		10 000	**diecimila**
13	**tredici** *traydeechee*			*deeaycheemeela*
14	**quattordici** *kwattordeechee*		1 000 000	**un milione**
15	**quindici** *kooeendeechee*			*oon meelyonay*
16	**sedici** *saydeechee*		first	**primo** *preemo*
17	**diciassette** *deechassehttay*		second	**secondo** *saykondo*
18	**diciotto** *deechotto*		third	**terzo** *tayrtso*
19	**diciannove** *deechanovay*		fourth	**quarto** *kwarto*
20	**venti** *vayntee*		fifth	**quinto** *kooeento*
21	**ventuno** *vayntoono*		once	**una volta** *oona volta*
30	**trenta** *traynta*		twice	**due volte**
31	**trentuno** *trayntoono*			*doo-ay voltay*

three times	**tre volte**	*tray voltay*
a half	**mezzo**	*maytso*
half a(n) hour	**mezz'ora**	*maytsora*
a quarter	**un quarto**	*oon kwarto*
a third	**un terzo**	*oon tayrtso*
a pair of …	**un paio di …**	*oon paa-eeoo dee*
a dozen …	**una dozzina …**	*oona dotseena*

DAYS

Monday	**lunedì** *loonaydee*
Tuesday	**martedì** *martaydee*
Wednesday	**mercoledì** *mayrkolaydee*
Thursday	**giovedì** *jovaydee*
Friday	**venerdì** *vaynayrdee*
Saturday	**sabato** *sabato*
Sunday	**domenica** *domayneeka*

MONTHS

January	**gennaio** *jaynnaaeeo*
February	**febbraio** *faybbraaeeo*
March	**marzo** *martso*
April	**aprile** *apreelay*
May	**maggio** *madjo*
June	**giugno** *jooño*
July	**luglio** *loolyo*
August	**agosto** *agosto*
September	**settembre** *sehttehmbray*
October	**ottobre** *ottobray*
November	**novembre** *novehmbray*
December	**dicembre** *deechehmbray*

DATES

It's …	**È …** *eh*
July 10	**il dieci luglio** *eel dee-ehchee loolyo*
Tuesday, March 1	**martedì, primo marzo** *martaydee preemo martso*
yesterday	**ieri** *ee-ehree*
today	**oggi** *odjee*
tomorrow	**domani** *domaanee*
this/last …	**questo(-a)/l'ultimo(-a) …** *kwaysto(-a)/loolteemo(-a)*
next week	**la prossima settimana** *la prosseema saytteemaana*

SEASONS

spring	**la primavera** *la preemava̲y̲ra*
summer	**l'estate** *laysta̲a̲tay*
fall/autumn	**l'autunno** *lowto̲o̲nno*
winter	**l'inverno** *leenva̲y̲rno*

GREETINGS

Happy birthday!	**Buon compleanno!** *bwon komplayanno*
Merry Christmas!	**Buon Natale!** *bwon nata̲a̲lay*
Happy New Year!	**Felice Anno Nuovo! Buon anno!** *fayle̲e̲chay anno noo-o̲v̲o/bwon anno*
Happy Easter!	**Buona Pasqua!** *bwona paskwa*
Best wishes!	**Tanti auguri!** *tantee owgo̲o̲ree*
Congratulations!	**Congratulazioni!** *kongraatoolatseeonee*
Good luck!/All the best!	**Buona fortuna!** *bwona forto̲o̲na*
Have a good trip!	**Buon viaggio!** *bwon veea̲djo*

PUBLIC HOLIDAYS

There are a number of regional holidays observed in Italy. National holidays are listed below.

January 1	**Capodanno or Primo dell'Anno**	New Year's Day
January 6	**Epifania/Befana**	Epiphany
April 25	**Anniversario della Liberazione (1945)**	Liberation Day
May 1	**Festa del Lavoro**	Labor Day
August 15	**Ferragosto**	Assumption Day
November 1	**Ognissanti**	All Saints' Day
December 8	**L'Immacolata Concezione**	Immaculate Conception
December 25	**Natale**	Christmas
December 26	**Santo Stefano**	St Stephen's Day
Movable dates:	**Lunedì di Pasqua/Pasquetta**	Easter Monday

Except for April 25, all Italian holidays are celebrated in the **Ticino** (Italian-speaking Switzerland), as well as: March 19 (**San Giuseppe**), August 1st (National Holiday), and the holidays of **Ascensione** (Ascension Day) and **Corpus Domini**.

TIME

The official time system uses the 24-hour clock. However, in ordinary conversation, time is generally expressed as shown below, often with the addition of **di mattina** (morning), **di pomeriggio** (afternoon) or **di sera** (evening).

Excuse me. Can you tell me the time?	**Scusi, può dirmi che ora è?** *skoozee pwo deermee kay ora eh*
It's five past one.	**È l'una e cinque.** *eh loona ay cheenkway*
It's …	**Sono le …** *sono lay*
ten past two	**due e dieci** *doo-ay ay dee-ehchee*
a quarter past three	**tre e un quarto** *tray ay oon kwarto*
twenty past four	**quattro e venti** *kwattro ay vaynte*
twenty-five past five	**cinque e venticinque** *cheenkway ay vaynteecheenkway*
half past six	**sei e trenta** *seh-ee ay traynta*
twenty-five to seven	**sei e trentacinque** *seh-ee ay traynta cheenkway*
twenty to eight	**otto meno venti** *otto mayno vayntee*
a quarter to nine	**nove meno un quarto** *novay mayno oon kwarto*
ten to ten	**dieci meno dieci** *dee-ehchee mayno dee-ehchee*

222

It's twelve o'clock (noon/midnight).	**È mezzogiorno/mezzanotte.** *eh maytsojorno/ maytsanottay mittaag/mitternakht*
at dawn	**all'alba** *allalba*
in the morning	**al mattino** *al matteeno*
during the day	**durante il giorno** *doorantay eel jorno*
before/after lunch	**prima di pranzo** *preema/dopo dee prandzo*
in the afternoon	**nel pomeriggio** *nayl pomayreedjo*
in the evening	**di sera** *dee sayra*
at night	**di notte** *dee nottay*
I'll be ready in five minutes.	**Sarò pronto(-a) fra cinque minuti.** *saro pronto(-a) fra cheenkway meenootee*
He'll be back in a quarter of an hour.	**Ritorna fra un quarto d'ora.** *reetorno fra oon kwarto dora*
She arrived half an hour ago.	**È arrivata mezz'ora fa.** *eh arreevaata maytsora fa*
The train leaves at ...	**il treno parte ...** *eel trayno partay*
13:04	**alle tredici e zero quattro** *allay traydeechee ay dzayro kwattro*
0:40	**alle zero e quaranta** *allay dzayro ay kwaraanta*
10 minutes late/early	**con dieci minuti di ritardo/di anticipo** *kon dee-ehchee meenootee dee reetaardo/dee anteecheepo*
5 minutes fast/slow	**cinque minuti avanti/indietro** *cheenkway meenootee avaantee/eendeeaytro*
from 9:00 to 5:00	**dalle nove alle cinque** *dallay novay allay cheenkway*
between 8:00 and 2:00	**fra le otto e le due** *fra lay otto ay lay doo-ay*
I'll be leaving by ...	**Partirò entro ...** *parteero ayntro*
Will you be back before ...?	**Ritornerà prima di ...?** *reetornayra preema dee*
We'll be here until ...	**Saremo qui entro le ...** *saraymo kwee entroh leh*

AUSTRIA

SWITZERLAND

Trento

Milano

SLOVENIA

Venezia   Trieste   CROATIA

Po

Po

Golfo di
Venezia

Torino

BOSNIA
AND
HERZEGOVI

Genova

Bologna Forlì

Golfo di Genova

Firenze

SAN MARINO

FRANCE

Pisa

Tevere

Ancona

Mare Ligure

Perugia

MONTENE

CORSICA
(FRANCE)

Mare Adriati

Roma

Campobasso

Napoli

Bari

Mare Di
Sardegna

SARDEGNA

Mare Tirreno

Golfo
di Taranto

Cagliari

Catanzaro

Mare

Mare Mediterraneo

Reggio di Cale

Palermo

SICILIA

ALGERIA TUNISIA

ITALIA

224